PRAISE FOR
OPERATING MODELS

"In a world where organizations are constantly evolving, this book is a must-read for business leaders and HR practitioners. It outlines structures and operating models that leverage technology, enhance agility, accelerate growth and address the challenges of today's complex business environment. The authors provide practical strategies to navigate global disruptions and drive transformative growth."
Karen Mattimore, SVP and Chief Human Resources Officer, Honeywell

"For leaders tackling growth, agility and transformation, this book offers a structured approach to designing operating models fit for today's challenges. Practical and relevant across industries."
Stan Zurkiewicz, Chairman of the Management Board and Chief Executive Officer, DEKRA

"Enterprise reinvention includes a thoughtful strategy for talent and organization. This book provokes us to rethink operating models for the future, highlighting the importance of a proactive approach and multiple iterations in order to unleash extraordinary growth opportunities and achieve even higher levels of performance."
Suzana Kubric, CHRO, Nubank

"*Rethinking Operating Models* offers an up-to-date roadmap for navigating today's complex business landscape. Tackling how to organize for innovation, cost, M&A and closing the gap on environmental sustainability, this is a must-read for those aiming to thrive in a rapidly changing world of data, technology and work."
Jean-Marc Duvoisin, Former CEO of Nespresso and Nestle Executive Board Member, and Active NGO Board Member

"Never have we seen the level of disruption we are facing today. This book takes a pragmatic approach to operating model design in light of the rapid advances in data, technology and ways of working. Providing frameworks for the big operating model challenges, but also inspiration on what the next generation of organization will look like. Sneak preview, it will require a new human and machine relationship."
Dimitra Manis, Former Chief Purpose Officer (Chief People Officer), S&P Global

"The book provides a practical set of frameworks and techniques to work through common challenges many executives face, brought to life with examples from many real-life projects, organizations and industries. With an eye on the future in this period of significant organizational change, it's a very helpful addition to the toolbox."
Ben Gaunt, SVP Group Transformation, BP

"This book is an important guide for organizations looking to effectively integrate sustainability into their core operations. With practical advice on implementation, strategies to mobilize teams and insights on the highest-value areas to focus, it empowers leaders to go beyond incremental changes."
Whitney Mayer, Head of Global Sustainability & ESG, Hershey

"The authors take a thoughtful and holistic approach to the perennial challenge of managing cost and complexity whilst enabling innovation-led growth. Going beyond simple top-down cost levers, they explore the balance of strategic operating model choices and operational tuning, and how data and technology are shifting the dials, combined with a continuous focus on unlocking productivity through aligned ways of working."
Andy Banfield, VP Organization Development & People Analytics, Unilever

"A profound read for both current and aspiring leaders, this book delves into the delicate balance between reflection and action necessary to adapt organizations in the digital age. It provides a powerful yet simple blueprint for transforming them into 'reinventor organization'. It also underscores the importance of customer focus, continuous learning and collaboration to foster innovation and agility."
André Santos, HR Center of Expertise Director, Vale

"Written by a series of practitioners with decades of hard-won experience, this book will teach you how to leverage organization design as a pillar of strategy execution while simultaneously addressing the most typical set of challenges CEOs face today. Thought provoking, tangible and enjoyable to read for CEOs, management teams and all those involved in making organizations more effective."
Rupert Morrison, Founder of Orgvue and Arahi, and author of Data-Driven Organization Design and Strategic Value Creation

Rethinking Operating Models

Designing people and technology powered organizations

Kent McMillan, Greg Kesler, Amy Kates

KoganPage

First published in Great Britain and the United States in 2025 by Kogan Page Limited

Kogan Page
Kogan Page Ltd, 2nd Floor, 45 Gee Street, London EC1V 3RS, United Kingdom
Kogan Page Inc, 8 W 38th Street, Suite 90, New York, NY 10018, USA
www.koganpage.com

EU Representative (GPSR)
Authorised Rep Compliance Ltd, Ground Floor, 71 Lower Baggot Street, Dublin D02 P593, Ireland
www.arccompliance.com

Kogan Page books are printed on paper from sustainable forests.

ISBNs

Hardback   978 1 3986 1798 8
Paperback   978 1 3986 1796 4
Ebook   978 1 3986 1797 1

British Library Cataloguing-in-Publication Data
A CIP record for this book is available from the British Library.

Library of Congress Cataloging-in-Publication Data
2025930254

Typeset by Integra Software Services, Pondicherry
Print production managed by Jellyfish
Printed and bound by CPI Group (UK) Ltd, Croydon CR0 4YY

CONTENTS

07   The Reinventor Organization 207
Sanam Gill, Kent McMillan
Contributor: Yaarit Silverstone

LIST OF FIGURES

LIST OF TABLES

ABOUT THE EDITORS AND LEAD AUTHORS

Kent McMillan

Kent McMillan is a consultant, innovator, and educator in operating model and organization design based in London, UK. With a wealth of experience advising CEOs and executive teams, he shapes and activates enterprise-wide operating model transformations that help his clients deliver on their ambitious growth, profitability, and sustainability objectives.

He has led iconic programs for some of the world's most recognized brands, solving for their most complex challenges such as new business strategies, cost optimization, mega-mergers, enterprise agility, and digital transformation across Europe, North America, Africa, the Middle East and Asia.

Kent has held multiple practice leadership roles at the European and global level for Accenture, and is one of the founders of its Operating Model & Organization Design practice. He has built a sought-after team who employ market-leading methodologies and cutting-edge data and analytics to deliver transformative results.

A passionate innovator, Kent has shaped novel operating model solutions for clients and advanced approaches to large-scale organizational change. He holds two US patents for Accenture's organization analytics and design platform and is a recognized thought leader and guest lecturer. Kent has spent over two decades at the intersection of people and technology, shaping future-ready organizations that are built to thrive in a rapidly evolving world.

Greg Kesler

Greg Kesler is a consultant, researcher, writer, and public speaker in operating model and organization design and activation, based in Easton, USA. He co-founded Kates Kesler Organization Consulting, acquired by Accenture in 2020, and until recently was the global leader of Accenture's Operating Model & Organization Design practice. Greg continues as a senior luminary advising CEOs and other client senior executives in organization design and executive talent. He and Amy Kates worked with senior leaders at

Accenture to build a global team that utilizes the market-leading methodology for operating model and organization design.

Leading transformative redesigns at global, enterprise-level, Greg has advised CEOs on team alignment around transformative goals and new business models. His expertise spans consumer goods, capital equipment, healthcare, and life sciences. Greg has also developed succession planning and executive assessment practices across multiple firms. In addition, he has held senior positions in multinationals based in the United States and Europe.

Greg is co-author of three influential organization design books, as well as a contributor to numerous articles and book chapters, and regularly speaks to and teaches executives.

Amy Kates

Amy Kates is a consultant, educator, and author in operating model and organization design, based in New York, USA. She co-founded Kates Kesler Organization Consulting, acquired by Accenture in 2020. As a senior luminary in Accenture's Operating Model & Organization Design practice, she continues to advise CEOs, while building a global team using common, market-leading methodology. Amy has authored five of the leading books in the field of organization design.

The organization design approach and tools Amy has developed with her colleagues have become the standard design methodology around the world. LinkedIn selected her to produce its organization design video series, which has reached over 130,000 learners.

In addition to her consulting work, Amy teaches organization design through Cornell University. She is an advisory board member of the two leading organization design professional associations, Organization Design Forum and the Organization Design Community. She was appointed a Visiting Fellow to the government of Singapore for 2018 to 2020. In 2019, she joined the board of Educate!, a non-profit organization focused on secondary school curriculum reform in East Africa. Amy is based in New York City.

FOREWORD

Organization patterns are surprisingly predictable. Individual and even small team behavior can be quite diverse. But as an organization grows in size and strategic complexity, we can anticipate the consequences of choices that leaders make.

Human behavior in large groups was studied throughout the 20th century. But it was the pioneering work of Jay Galbraith in the 1970s and 80s that showed how decisions around structure and power, processes and decision-making, metrics and rewards, and people practices, can be made to intentionally shape human behavior at scale. Jay's work combined an engineer's curiosity for complex systems with a deeply humanistic approach.

For the past 30 years, we have built on Jay's work to bring his foundational thinking to broader audiences. The Star Model is our mental model for holistically diagnosing and designing organizational systems. We've also been deeply influenced by the thinking of Peter Drucker, Walt Mahler, Paul Lawrence and Jay Lorsch, Dick Axelrod, Steve Drotter, Ed Schein, and many others. We have enjoyed the creative challenge of translating formidable theory into practical frameworks, tools, and methods. We believe in the power of thoughtful organization design, well executed, to create successful businesses that are rewarding places to work.

While humans have not evolved over the last 30 years, we have seen a drastic change in the environment that defines business and the workplace. Advances in information technology, data, and communications have made the ability to collaborate across the boundaries of time, language, and culture possible in ways that were not imaginable when Galbraith did his early work. The effect is dramatically compressed change across the entire business environment, from customer expectations to new business models, faster insight-led innovation, deep consumer engagement, supply-chain agility, and so much more. Today's breakthroughs in artificial intelligence are changing not just how work is done, but also fundamentally how decisions are made.

The organization's operating model and the design of the system must keep pace with this compressed transformation. And since there are so many unknowns about what the future looks like, the change must be continuous. What has not changed—and in fact is becoming more critical—is understanding human behavior within and across groups. The new work of the organization designer is to motivate and channel the energy of the people in the company in what are likely to be radically new ways of working.

There is an ambitious narrative today that argues that smart companies will use artificial intelligence (AI) to augment rather than replace human capability. Many claim business leaders will be able to create a more inclusive and innovative workforce in this new world. But these sanguine predictions are yet to be seen and will require transformation that is rooted in levels of trust that will not be easy to nurture and sustain without deliberate, purposeful organization strategy.

In 2020, our firm, Kates Kesler, was acquired by Accenture. We were given the opportunity to create the first global practice for organization design built on a common theory-based methodology, grounded in human behavior and participative consulting. Equally, we had the opportunity to enhance and improve our methodology. Today's companies are integrating data and technology into every facet of their business—and in their operating models and organizations. And so, organization practitioners are quickly employing assets and know-how deeply embedded with technology-powered frameworks and data-driven organizational analytics.

From this experience comes this book. It extends the work of the Kates Kesler firm in a way that would not have been possible before becoming part of Accenture and the having access to the exceptional collection of capabilities of our colleagues. Each chapter is written by Accenture strategists who bring a passion for organization design and deep expertise and wisdom that comes from working with great companies across the world.

Each chapter is aligned around a client challenge, one of six business problems at the center of our work. Collectively they represent a call for growth that incorporates sustainability, innovation, and productivity, and embraces the promise of technology and data with greater enterprise agility. The focus of the narrative is aimed at senior-most executives, including the CEO who knows that enterprise reinvention includes a thoughtful strategy for talent and organization.

We feel privileged to have worked with and learned from these seasoned strategists during our time at Accenture. These colleagues have made our own work better, and it has been a pleasure to support them in writing this next chapter in what will continue to be a vigorous topic of discussion over the coming years.

Greg Kesler
Amy Kates

ACKNOWLEDGMENTS

The editorial team extends our deepest gratitude to the 32 authors and contributors who have generously shared their expertise and collaborated with us through the editing and publishing process to bring this work to life. It has been a privilege to work with such a diverse and experienced group of practitioners from across Accenture's Operating Model & Organization Design practice and beyond.

We would also like to thank our many clients who have inspired our work, as well as our colleagues and personal networks who have acted as sounding boards and shared their expertise and experience. Without their invaluable input, this book would not have reached its full potential.

Special thanks go to Accenture leaders Muqsit Ashraf, Jack Azagury, and Karalee Close who have sponsored this book, and for their thoughtful reviews.

We are grateful to Lucy Carter and Joe Ferner-Reeves for their unwavering belief in this book, their insightful feedback, and their patience throughout its development.

A heartfelt thanks to Nicole Lehman, Bernd Muller, and Craig Roach for their exceptional project management skills, as well as to the many who helped manage the process and make this happen.

Our appreciation also goes out to the entire Accenture Operating Model & Organization Design practice. Your curiosity, creativity, and courage in delivering the best for our clients are the foundation of our thinking and the driving force behind this book.

Lastly, a big thank you to our families and friends, and the families and friends of the authors, for their support and understanding during the long nights and missed weekends. Without your encouragement and patience, this book would not have been possible.

LIST OF AUTHORS AND CONTRIBUTORS

This book is authored by a global team of Accenture strategists who combine their passion for organization design with extensive experience collaborating with leading companies worldwide. Together, they offer a wealth of actionable insights to guide readers in navigating the complexities of modern business.

Foreword

Amy Kates, Senior Luminary Advisor and former Senior Managing Director, Operating Model & Organization Design, New York City, USA
Greg Kesler, Senior Luminary Advisor and former Senior Managing Director, Operating Model & Organization Design, Connecticut, USA

Introduction

Paul Jeruchimowitz, Senior Managing Director, Operating Model & Organization Design, New York, USA
Sam Holmes, Managing Director, Operating Model & Organization Design, London, UK
Kent McMillan, Managing Director, Operating Model & Organization Design, London, UK

Chapter 1: Fuel Innovation-led Growth

Katherine Mohrig, Managing Director, Operating Model & Organization Design, Philadelphia, USA
David Price-Stephens, Managing Director, Operating Model & Organization Design, London, UK

Contributors:
Greg Kesler, Senior Luminary Advisor and former Senior Managing Director,
Operating Model & Organization Design, Connecticut, USA
David Kidder, Managing Director, Song, New York, USA

Chapter 2: Manage Cost & Complexity

Cherene Powell, Managing Director, Operating Model & Organization
Design, Minneapolis, USA
Rob Rubin, Managing Director, Operating Model & Organization Design,
Minneapolis, USA
Contributors:
Thomas Haslinger, Managing Director, Operating Model & Organization
Design, Vienna, Austria
Chris Roark, Senior Managing Director, Americas Strategy, Chicago, USA

Chapter 3: Execute Mergers, Acquisitions, & Divestments

Steve Giles, Managing Director, Operating Model & Organization Design,
Brisbane, Australia
Lynn Gonsor, Managing Director, Operating Model & Organization Design,
New York, USA
Greg Kesler, Senior Luminary Advisor and former Senior Managing Director,
Operating Model & Organization Design, Connecticut, USA
Contributors:
J. Neely, Senior Managing Director, Mergers & Acquisitions, Cleveland,
USA
Andrew Sinclair, Managing Director, Technology Strategy, Denver, USA

Chapter 4: Reinvent with Data and Technology

Tom Falkowski, Managing Director, Operating Model & Organization
Design, Boston, USA

Kent McMillan, Managing Director, Operating Model & Organization Design, London, UK
Gerd Saalfrank, Managing Director, Operating Model & Organization Design, Munich, Germany
Contributors:
Ashwin Acharya, Managing Director, AI for Talent & Organization, San Francisco, USA
Adam Burden, Managing Director, Technology & Innovation, Tampa, USA

Chapter 5: Achieve Enterprise Agility

William Carberry, Senior Manager, Operating Model & Organization Design, Charlotte, USA
Kent McMillan, Managing Director, Operating Model & Organization Design, London, UK
Contributors:
Neetu Mishra, Senior Manager, Operating Model & Organization Design, London, UK
Kestas Sereiva, Managing Director, Operating Model & Organization Design, Boston, USA
Megan Tyler, Managing Director, Operating Model & Organization Design, Melbourne, Australia

Chapter 6: Close the Sustainability Execution Gap

April LaCroix, Senior Manager, Sustainability, Chicago, USA
Jenna Trescott, Managing Director, Sustainability, New York, USA
Contributors:
Ellie Azolaty, Senior Manager, Sustainability, Houston, USA
Tim Henshaw, Managing Director, Operating Model & Organization Design, London, UK
Jens Laue, Managing Director, Sustainability, Dusseldorf, Germany
Cyrus Suntook, Senior Manager, Operating Model & Organization Design, London, UK

Chapter 7: The Reinventor Organization

Sanam Gill, Managing Director, Operating Model & Organization Design, London, UK

Kent McMillan, Managing Director, Operating Model & Organization Design, London, UK

Contributor:

Yaarit Silverstone, Senior Managing Director, Talent & Organization, Atlanta, USA

Introduction

PAUL JERUCHIMOWITZ, SAM HOLMES, KENT MCMILLAN

The first decades of the 21st century have seen durable economic expansion driven by a dazzling wave of technology and connectivity. Frontiers abound, thanks in large part to a new generation of artificial intelligence, but every business operates in context of challenge and uncertainty. The cost of capital, international trade policies, social politics, new regulation, inflation and deflation, supply chain turbulence, migration waves, war and geopolitical instability, and even pandemics such as Covid-19 impact regions and sectors unequally.

Growth champions that benefited from the flood of sales related to the pandemic face pressures to maintain those levels of revenue and market capitalization growth. In 2024 Pfizer and Moderna were working to close revenue gaps of 40 percent after a collapse in vaccine uptake.[1] This challenge can be seen beyond the pandemic. For instance, Novo Nordisk saw sales growth in 2023 of more than 30 percent reaching \$33.7 billion,[2] driven by extraordinary demand for GLP-1 therapies, while a threat of loss of exclusivity on the not-so-distant horizon is already creating a challenge to these companies of reinventing their businesses in hopes of finding the next mega-growth engine in other therapeutic areas.

Companies known for decades of consistent execution of growth commitments and accompanying premium stock prices are facing new obstacles and market ambiguity. A scan of shareholder and analyst reports, as well as comments in the public domain from some top leaders of these companies, render surprising levels of uncertainty as this book is being written. Apple, Nike, P&G, Unilever, Disney, and Honeywell are just a few examples of companies across diverse industries managing sales and profit margin pressure.[3, 4]

While environmental policies in Europe maintain a mostly steady path, the United States remains behind on climate goals. The financial and environmental regulatory environment is constantly changing as policies are increasingly politicized. Consider too the uncertainty in the automotive industry around electrification. Should traditional car makers be placing their bets on all-electric or on hybrid automotive technology when electric vehicle sales are slowing? Are consumers hesitating to commit to all-electric vehicles, or just waiting for more affordable options?[5] Many of today's uncertainties will be seen in the rearview mirror as extraordinary growth opportunities. Boards of directors want to know now how company leaders are incorporating innovation and adaptability into their strategies and organizations.

Transformation and reinvention

Nearly every major company has recently worked its way through an ambitious transformation program of some kind as a way to respond to or ready themselves for a changing context. Research indicates that 80 percent of organizations have made change a part of their long-term vision, while 95 percent have already undergone two or more transformation initiatives over the past three years.[6] The impact of these efforts continues to be unimpressive, however, with recent figures suggesting only around 12 percent of these programs produce lasting results.[7]

Bold strategies for growth and new business models are the foundations of successful transformation, but it is a set of smart connections among technology, organization, leadership, and talent, anchored to a clear ambition, that brings deep change. In the face of continued uncertainty, having a compelling purpose behind the transformation and knowing what it will deliver to customers, to owners, and employees has never been more important.

This book is focused on innovation in operating models and organization design. We hope to make the case for a more integrated approach to this work that closely ties together business strategy, the design of the organization and ways of working, the blueprinting and activation of technology and data, and ambitious talent agendas.

The democratization of data and advances in technology such as generative AI (GenAI) make it easier every day to achieve this kind of change. Work is powered by algorithms, and the transparency of data and insights enables decisions to be made anywhere in the organization.

This book is grounded in a few key principles that we believe will guide transformation over the next few years.

Reinvention is end to end

Priorities and initiatives are integrated across an enterprise, led from the center by the top executive team, who work together as enterprise leaders and deeply engage a broad base of the organization. The CEO is actively orchestrating a company-wide change. The leadership team is fully engaged, but leadership responsibility for reinvention is not delegated.

Technology-driven initiatives can only be part of an end-to-end approach to reinvention when they are connected to a clear growth strategy, new business model, or expansion into new markets. Three-year master plans for migration to cloud or moving to the next version of SAP, the enterprise resource-planning software, do not deliver transformation when viewed with a pure technology lens. It is impossible to maintain enterprise focus on these programs when they are not producing outcomes that matter to the businesses. Technology blueprinting is a critical element of business strategy, but not an aim in itself. Organization, operating models, and talent initiatives are interlocked with the technology blueprint to engineer new ways of working that technology and data will power.

The organizational chassis, comprising its tech-enabled business processes, decision-making forums, metrics, and talent deployment, is a woven fabric that must be flexible, binding together people and purpose, over time. The shift from chasing use cases for generative artificial intelligence to end-to-end transformation of entire value chains will require rethinking of organized ways of working and all elements of the operating model.

Rapid-path initiatives with a North Star

Companies that make the most progress in transformation drive smaller, faster initiatives that enable rapid adoption and quicker time to value. Top leadership of these companies think beyond change events by establishing a vision for the future operating model, then manage a connected set of innovation, commercial, technology, and organizational initiatives. Companies that do this well take a proactive, rather than reactive, stance and organizational design and activation are considered a distinctive capability.

Leaders of organizations that embrace this approach don't fret that business units and functions are iterating and transforming their operating models. They recognize this as healthy and that it takes multiple pathways of exploration and change to achieve ever-higher levels of performance. Nor do they leave the operating model changes to chance or the whim of each organizational unit leader; they set the conditions for success, grounded in the company's strategy.

The North Star creates a direction and structure that guides a diverse set of initiatives over time, often through high degrees of uncertainty. Artificial intelligence adds to short- and mid-term ambiguity as well as to potential opportunities. At its best, a North Star vision lays out a path that connects the growth strategy, an organization and talent plan, and a fully connected technology roadmap. This future-looking commitment serves as the anchor for a diverse set of rapid path initiatives. It is the thread that holds the parts together, bound to a strategy and clear set of outcomes.

Target priorities for change are purposefully set. Experiments are designed, such as applying AI to speed investment decisions, or to scale fraud prevention, or to enable more personalized shopping experiences. The North Star may include external partners to leapfrog ahead when internal capability is low and speed is of the essence. Teams are taught to seek opportunities to experiment, produce outcomes quickly, and learn and scale those early wins, adjusting priorities as the process unfolds, always aligned to the North Star.

Adaptive organization design is continuous

Organizational restructuring "events" will give way to more nuanced changes in strategy, organization, and talent, which, taken together, create the performance system that CEOs and their teams own.

Research indicates that the level of disruption CEOs must navigate is at an all-time high, up 200 percent between 2017 and 2022. The great majority of companies report dealing with 10 or more global challenges to their business.[8] A powerful set of disruptive forces has tasked CEOs with steering a course through a complex web of obstacles and opportunities, whether political and shareholder expectations at Disney or explosive growth at Novo Nordisk.

These shifts in the landscape will require continuous reviews of where people and capital are allocated, where decision-making authority should reside, how accountability is measured and aligned within and across boundaries, and what areas of deep expertise must be built. New capability is both an outcome of effective organizational change and, increasingly, it is the critical means by which strategy, organization, and talent are aligned in a technology-powered world.

A stable center of organizational gravity is critical to making this more continuous model work. Building blocks such as functions and centers of expertise can serve as a home for employees, while horizontal mechanisms are used to flex to customer and market needs. The true reconfigurable organization uses value streams and agile ways of working as mechanisms to assemble teams and talent around multiple dimensions of product, channel, segment, and experience.

This book will demonstrate that both strength and flexibility are features of the adaptive operating model. Companies will continue to invent entirely new business models, focused on data-based services and integrated customer solutions, often reaching across complex ecosystems. They are engaging customers and consumers in direct and personal ways. They are investing massive amounts of capital in digital-core assets, precursors to strategic bets in AI, and they are fundamentally rethinking ways of working in order to attract and engage talent across the entire value chain of the enterprise.

The six business challenges

While no CEO will speak openly about feeling overwhelmed by these challenges, it is easy to see how many may experience a sense of vulnerability. The median CEO tenure among the S&P 500 companies decreased 20 percent, from 6 years in 2013 to 4.8 years in 2022.[9] Furthermore, a recent study found that 69 percent of executives believe their operating model is unable to continuously adapt to disruptive forces,[10] and 73 percent perceive at least some risk to growth and performance if they do not rethink their operating model.[11]

We believe that the intentional design of the company's operating model, aligned with the strategic ambition and capability of sensing and responding to external change is the CEO's strongest lever for managing uncertainty.

To help leaders make sense of the operating model choices available, we have aligned our work, and the structure of this book, around six business challenges that most companies face today and which require a strategic and organizational response. The first three challenges concentrate on the drivers of profitable growth; the second three emphasize building the essential capabilities needed to succeed. To be clear, few companies have the luxury of facing these challenges one at a time, and many face all of them at some point or another.

Although these challenges are not entirely new, they have become more complex, and solutions must adapt accordingly. Samuel Hammond, senior economist at the Foundation for American Innovation, argues that the disruptive force of AI could be as transformative as the printing press was in the 15th century. Digital disruption is revolutionizing how companies operate and create value. The operating model of the enterprise, its businesses and its functions, are at the center of the systemic change now required. Leaders are challenging conventions and traditional organizational trade-offs, such as scale versus agility, enabling more boundaryless ways of working, and radically reducing unrewarded complexity.

Our authors explore the new terrain of these six business challenges and examine how companies are harnessing the muscle of people and organization, powered by digital technology and data, to expand sources of growth and execute complex strategies with sustainable results.

1: Fuel innovation-led growth

Growth is the central task of all businesses, and the first step in organization design is to explore choices around driving growth. These choices are translated into capabilities that power execution. Through this logic, all elements of the organization's operating model—structure, process, metrics, and talent—along with technology, are purposefully aligned to build those capabilities.

Companies with long track records of growth skillfully align all elements of their operating models to manage short-, medium- and long-term growth prospects over time as well as tensions between the core business and the new—mastering the paradoxes that innovation brings. Today, companies are experimenting with more nuanced approaches, gaining the benefits of both separation and integration.

Chapter 1 of this book explores how to build operating models to drive innovation-led growth powered by new forms of technology and data-driven insights.

2: Manage cost and complexity

No businesses today can ignore the embedded cost structures of their operating models. Some of this is fixed cost, an attractive target for reduction programs, but direct costs of production and distribution are also front and center today. All companies should have some focus on efficiency and productivity even as they continue to innovate and grow.

A major driver of cost is the internal complexity that tends to build over years of growth. Narrow spans and deep layers are obvious culprits, but so is overreliance on profit-and-loss centers intended to create accountability but which also result in duplication. Business portfolios that have not been pruned on any regular basis, and acquisitions that have never been effectively integrated, are sources of complex geographic footprints, duplicated functions, and complex decision-making processes.

Chapter 2 brings a strategic organization view to the task of reducing cost and complexity in a manner that is anchored to a growth.

3: Execute mergers, acquisitions, and divestments

Optimizing the business portfolio through merging, acquiring, and divesting businesses creates a unique set of organization challenges for leaders to manage. Surveys indicate that executives expect to see a continued increase in mergers and acquisitions (M&A) activity through the current decade, particularly in sectors where scale and efficiency are sources of strategic advantage.[12]

The mixed track record for returns in M&A activity is well documented.[13] Lack of due diligence, overpayment, and miscalculation of synergies are strategic errors, but poor integration is often a major factor in achieving the pay-off for even a sound business case. The central integration design issue is understanding what the value driver of the deal is in order to ensure it is protected in the new arrangement. If that value driver is not effectively scaled, or does not bring growth synergy to the marriage, then no new value has been created, and shareholders will gain little from the transaction. The wrong integration program can easily destroy value.

Chapter 3 explores how to integrate and divest organizations from day one and for the long term to deliver on the true intent of the deal.

4: Reinvent with data and technology

Boards are placing great pressure on CEOs to understand and prepare to unlock the potential of GenAI and other technology disruptors. Pharmaceuticals and life sciences, banking, media, and retail may be among the first to be disrupted, but the impact of this next wave of digital transformation will soon reach all segments, including manufacturing. Companies with strong digital cores will be able to move faster in realigning operating models and talent to build new capabilities in business-model innovation, service delivery, customer marketing, and resilient supply chain management.

The only way to realize the real promise of data and technology versus incremental value will be to rethink your organization structure, processes, metrics, and talent, while reimagining and building new capabilities married to a foundation of data and a powerful technology backbone. While early applications will target specific activities and functions, the impact of technologies such as GenAI will play out in end-to-end capabilities, such as customer engagement and new product innovation and launch. Anticipating this now in the way we think about organizations will provide an advantage for some companies over others.

Chapter 4 addresses how to design an organization's operating model to fully capitalize on advances in data and technology to drive competitive advantage.

5: Achieve enterprise agility

Few topics in the field of organization design have gained more attention in the recent past than creating an agile organization. Technology has allowed entry barriers to drop in many industries, and size alone is no longer a guarantee of sustainable market dominance. The imperative to build agility into the operating model has reached nearly all corners of business, not just those companies that have grown up around technology. By now, most organizations have experience with agile teams and related ways of working, but we will make the case that team interventions alone are not enough to create an agile enterprise.

Chapter 5 assembles a framework that shows how portfolio, organization, and team agility combine to create a system that allows an organization of any size to gain the dual advantages of size and speed.

6: Close the sustainability execution gap

Sustainable business is creating a lot of discussion. However, climate and environmental pressures, as well as the concerns of a new generation of consumers, continue to push it up on the business agenda. Compliance requirements are increasing in Europe and North America,[14] and the imperative for green business is growing in Asia. Governments are also introducing regulations and initiatives on the production and consumption sides.

The challenge for many companies today is to effectively link sustainability goals to business strategy and set up the organization to deliver and measure impact.

Chapter 6 explores what is needed for companies to deliver on their sustainability strategies to both manage new requirements of data reporting and compliance and use sustainability as a catalyst for differentiation and growth.

The reinventor organization

We conclude the book with a look ahead. With the advent of advanced technologies and an ever-increasing pace of change, we explore what it will take to rethink operating models for the future. Chapter 7 emphasizes the importance of moving beyond revolutionary ideas towards the implementation of practical and innovative ways of working. While it draws on the inspiration of pioneers such as Haier, Amazon, and Ocado, the focus is on understanding the principles behind their success rather than mere imitation.

Rethinking operating models in this context is not merely about adopting new structures and systems; it is also about embracing a reinvention mindset—one where organizations don't seek simply to achieve the benchmark, but rather continuously seek a new performance frontier for themselves and their industry. This final chapter explores seven features that offer a blueprint for a new type of organization that continuously reinvents itself, morphing with market dynamics, embracing new technology and staying in tune with customer, employee, and societal expectations.

Navigating the six challenges

As we have pointed out, these six challenges rarely appear one at a time, and there are cause-and-effect relationships across them. A merger or major acquisition will require attention to cost and complexity. Adoption of new technology will open opportunities for enterprise agility. Growth strategies may lead to sustainability challenges or open doors for new business models that help solve environmental problems. The precise form these varied combinations take, and their importance, will vary by industry.

The theme across all the chapters is the need for a system view of the organization, recognizing that changes to strategy require new capabilities and adaptive arrangements of roles, process, and metrics, vertically and horizontally. Along with an enterprise-systems approach, we encourage our readers to take a fact-based perspective. When data is surfaced around the case for change, and a range of options are generated, debated, and evaluated, this deep analysis will turn up the right priorities for reinvention. Design is not a benchmarking exercise. It must fit the context of company and environment. It is core work for leaders.

Every company must determine how each challenge affects its ability to execute its business plans, and how it will assemble a reinvention strategy with the right operating model choices that reconcile competing pressures and build new capabilities to create value.

On reading this book, we hope you will recognize the urgent need to rethink operating models for the modern age. Our goal is to equip you with practical frameworks and insights that help demystify these challenges and offer effective solutions.

Looking ahead, if you take away only three key points, our authors believe that leaders need to:

- Build a highly adaptive organization that challenges traditional trade-offs and continuously reinvents itself to respond to dynamic market conditions and ever-more demanding customer needs.

- Put data and technology at the heart of operating model design. Achieving more than incremental results requires fundamentally reimagining customer journeys and workflows, with humans and machines working in harmony.

- Revisit the operating model design more frequently, or even better, continuously. The accelerating pace of disruption and the emergence of new technologies, such as GenAI, demand faster iteration cycles.

Notes

1 Reuters (2023) Pfizers 2024 Revenue Forecast Below Wall Street Estimate, MarketScreener, December 13.

2 Fierce Pharma (2024) Novo Nordisk and Eli Lilly Lead Industry Wide Sales Survey in Fourth Quarter, February 22.

3 *Forbes* (2023) How Retailers are Battling Slowing Sales Growth and Tightening Margins, September 25.

4 Daniel, W. (2023) Record Revenues But Plummeting Profits: The Fortune 500 is trying to tell us something about the state of the economy, *Fortune*, June 10. fortune.com/2023/06/10/fortune-500-falling-profits-telling-something-economy-recession-return-to-normal (archived at https://perma.cc/9WRF-TG72).

5 Goldman Sachs (2024) Why are EV Sales Slowing? May 21.

6 Accenture (2024) *Change Reinvented.*

7 Mankins, M. and Litre, P. (2024) Transformations That Work: Lessons from companies that are defying the odds, *Harvard Business Review*, May–June.

8 Accenture (2023) *Reinventing for Resilience: A CEO's guide*, Accenture research report.

9 Chen, J. (2023) CEO Tenure Rates, Harvard Law School Forum on Corporate Governance, August 4.

10 Accenture (2023) *The Tech-Powered Operating Model*, Accenture research report.

11 Accenture (2021) *Accenture CXO Survey, 2021*.

12 Deloitte (2024) *Mergers & Acquisitions Market Outlook 2024: Your latest deals market update.* deloitte.com/uk/en/services/financial-advisory/collections/mergers-and-acquisitions-market-outlook.html (archived at https://perma.cc/S7JE-XKZX).

13 Accenture (2021) Making M&A Pay, July 15.

14 Meynier, T., Mishkin, S.H., and Triggs, M. (2023) EU Finalizes ESG Reporting Rules with International Impacts, Harvard Law School Forum on Corporate Governance, January 30.

Fuel Innovation-Led Growth

KATHERINE MOHRIG, DAVID PRICE-STEPHENS

Contributors: Greg Kesler, David Kidder

The ability of a company to create new products, services, markets, and business models is still one of the most important reasons shareholders choose to stay invested, and being part of a winning team is the main reason great talent chooses to join a particular company.

Innovation has always played an important role in business growth. Many successful companies have long incorporated ways to sustain and foster disruptive innovation into their plans. Different today are the increasingly difficult choices leaders face in funding innovation-led growth in the mid-to-longer term while delivering on short-term commitments.

New technologies and the power of data are driving business model innovation at an unprecedented rate, with 93 per cent of executives believing that rapid technological advancements have made purposeful innovation more important than ever.[1] Many technology observers argue that companies with a major role in GenAI applications across the entire value chain may still be undervalued.[2]

These disruptive changes are causing companies to fundamentally rethink growth and innovation. The effects are only now beginning to materialize, but are already elevating conversations about effective enterprise operating and organization models. Let's look at a few examples of legacy businesses that are reinventing business models and therefore rethinking their operating models.

Stories of innovation-led growth

CVS Health

Through its diverse businesses and technology-powered approach to care, this healthcare giant engages with more than 100 million consumers, patients, and members through corporate and government-sponsored health plans.[3] The challenge is to combine its newly acquired care-delivery businesses, such as Oak Street and Signify, with its risk-based businesses (Aetna), and its expansive retail and mail-order pharmacies (CVS and Caremark) to bring fully integrated and innovative care solutions to the market. The strategy is clear, but the challenge is building an operating model that maintains focus, decision rights, and metrics for profitable growth in these very large, core businesses—while creating something new and truly innovative that requires wiring hard linkages across all parts of the enterprise. Shared technology and data mean that innovating new integrated products and solutions cannot happen in the way of the past by standing up a new vertical organization.

Live Nation

The largest live entertainment company in the world is now focused on moving beyond its impressive scale in booking concerts and tours and managing ticket sales for over 145 million fans a year.[4] The strategy is to innovate the concert-goer and artist experience, to shift from transactions to a broader set of products and experiences, including new venue design, enhanced ticketing and premium hospitality, merchandise, parking, and security.

An experience-based business requires designing the end-to-end value chain around customer journeys and sophisticated operating model arrangements, held together with metrics to manage potential business-model tensions. A substantial investment in cloud computing enables data-driven insights and enterprise coordination for what remains a delivered experience that is highly local.

Medtronic

The successful medical devices leader has discovered the growth potential of bringing new clinical services to market based on the data that surgical equipment and devices ingest during medical procedures. Surgeons and other clinicians can now benefit from real-time, AI-enhanced guidance from cloud-based data generated over thousands of procedures.[5] Medtronic's opportunities are many, but its current device offerings are owned by more than 20 diverse business units. The organizational challenge is to empower each business to create its own data-based offerings with coordinated medical and clinical guidance from the center to protect the enterprise from the risk inherent in democratized decisions across the business units.[6]

The ability to define, prioritize, manage, and deliver a portfolio of projects and innovation ventures is one of the key factors that turn insights and ideas into profitable products. For many companies, this is a new capability and new muscle that must be built.

A structured approach to innovation-led growth

In the book *New to Big*, David Kidder and Christina Wallace describe the need to install a "growth operating system" within the organization.[7] They use the image of building a ladder to the moon, rather than pursuing speculative one-off innovation moonshots. A core tenet of this argument is the need to build and embed an organizational system that maintains the precarious balance between the strengths of the established organization and new entrepreneurial teams.

Many companies try to push disruptive innovations though their existing operating model, and they struggle to deliver. Executives have discovered that capabilities that served the past are less relevant, and entirely new capabilities are required to execute innovation-led growth. The profit-and-loss business units that are such powerful, predictable drivers of accountability lose relevance in a growth strategy that is centered on bringing integrated offerings to customers from across legacy businesses, as well as business partners, in the wider ecosystem. The problem of highly accountable, but also highly autonomous, business units is that white space for innovation isn't owned by anyone and goes unattended.

This chapter explores how choices in operating model and organization design must change to execute innovation-led growth strategies. The discussion is framed around a cyclical view of activities, from sensing an opportunity, to testing new ideas, to scaling new products, services, and go-to-market models at the enterprise level:

1 Find the next growth frontier.

2 Build the capability to innovate.

3 Design the innovative enterprise.

We present examples to show what can be learned from the maturation of digital-native technology companies. Many of the examples focus on how to preserve the ability to innovate successfully as operating models have evolved to look more like the traditional corporate models that they once challenged. Conversely, traditional industries, such as consumer products and automotive, provide valuable lessons in adapting an operating model in order to embrace new capabilities and consumer expectations.

Find the next growth frontier

The central operating model challenge for identifying the next growth frontier is business decision-making with an eye to the future. Drucker argued that this is most difficult in the multi-product, global enterprise that seeks an enterprise approach to portfolio management in order to increase the return on its innovation investments.[8] We suggest this is a distinct capability that must be built with high collaboration across finance, strategic planning, product and market management, and enterprise technology.

The Covid-19 pandemic, economic uncertainty, and extraordinary waves of technology development have pushed many businesses to rediscover their customers' expectations and ensure that their offerings, go-to-market processes, and even values are aligned with current realities. Innovation sensing and insight has never been more important.

Large corporations are not generally set up to invent the next frontier. They face headwinds in terms of decreased agility, difficult funding trade-offs, relentless quarterly shareholder expectations, and new wars for technology talent. Executives in these companies often hesitate to fund innovation at scale because of the uncertainty in the environment; however, by investing in and organizing the businesses and the corporate center for discovery, the confidence for investing in trends as well as what is trending increases. Every customer touchpoint is an opportunity to learn, but until the data is effectively analyzed and accessed by the right people, little is accomplished. Companies that are especially effective at "sensing" integrate direct interactions with customers as part of the value delivery process, including dialogue on what is working and what is not in the current offering.

Established companies determined to grow through innovation should focus on rapidly identifying opportunities, building repeatable capabilities, and scaling the next frontier—not necessarily on inventing it. Microsoft was not the first to market with cloud services—in fact, it was four years behind Amazon's launch of the first commercial cloud in 2006.[9] Even before then,

Salesforce leveraged cloud technology to offer the first software-as-a-service in 1999—nearly 15 years before Microsoft would launch its now industry-leading cloud business.[10]

Azure has been the growth and reinvention driver for Microsoft for nearly a decade, helping to move its market cap from $300 billion to nearly $3 trillion.[11, 12] Satya Nadella, the current CEO of Microsoft, placed a big bet on cloud, and this business model shift, and the cultural and operating model transformation he led to enable it, brought Microsoft back to innovation and strong growth even though Microsoft entered the market later than competitors.

Willingness to experiment

While large corporations aren't likely to invent the next frontier, they do need to discover it. This doesn't mean avoiding investment in research and development; it actually makes research, data and analytics, and product development even more important to identify the next frontier. Both business and executive leadership need to be involved in the process of experimentation, testing, and developing new products and services by asking the right questions.

Let's come back to Microsoft. How did Nadella know that making the pivot from the PC-based business to cloud and mobile was worthwhile? Microsoft saw the transformative power of cloud through its active investments in others who were developing cloud services, and in understanding the research coming from universities, technology corporations, and competitors. Experts in the business were experimenting, learning, building, and, importantly, senior executives were deeply involved.[13] Nadella established Azure before his rise to CEO.

Experimentation isn't always easy within a large corporation, however. Corporations are often constrained by the need for short-term payoffs and quarterly earnings increases, and don't feel that they can afford to invest in pipelines of opportunities with high failure rates. Even so, companies can still foster experimentation within their own walls and through ecosystem partnerships with academic institutions and others, as we will see later in this chapter. The operating-model question then becomes where experimentation should live in the company: is it embedded in business unit product development or is it consolidated into an enterprise center? The answer is that it is inevitably a combination of both, but it needs to be designed with deliberate intent to be able to work effectively within the company context.

Medtronic pushes data out to the edge and brings it back to the center. The center makes sense of the data, but the business units then use it to create commercial solutions. Competitor W.L. Gore treats innovation and experimentation as a core competence.[14] Its vastly diverse product set derives from experimenting to find new applications for a common polymer. Innovation has allowed it to expand from one of its earlier and best-known products—Gore-Tex Fabrics, used to make fabrics water and flame resistant—into medical products embedded into the body. The growth frontiers are developed through a combination of an integrated research and development organization and small business teams close to customer applications and needs.

Extensive use of data

Data is both an input and an output of experimentation. Data is the way a corporation identifies an opportunity that could potentially be the next frontier to begin testing, and a vast amount of data is also generated through the experimentation process.

Let's take an example from the automotive industry to illustrate the importance of data in identifying new growth frontiers. In the United States, consumers have historically purchased vehicles through dealerships rather than directly from the original equipment manufacturer (OEM)—companies like Ford and General Motors. This practice originated to protect consumers from price-fixing and unfair business practices when the market was still young and with limited options. Although market conditions have changed, until recently, the channel to interact with consumers has not. US consumer data showed that auto shoppers disliked the pressuring sales tactics,[15] opacity of processes and negotiations, lengthy paperwork, and complex financing options, but, for years, no one seriously tried to disrupt the dealer franchise model.

As Tesla prepared to enter the car market, it was researching electric vehicle battery technology, but it was also studying consumer sentiment and market trends. Founder Elon Musk saw an opportunity not only to revolutionize the product offered but to transform the channel and experience by creating a direct-to-consumer model with quick, digital interaction, consistent pricing, salaried sales advisors not hunting for commissions, and simple financing.[16] By selling directly to consumers, Tesla has more control over brand identity. Tesla's explosive growth hasn't been exclusively based on product; the buying experience the company has created has been a foundational part of the brand—and this was designed around the customer by leveraging a wealth of consumer data.

Pepsi provides an example of using real-time data and AI to inform innovation. Rather than relying on the traditional approach of researchers and surveys, where people's responses might not be strong predictors of year-over-year buying behaviors, Pepsi has used AI analysis of social media.[17] The company collects data on what people are searching, what they are eating, what recipes they are saving and what they are discussing about food broadly. This allows the company to uncover innovations such as unexpected flavor profiles to incorporate into snacks, or beverages infused with immunity ingredients.

Another example is Volition,[18] a sustainable beauty brand that solicits product ideas from the public. Individuals with promising ideas are paired with internal research and development teams to create prototypes. Members of Volition's customer community then vote on the products, which is supplemented by rapid experimentation and testing to determine which products are possible to manufacture and commercialize effectively. This creates a process of perpetual design and refinement that provides consumers with products that evolve in lockstep with their preferences.

Robust data operating model

AI is a critical growth enabler, and high-quality, accessible data is its foundation. As business and operating models evolve, data and AI converge processes from a series of linear steps to consolidated, dynamic capabilities. In this new reality, data becomes central, processes are automated and augmented, and the remaining work is completed by people, both workers and customers.

The effective use of data requires a defined data operating model—strategy, roles, processes, policies, standards, metrics, skills, and technologies—to effectively gather and use data. Data operating models typically follow a hub-and-spoke model, where the weight towards hub or spoke is determined by data and analytics maturity, resourcing and scale, and business unit complexity or differentiation from each other. Table 1.1 summarizes the elements of the data operating model.

Table 1.1 Data operating model elements

Data organization	Data governances	Data architecture
• **Data organization**: Defining roles, responsibilities, and capabilities for data management (data owner, data steward, etc.) • **Data governance**: Policies, procedures, and decision-making processes for managing data assets, ensuring data quality, integrity, security, and compliance with regulations and standards • **Data culture**: A data-driven culture within the organization where data and data integrity add value, and where data literacy and data collaboration are fostered across the enterprise	• **Data management**: Processes and workflows for data collection, storage, processing, analysis, and dissemination throughout the data life cycle • **Data quality management**: Standards, metrics, and processes for assessing and improving the quality of data to ensure its accuracy, completeness, consistency, and reliability	• **Data architecture**: Structure, organization, and integration of data assets across the organization, including databases, data warehouses, data lakes, and other data repositories • **Data integration**: Methods and technologies for integrating disparate data sources and systems to enable data sharing, collaboration, and interoperability across the organization • **Data security**: Controls, policies, and measures to protect sensitive data from unauthorized access, breaches, and misuse, as well as ensuring compliance with privacy regulations and laws

Data reporting, analytics, insights: Strategies, tools, and processes for leveraging data to drive actionable insights, support decision-making, and drive business outcomes

A *thick hub model* is one in which tools, processes, governance and advanced analytics capabilities are centrally housed, with basic reporting and simple analytics functions residing in the business units and functional teams. Companies lean towards a thick hub model when there is limited

Figure 1.1 Data operating models

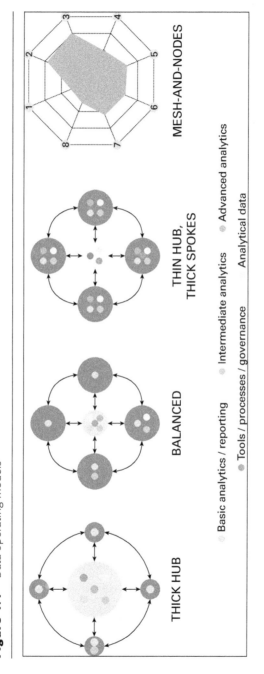

THICK HUB

BALANCED

THIN HUB,
THICK SPOKES

MESH-AND-NODES

- Basic analytics / reporting
- Intermediate analytics
- Advanced analytics
- Tools / processes / governance
- Analytical data

data and analytics maturity as well as limited resourcing that must be centrally managed and allocated to top strategic priorities.

By contrast, the *thick spoke model* is one in which even data science capabilities sit within the functional or business unit teams. The central data organization focuses primarily on setting standard data processes, tools, and governance. Some advanced modeling and niche skills may still reside centrally, and the hub still serves as a place to incubate new skills and AI advancements before they reach scale. A thick spoke model is typically chosen when business units are highly autonomous, when data and AI are prioritized as a competitive advantage in the market, and when data and analytics skills and rigor are very mature across the enterprise.

Most companies sit between these ends of the spectrum. Companies such as Tencent have successfully embedded a shared data profile across all of their businesses and extended ecosystem of partners, and this connects them in a way that was not previously possible.[19]

Some take a more balanced approach, where the central organization leads knowledge sharing and best practice development, or even manages spoke resourcing to centrally allocate resources to highest priority projects. In addition, not all spokes need to have the same capabilities: an organization might choose to have some business unit or functional spokes thicker than others, perhaps when a function such as marketing has very mature data science capabilities. Figure 1.1 illustrates the design options.

Some companies with very mature data governance, where data is also a product, can evolve past a thin hub, thick spoke model to an even more decentralized approach called "mesh and nodes". In this model, data domain ownership is decentralized, data is accessible across the organization in a self-service manner, and computational governance is federated and highly automated. (Chapter 4 offers more detail into data operating model options and choices and provides more information on the mesh and nodes model specifically.)

What matters most for enabling growth through innovation is not the specific data operating model you choose, but that you intentionally choose a model that fits your needs and maturity—and that you secure enterprise-wide buy-in and fully implement the model. Connecting data sources and maintaining high-quality data is no small feat. The experimentation function will not be the owners of the data within the customer 360—this requires owners and stewards across all sales interactions, service interactions, or product telemetry that might describe a customer's experience even if they don't formally interact with a company. The experimentation function, however, needs defined roles within the data operating model and the people in those roles need to be able to reply upon integrated, high-quality data from the organization.

Build the capability to innovate

As Clay Christensen puts it, "The very capabilities that propel an organization to succeed in sustaining circumstances will systematically bungle the best ideas for disruptive growth... An organization's capabilities become its disabilities when disruption is afoot."[20]

Discovery—through sensing internally and externally, turning data into insights, and center-supported experimentation—is the start. Turning this into a repeatable capability that can turn promising experiments into profitable products requires an additional set of capabilities and design choices.

Companies that consistently grow over time have been well studied to understand what makes them different.[21] A recent review of more than 2,000 companies by Blasé and Leinwand revealed unsurprising findings:[22] "The highest-performing organizations invested in a *growth system*, an integrated collection of capabilities and assets that drive both short-term and long-term growth." The power of deliberate assemblage of a growth engine enables these companies to escape the treadmill of incremental brand extensions, discounting and promotions, and investments that simply return too little to shareholders. Many companies do not succeed at building these muscles because it is difficult to do.

The operating model must build these capabilities, and it is important to establish clear ownership or sponsorship for each. Examples of the kinds of capability that companies are building or enhancing today, and where they are often owned, include:

- Ideation, co-creation of personas and concepts (strategy or customer marketing)
- Innovation pipeline and lean portfolio management (the CEO and team, supported by program management)
- CX (customer experience) visioning and customer journey development (marketing)
- Product and service-offering development (the business unit)
- New product and service launch in specified channels (sales, marketing, and/or product management)
- Brand innovation and consumer engagement (brand marketing)
- Digital commerce (the commercial organization)
- Supply chain agility (supply chain management).

Where these capabilities live, who sponsors them, and how they are developed and governed over time are important operating model questions. Considerations for making foundational choices are explored in the following sections.

Innovation centers

Companies that have little variety in products and low product development velocity are candidates for separate innovation structures. Concentration of revenue in a narrow offering is meaningful because a dominant product or service offering tends to dominate innovation funding. These core, long-lasting products often have a long list of incremental investment projects that consume large sums of capital.

An example of a company with low product variety is a high-tech company that historically has focused on products such as two-way radios, body cameras, push-to-talk cellular devices, and in-car camera systems. While these products do serve a variety of industries, including military, law enforcement, mining, and oil and gas, the range of product technology is very narrow. When this company entered the as-a-service market, it needed to create a separate innovation engine to ensure that investment in developing completely new data-as-a-service, software-as-a-service, and other offerings were not overshadowed by investment in improving the core product and multi-billion-dollar business.

The other consideration, product development velocity, is the speed with which products generally progress through the product development life cycle or innovation funnel. A low product development velocity is measured in months and years, typically due to factors such as regulation.

A consumer goods company, with a single-category business in a market that demanded fast product development cycles, faced stalled growth and a troubling history of failed innovations driven from inside the brand groups. Executives opted to establish a growth and innovation incubator that would own category extensions, both organic and acquired. New capabilities and talent were placed in the center, reporting to the CEO. Within two years, the business successfully launched a new product and scaled it in a disciplined way in selected markets.

Innovation embedded in the businesses

When product variety and product development velocity is high, it is often best to embed innovation responsibilities within the business units. A company with a high diversity of products typically has had to experiment across industries, segments, and channels to end up with such a diverse product and has thus developed experimentation as a strong competency within the core business.

Mature product stage gates and exit criteria, lean portfolio management, and frameworks for connecting strategic goals with a specific product's performance during testing are all important for a mature experimentation function. These capabilities also all correlate to a high product development velocity. Center-led, advanced development teams often support these business unit groups, bringing best practices and specialized technical skills to the process. They may also develop new product platforms that serve as integrators across separate but related product lines.

RTX, the aerospace and defense company assembled through the merger of United Technologies aerospace and Raytheon defense business, operates through three powerful product divisions, each with its own deep engineering organization, reflecting the diversity of technologies in its products (GPS and communications, missiles, jet propulsion, and aerospace componentry).[23] A robust and well-resourced engineering organization delivers advanced innovation platforms that are key to developing the "connected battlefield" vision of the future. AI-enabled communications and gateway technology systems rapidly distribute data across componentry and, ultimately, coalition partners.

Connecting center and business-led innovation

When a company launches an ambitious new product, it may make the most sense to start with a focused innovation organization and then embed this newly established set of capabilities back in the business unit. This is where Accenture's concept of the *wise pivot*[24] becomes an important consideration—knowing how to gradually invest more in the new products and services without prematurely diminishing the core business. The balance and timing for the pivot will be different for all organizations, but the conditions to drive decision-making around the pivot must be defined and understood.

For example, a high-tech company was able to grow billions in revenue by successfully disrupting established brands through premium products and design. It started with a powerful and independent research and innovation unit. This function was intentionally independent from the sales and marketing organization so that it could focus on driving breakthrough innovation protected by long-term KPIs and significant budgets. However, as the company grew globally and competitors quickly copied features, the need arose to become more consumer-insight-driven, with faster incremental innovations and greater discipline around innovation budget return on investment. Leaders evolved the innovation model to become much more closely integrated to the core business. In parallel, the independent model was maintained to drive breakthrough innovation in line with the overall strategy. Portfolio management was used at the enterprise level to inform priorities across a much more complex innovation plan. To date, this multi-speed model has enabled the organization to achieve double-digit growth, both in existing and new categories.

Sometimes an innovation center serves a useful purpose and can then be disbanded. An example is the approach that Accenture took in building its digital business footprint over seven years. In 2013, Accenture proclaimed that every business was a digital business[25]—a statement that now seems obvious, but back then was considered bold (the US census estimated that, in the US retail market in 2013, e-commerce accounted for only 5.8 percent of total sales). Accenture believed that digital, data, and analytics were the next growth frontier. It had acquired, as well as organically grown, analytics and digital capabilities and, rather than keep these teams small with minimal support infrastructure, Accenture formalized them into a business.

In 2014, Accenture established a new business unit called Accenture Digital, which included Accenture Analytics (data and analytics services to drive insights at scale), Accenture Interactive (marketing and digital transformation solutions), and Accenture Mobility (mobility solutions for connected product offerings). This new business unit was to collaborate with and serve consulting, technology, and operations. It was given dedicated corporate functional support to reflect the differences in business model from the core divisions. Processes and policies, interaction models between other business units, metrics, and culture were defined and implemented. In 2020, the business had scaled sufficiently that Accenture broke apart the unit and integrated components back into its core business. Data, AI, and mobility became part of the core businesses, while the marketing-specific offerings stayed together and became their own business unit, now called Song.

Finally, the idea of using an acquisition as the innovation center and connecting it to business unit innovation is a powerful idea and can avoid the need to start up a center capability, but is not easy to execute. The Mars confectionary business found its way into "healthy" snacking by acquiring a "better-for-you" snacking platform in its Kind-branded cereal bars.[26] The acquired business, with its unique consumer proposition, has become an innovation center for the legacy business—a place to plug in other acquisitions and develop new product ideas. Kind is run relatively separately from the core candy and chewing gum brands, but there is intentional integration in the commercial front-end with channel management organization in order to gain benefits of scale with trade partners. The intention is to move towards a harmonized approach to managing elements of the supply chain to bring benefits of scale to the healthy snacking business while retaining the ability of the supply chain to flex to meet distinct differences required of the powerful Mars brands.

Design the innovative enterprise

Growth through innovation is not just about new products and services; it is about how the entire organization operates and delivers. When and how to integrate across organizational boundaries between the new and the core is a central problem to solve. We have looked at how data can be a powerful mechanism to make stronger connections and to find deeper and more relevant insights into customers. In addition, a culture of organizational learning and the capacity to "absorb" changing customer expectations and new, tech-enabled ways of working are key enablers. The enterprise operating model components of structure, business process, talent, metrics, and incentives all need to be aligned with the bounds of the firm, as well as with ecosystem partners.

Connecting the core to the new

We have looked at considerations for designing data capability and how to link center and business unit innovation activities, so now we extend our thinking to what needs to change across the enterprise to support truly new business models.

Figure 1.2   The front/back organizational model

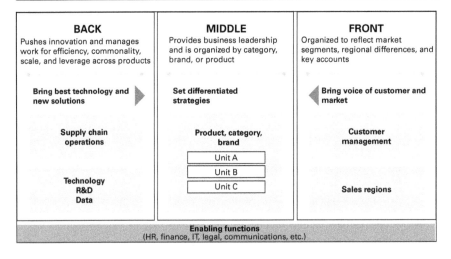

BACK	MIDDLE	FRONT
Pushes innovation and manages work for efficiency, commonality, scale, and leverage across products	Provides business leadership and is organized by category, brand, or product	Organized to reflect market segments, regional differences, and key accounts
Bring best technology and new solutions	Set differentiated strategies	Bring voice of customer and market
Supply chain operations	Product, category, brand	Customer management
	Unit A	
	Unit B	
Technology R&D Data	Unit C	Sales regions

Enabling functions
(HR, finance, IT, legal, communications, etc.)

We start with understanding the overall architecture of the business. It is helpful to consider the three major operating model components of a business[27] when choosing where to separate and where to integrate new business models into the legacy corporate structure. Nearly every company is built, by design or by happenstance, around three major sets of responsibility, as shown in Figure 1.2:

- Commercial **front** end (sales, market, and customer management)
- Lines of business—the strategic **middle** (product, brand, category management business units)
- Platforms and **back**-end services (technology, fulfillment, shared services).

This framework allows leadership to take a modular and systematic approach to alternatives. Leaders can readily test options by moving organizational components in and out of the three major blocks of responsibility, then create scenarios for wiring close collaboration across the boundaries through horizontal ways of working, different metrics, and aligned incentives.

The central questions around the enterprise-level view of the growth-oriented operating model include:

- Who should own the overall business plan and offering strategy?
- Where does profit and loss (P&L) accountability reside?
- How unique and differentiated, by line of business, will the commercial business process need to be in order for the new offering to succeed in the market (versus remaining within a consolidated front end)? What efficiencies will we trade for focus?
- How differentiated does supply chain and fulfillment need to be for our ventures and fast-growth businesses?
- To what extent can all digital capabilities be centrally managed and delivered to support this new business versus the need for dedication? If dedicated, for how long?
- What shared services at the enterprise level should be leveraged across core and new lines of business?

We have seen a common trend emerging across multiple industries where organizations are combining hardware (which may have been the traditional "products") with digitally enabled software (services) to provide customers with enhanced, more expansive, data-rich, and personalized solutions. Particularly interesting here is that this shift has been successfully delivered without the need for a fundamental change in the operating model. In many cases, the lines of business or divisions that deliver the core products have remained intact to ensure focus is retained on evolution and continuous improvement. New capabilities have been built to complement the existing business and to focus on developing digital technologies that become the foundation for joining up across the products and delivering services and solutions. The commercial teams at the front end of the organization, often organized geographically, have then evolved from selling conventional products to tailoring and selling bundled services and solutions to customers (and to understanding their precise requirements so these can be personalized).

What has changed and has required significant investment is that the skills and experience required to engage with customers around bundled solutions are very different from those required to drive basic product sales. This evolution towards greater focus on services and solutions has also necessitated a shift in P&L accountability away from lines of business and divisions towards the front of the organization. A further enabler of this model is ensuring a shared back-end of the organization and common platforms that support the entire business.

The strategic middle is largely associated with product management and is usually where the offering is conceived, developed, and managed for profitability across the life cycle of the offering. This is where traditional product and service innovation takes place. The key design question for new business models and truly innovative products is whether a heavyweight business unit is needed (with dedicated strategy, marketing, product management, supply chain, and finance) or whether this new line of business can be managed within an existing line of business. Degrees of dedication are determined largely by the same criteria we have previously outlined relative to benefits of separation versus integration into the core. When the new business model is radically outside the culture and cadence of the core business, a separate strategic middle or business-line organization makes sense. Deere and Co. succeeded fully with this approach in standing up its precision agriculture data-based business unit—a data services business that would likely not have succeeded had it remained in a core equipment division.

When a company has a portfolio of products and services, the work of leaders is to design the right focus for each line of business and the right weight of connections. This sophisticated enterprise model may create complexity for leaders, but also creates a clear logic and competitive advantage that a simpler, one-size-fits-all approach lacks.

Building absorptive capacity

Sophisticated enterprise models designed to support growth through innovation put stress on leaders. Cohen and Levinthal, economists and professors who conduct organizational research, have found that "absorptive capacity" is a useful predictor of a company's ability to grow and innovate.[28] They define absorptive capacity as the ability of an organization to recognize the value of new information, assimilate it, and apply it to commercial ends. Absorptive capacity has traditionally focused on R&D capabilities, but there is applicability for the whole enterprise when considering what is required to successfully integrate and scale new frontiers. Let's look at one very practical way of building absorptive capacity.

Scaling innovation at the enterprise level is an ambitious task. The challenge is sustaining energy on growth ideas when metrics and past successes direct management focus to legacy profit centers. Kates and Kesler[29] have argued that enterprise operating models should tailor and line up all elements of Galbraith's Star Model[30]—strategy, structure, process, metrics, rewards, and people practices—to enable the organization to flex around the different stages of new product and brand innovation. Building on the work of Geoffrey Moore,[31] the authors take an organizational view of the challenges that large companies face in managing competing priorities that get in the way of taking risks on new ventures that may not produce measurable returns in the near term. Solving the innovator's dilemma[32] requires enterprise-level change in fundamental ways of working across boundaries, changes in what is measured and what is incentivized, and changes in the way data and technology are incorporated into the business, ultimately leading to a different mindset and collective know-how across the leadership team.

Based on his years of advisory experience with Silicone Valley startups and digital natives, Moore, in his book *Zone to Win*,[33] lays out a thoughtful framework for managing a very focused portfolio of investments, aimed at moving disruptive innovations through four phases of an innovation cycle—while maintaining necessary focus on the core business. As shown in Figure 1.3, this framework provides the foundation for organization strategists to configure structure, process, and metrics that drive the right agile behaviors and decision-making in the face of competing priorities across all four innovation phases:

1 **Incubation**—nurturing the very new venture

2 **Transformation**—beginning to scale the new in a still fragile state

3 **Performance**—transitioning to full commercial scale

4 **Productivity**—managing the asset for maximum profitability in order to fund next-generation ventures.

Figure 1.3   Innovation zones

	DISRUPTIVE INNOVATIONS	SUSTAINING INNOVATIONS
REVENUE PERFORMANCE	*Transformation zone* *Horizon 2*	*Performance zone* *Horizon 1*
ENABLING INVESTMENTS	*Incubation zone* *Horizon 3*	*Productivity zone* *Horizon 1*

Management decisions and behaviors need to adapt to the varied nature of the task in each zone. Timing of moves is a critical part of this approach:

- What elements of the new venture should be structurally separated and what portions should be integrated with the core, and when, across the four zones?
- What talent and resource dedication are needed in each zone?
- What level of autonomy and decision rights should be granted to the team managing the venture in each zone?
- What metrics for customer uptake, technical viability, sales, profitability, and return on investment should be applied, and when?
- What decision forums and venture sponsorship will be needed to maintain the right management attention to this venture over time?
- What support and know-how (data, analytics, insights, scientific staff, and so on) will be required from other parts of the organization?

The ability to flex the arrangement of roles, processes, data, talent, and metrics over time, across the four zones (the development cycle) enhances the capacity of the company to absorb innovation. The role of senior leaders is to orchestrate investment, management focus, and timing so that the core organization avoids becoming overwhelmed and distracted.

Identifying and managing the tipping point in the transition from incubation to transformation is the most complex part of the journey and the most difficult one for most companies. The transformation zone is not a place on the organization chart but a distinct leadership focus, owned at the top. It is both art and science; data informed, but requiring wisdom and judgment. Creating the right linkages to core functions and value-stream elements, such as supply chain in the back and field sales at the front, is important in setting a path for scaling the venture.

The idea is to replicate the system for multiple ventures with the process and decision-making getting better with practice. With the right leadership engagement at the top, these become deeply seated ways of working. The culture begins to change. The ability to absorb new data and ascribe new meaning, to place customer value in the center of decision-making, and to reprioritize investments are realized through repetition, channeled through a new mental model.

Aligning metrics for growth

Metrics and incentives are a critical, and often overlooked operating-model component for building the innovation-led growth system. Horizontal ways of working—collaborating at scale across business units, functions, and geographic markets—are nearly impossible with conventional, individually oriented metrics and incentives. What rational executive would invest in a potentially disruptive new product that will not quickly deliver profit consistent with today's expectations and requires investment in production equipment that replaces fully depreciated machinery? The answer depends on how the executive is measured and rewarded.

Often, new products and new business models must be sheltered from the destructive effects of P&Ls and return-on-asset measures. Moore argues that these early-stage opportunities should instead be measured on the basis of technical viability and customer uptake.[34] The sales force expected to bring new products to market must be measured on the right mix of new and core offerings, rather than a single overall target that allows them to sell what is easiest in order to achieve their goal.

It is important for companies to be granular and specific about the new business outcomes that the organization wants to deliver, and to make real-time data part of the review process. Organizations must set near-term targets to track progress and be able to make quick course corrections in scaling new products. New metrics and data will prompt the right conversations, with shorter cycle times and a willingness to make hard decisions to cancel sprints or programs that are not likely to be successful.

For example, the Diageo-backed accelerator program, Distill Ventures, invested in Seedlip one year after the company was created. Two years later, this led to Diageo acquiring the alcohol-free spirit brand, and establishing itself as a leader in the low-no alcohol category.[35] Diageo had a playbook for newly integrated businesses and brands, which allowed acquisitions to rapidly access Diageo's core competitive advantages en route to market, supply chain, and marketing. The parent company provided investment relief for general managers to support growth of the new brand, while also applying a different set of metrics to the newly acquired business.

OKRs

Objectives and key results (OKRs) were popularized by Google, but they have been used since the 1970s. OKRs comprise an objective and goal-setting system driving delivery of specific outcomes in a defined period of time (which is often shorter than the time frame required to get real insight from a more traditional functional metric). The approach is to define a concrete objective and three to five measurable results. Teams working cross-functionally on projects appreciate the system's simplicity and relevance to outcome delivery. Google has said that use of OKRs has had a 10-times multiplier on their ability to drive growth.[36]

From an innovation perspective, OKRs can be useful to align functions that play a role in the success of the new venture. Each function may have different deliverables that are role-specific, but all key results must converge on the new venture's outcomes and timelines. All senior leaders across the organization must be aligned and committed around the new business outcomes. The bigger the bet, the more presence venture-type targets will have in the overall measurement mix.

Executive metrics

Shared executive metrics is another way to support innovation and new ventures. Accenture is one of many companies today that have established a strong innovation and growth culture by changing the way senior leaders are recognized and rewarded for "shared success". Top leaders are expected to work across services business units, geographic market units, and industry-focused teams to serve customers, create new solutions, and support new areas of growth—and their bonuses are directly tied to the overall business performance, not just their specific business line.

Some large and diverse companies, however, report that, even when compensation policy is changed and all top executive bonuses are based on enterprise-wide results, behaviors are slow to change. The consistent finding is that top executive routines, especially meeting agendas and quarterly business reviews and capital allocation sessions, continue to drive individual decision-making and recognition. Power and status motivators are real, and CEOs would do well to focus on breaking down these added barriers to innovation. The quality of conversations at the top and in the boardroom is both a leading indicator and an enabler of an innovation-oriented culture.

Creating a culture of continuous learning

Talent is always at the top of the growth company agenda. There is an increasing agreement among business leaders about the very real necessity to strengthen the connection of human and machine collaboration.[37] AI is both a problem to solve and a part of the solution. Human and machine and AI are recent examples, but whatever the skills needed for success at the next growth frontier are, they will almost always be in short supply. The key to rapidly adapting your business when skills are scarce is creating a culture of continuous learning. As a company navigates its way to a digitally literate workforce and culture, the ability to enable technical experts to upskill and integrate new technology into their work is foundational to innovation.

The concept of absorptive capacity—the ability of an organization to recognize the value of new information, assimilate it, and apply it to commercial ends—is useful again here. The idea of a continuous learning culture is once again popular. The design of the operating model can help create this culture.

Flattening the organization and removing layers can accelerate learning up and down the organization. Reducing barriers to information based on status can reduce bureaucratic burden, giving employees more time to collaborate on new ideas. Removing boundaries enables more horizontal ways of working that expose all employees to more elements of the business, including the voice of the customer. Engineers talking to marketers, finance, and sales and product people is an example of a path that leads to absorptive capacity through learning.

In a recent study, 94 percent of workers said they wanted to learn new skills to work with GenAI, but only 5 percent of organizations provide GenAI training at scale.[38] Accenture has addressed this issue with its own employees. On her first day in 2019 as the new CEO of Accenture, Julie Sweet announced the launch of Technology Quotient. All employees—today, a workforce of 725,000 people—are mandated to take an extensive curriculum of digital technology and data basics. Courses are continually added to reflect new technologies and advances. Many companies achieve similar benefits and encourage learning at work. 3M's "15% Culture", for example, encourages employees to set aside a portion of their work time to proactively cultivate and pursue innovative ideas that excite them.[39]

The shifting role and requirements of leaders must not be underestimated in these new models for growth through innovation. Many senior leaders have grown up in traditional functional and hierarchical models where the role of the leader is to drive steady year-on-year growth based on a consistent set of defined metrics. We are now in a world where the leader may own the accountability for delivery of an outcome but not the resource, where leaders have to embrace disruption and manage the impact on their organization, where answers are not always obvious and experimentation and failure have become part of the process, and where employee expectations of what they will get from their careers has evolved considerably.

Extending to the ecosystem

Increasingly, disruptive innovation capability is being extended to ecosystem partners as a way to manage risk and potentially increase return on investment. Pharmaceutical and biotech companies have been working in these extended models in recent years, exchanging mutually beneficial research and other resources, with big pharma benefiting substantially from biotech innovation, while the biotechs gain faster geographic market reach. Many of the OEMs in the automotive industry have built venture capital teams separate from the core business to invest specifically in future capabilities, creating value for all the participants in the ecosystem.

Businesses that seek the benefits of personalized digital connectivity with their customers often need to rely on partners to build these powerful links. An example is the relationship between technology providers and the strategic partners who configure and install the technology. Technology solution vendors, software vendors, systems integrators, resellers, and managed services partners work with technology suppliers. Cloud services from Microsoft, Amazon and Google in particular have created ecosystems where firms can be competitors, partners or suppliers, depending on the solution being created. This dynamic system leads to innovation across the players.

For example, VMware manages numerous co-innovation programs with its customers and thousands of provider partners, cultivating an internal culture of innovation and extending this cultural trait to its customers and partners in the ecosystem. In 2023, VMware and Nvidia debuted a joint offering for customers to unlock the power of GenAI, enabling customers to customize models and applications.[40] Leaders in this space note that it is impossible to invent in isolation today. When these providers invent something new, it will inevitably be extended across the peer community.

We also see consumers and customers playing a more active role in the innovation of new products and services. This not only results in more relevant innovations but creates a much stronger relationship between companies and their customers. For example, LEGO's Ideas platform allows consumers to submit ideas for new products, and to vote and provide feedback on others.[41] Ideas that receive over 10,000 votes are reviewed, and if selected, the submitter has the opportunity to work with the LEGO team to make their idea a reality, and receive royalties on product sales.

Consider too the case where a group of firms join forces to share a common platform for providing energy and resources for their export business. In *Designing Adaptive Organizations*, John Matthews describes the case of firms working together to create a solution to the shared need for water in the textile dyeing process in the form of a water-treatment plant that circulates 90 percent recycled water to all businesses.[42] The plant incorporates a solar facility for drying the sludge that is generated and then links with a nearby cement plant to supply the powder-dry sludge as an input to the cement-making process. The result means that firms are jointly operating a zero-liquid discharge system: the remaining 10 percent evaporates through solar means, and no wastewater is discharged into the environment. This switch from a linear to a circular flow applies innovative coordination mechanisms to gain both financial and sustainability benefits.

Innovation through ecosystem partnerships depends upon a strong set of partnering features that include:

- Joint business planning for alignment on goals, funding, and timelines
- Prioritization of funds on key areas of values streams that drive the most revenue and profit
- Different metrics and incentives to maximize the value of the ecosystem
- Wiring connections forward and backward with partner and customer teams to blur boundaries
- Orchestrating the whole and reducing friction across partner teams
- Shared data and technology integration where it makes sense.

Conclusion: Fueling innovation-led growth

Innovation has always played an important role in growth; different today are the pace of change and the degree to which new technologies and data are driving business model innovation. To succeed, companies need to identify and build the next growth frontier, then integrate the new business.

The first step to growth through innovation is the rapid identification of breakthrough business models. Innovation-led growth is not only about experimenting and inventing; for large corporations, it is also about identifying what is being invented elsewhere and quickly building, buying, or creating ecosystem partnerships to scale this new growth frontier.

Corporations should invest in experimentation and must extensively leverage data through a strong data foundation and democratized insights close to the customer. Data is critical to innovation-led growth: it allows companies to create more customer-centric and more integrated solutions, it becomes its own potential product with data monetization, and it enables corporations to test and learn. Effective and efficient data use requires an agreed data operating model across the full enterprise (technology *and* the business). The specific model chosen will vary by data maturity and business strategy; the key to success is not the specific model but that the model is implemented across the enterprise.

When building the capability to innovate, consider an innovation center separate from the core business when the corporation has low product variety and low product development velocity. Conversely, consider an embedded innovation capability when product variety and development velocity are high. Regardless of where the innovation capability is housed, connecting the center and business-led innovation capabilities is critical. The degree of integration should become tighter as the new growth frontier scales, but customer expectations require that the new business always has some connection to the core business (such as shared and integrated data for customers).

Finally, innovation at scale in the enterprise relies on the absorptive capacity and an enterprise-wide culture of continuous learning, aligned metrics for growth across all levels and functions, and strong ecosystem partnerships where co-innovation occurs.

Key takeaways

- The next growth frontier is identified through investment in experimentation, leveraging data extensively, underpinned by an enterprise-wide data operating model.

- The placement of the innovation capability is determined by product variety and development velocity—kept separate from the core business when both are low and embedded in the core business when both are high.

- Center-led and business-led innovation capabilities should be connected—the degree of integration should be tighter as the new growth frontier scales, but customer expectations require that the new business always have some connection to the core business.

- Absorptive capacity should be created through an enterprise-wide culture of continuous learning, aligned metrics for growth across all levels and functions, and a strong ecosystem of partnerships where co-innovation takes place.

- Targeted, strategic hires should be made but your talent should be brought along on the journey through the implementation of a thoughtful learning approach that extends beyond classroom curriculum—both enterprise-wide (e.g. data literacy) and function-specific (e.g. solution selling for sales).

Notes

1 Accenture (2024) *Technology Vision 2024. Human by Design. How AI unleashes the next level of human potential.* accenture.com/content/dam/accenture/final/accenture-com/document-2/Accenture-Tech-Vision-2024.pdf (archived at https://perma.cc/L5T4-5FQE).

2 Nasdaq (2023) Diving Deep into the AI Value Chain, December 18. nasdaq.com/articles/diving-deep-into-the-ai-value-chain (archived at https://perma.cc/CLE3-X76K).

3 CVS Health (2024) About. cvshealth.com/about.html (archived at https://perma.cc/LQ9V-4WDA).

4 Live Nation (2023) *2023 Annual Report.* https://d1io3yog0oux5.cloudfront.net/_166e4467cc2a54cd5a7f702f35e9b921/livenationentertainment/db/670/6302/annual_report/2023+Annual+Report.pdf (archived at https://perma.cc/JB78-ME5V).

5 Medtronic (2024) Our Company. medtronic.com/ uk -en/our-company.html (archived at https://perma.cc/C6PK-JP8V).

6 Research and Markets (2024) Medtronic Plc – Digital Transformation Strategies, May 2024.

7 Kidder, D. and Christina W. (2019) *New to Big: How Companies Can Create Like Entrepreneurs, Invest Like VCs, and Install a Permanent Operating System for Growth*, New York: Currency.

8 Drucker, P.F. (1967) The Effective Decision, *Harvard Business Review*, January. hbr.org/1967/01/the-effective-decision (archived at https://perma.cc/GB23-7XYW).

9   Amazon (2024) About AWS. aws.amazon.com/about-aws/#:~:text=Since%20
     launching%20in%202006%2C%20Amazon,and%20lives%20for%20
     the%20better (archived at https://perma.cc/8E83-DHJJ).

10 Forbes (2020) A Look Back at Ten Years of Microsoft Azure. forbes.com/sites/
     janakirammsv/2020/02/03/a-look-back-at-ten-years-of-microsoft-azure
     (archived at https://perma.cc/SF2K-6KP9).

11 Microsoft Source (2024) Microsoft Cloud Strength Fuels Third Quarter
     Results, April 25. news.microsoft.com/2024/04/25/microsoft-cloud-strength-
     fuels-third-quarter-results-3 (archived at https://perma.cc/NK2Z-SLUB).

12 Jowitt, T. (2021) Microsoft Thrives Thanks to Azure Growth. silicon.co.uk/
     workspace/operating-system/microsoft-azure-growth-408982 (archived at
     https://perma.cc/MV3P-VWRT).

13 Forbes (2020).

14 Gore (2024) The Gore Story. gore.com/about/the-gore-story (archived at
     https://perma.cc/T94H-QMM5).

15 CDK Global (2023) Dial Down the High-Pressure Sales Experience to Win
     Today's Car Shoppers, October 23. cdkglobal.com/insights/dial-down-high-
     pressure-sales-experience-win-todays-car-shoppers (archived at https://perma.
     cc/PNW6-QBE4).

16 *The Week* (2023) How Tesla's Direct Sales Model is Roiling the Car Dealership
     Industry, June 21. theweek.com/us/1024416/tesla- vs -car-dealerships (archived
     at https://perma.cc/E946-HMUQ).

17 Koetsier, J. (2023) Pepsi, Mobile, and Generative AI: Engaging with billions of
     customers one on one. *Singular*, November 27. singular.net/blog/ pepsi -mobile
     (archived at https://perma.cc/3F5H-JZ5D).

18 Volition Beauty (2024) About Us. volitionbeauty.com/pages/ about_us
     (archived at https://perma.cc/J2Y3-KNUC).

19 Forbes (2018) How Tencent is Using Closed Loop Data to Drive Better Insight
     and Engagement, January 9. forbes.com/sites/kimberlywhitler/2018/01/09/
     how-tencent-is-using-closed-loop-data-to-drive-better-insight-and-engagement
     (archived at https://perma.cc/3GMU-LWPP).

20 Christensen, C.M. (1997) *The Innovator's Dilemma: When New Technologies
     Cause Great Firms to Fail*, 1st edn, Cambridge, MA: Harvard Business Review
     Press.

21 Patrick, V., Smit, S., and Baghai, M. (2007) *The Granularity of Growth:
     Making Choices That Drive Enduring Company Performance*, Singapore and
     London: Cyan Books / Marshall Cavendish.

22 Blase, P. and Leinwand, P. (2024) Create a System to Grow Consistently: Five
     elements can move you beyond episodic success, *Harvard Business Review*,
     March–April.

23 RTX Corporation (2024) Our Businesses. rtx.com/who-we-are/our-businesses
     (archived at https://perma.cc/98PW-4PVM).

24 Abbosh, O., Nunes P., and Downes L. (2019) *Pivot to the Future: Discovering Value and Creating Growth in a Disrupted World*, New York: PublicAffairs.

25 Accenture (2013) Accenture Technology Vision 2013 Report Highlights, February 19.

26 Mars (2020) KIND and Mars Announce Next Step in Partnership to Build a Kinder World…, November 17.

27 Kates, A., Kesler, G., and DiMartino, M. (2021) *Networked, Scaled, and Agile: A Design Strategy for Complex Organizations*, London: Kogan Page.

28 Cohen, W.M. and Levinthal, D.A. (1990) Absorptive Capacity: A new perspective on learning and innovation, *ASQ*, 35, 128–152.

29 Kates et al. (2021).

30 Galbraith, J.R. (1995) *Designing Organizations: An Executive Briefing on Strategy, Structure, and Process*, San Francisco: Jossey-Bass.

31 Moore, G.A. (2015) *Zone to Win: Organizing to Compete in an Age of Disruption*, New York: Diversion Publishing.

32 Christensen (1997).

33 Moore (2015).

34 Moore, G.A. (2014) *Crossing the Chasm: Marketing and selling disruptive products to mainstream customers*, New York: Collins Business Essentials.

35 Diageo (2019) Diageo Acquires Majority Shareholding in Seedlip, the World's First Distilled Non-alcoholic Spirit, August 7.

36 Celen, S. (2021) *OKR. Master the Performance Framework that Google Perfected: Create & Achieve Your Top Startup and Personal Goals Using the Leading Innovation Management System*, self-published, July 6.

37 Accenture (2024) *Technology Vision 2024*, January 9.

38 Accenture (2024) Work, Workforce, Workers: Reinvented in the age of generative AI. accenture.com/content/dam/accenture/final/accenture-com/document-2/Accenture-Work-Can-Become-Era-Generative-AI.pdf (archived at https://perma.cc/W7S8-EJX9)

39 3M (2024) 3M's 15% Culture. 3m.co.uk/3M/ en_GB /careers/culture/15-percent-culture (archived at https://perma.cc/Y7F4-L72W).

40 Himanshu, S. (2024) Announcing Initial Availability of VMware Private AI Foundation with NVIDIA, VMware blog, March 18.

41 LEGO (2024) LEGO Ideas. ideas.lego.com (archived at https://perma.cc/7ZJF-Q957).

42 Matthews, J.A. (2024) *Designing Adaptive Organizations* (Chapter 6: Circular Organizing), Cambridge: Cambridge University Press.

Manage Cost and Complexity

02

CHERENE POWELL, ROB RUBIN

Contributors: Thomas Haslinger, Chris Roark

Cost comes from many sources, including procurement of goods, facilities, infrastructure, vendors, and partners. But the largest cost for many companies remains people. Not only the direct costs of compensation but also the indirect costs of management and internal support. On top of these are the invisible coordination and unrewarded complexity costs that head-count growth often brings.

When times are good, organizations tend to become bloated. Jobs are added ahead of growth, projects are launched, performance management is lax, and acquisitions aren't integrated with discipline. Expenses rise and having too many units and people involved in decisions slows output. At some point, the pain becomes great enough that something must be done.

When a company's executives realize they must reduce labor costs, the collective feeling is usually a combination of frustration, fear, and anxiety. Most senior leaders have gone through at least one experience where costs were cut from the wrong places or from the right places in the wrong way. Often, cost-reduction targets are created using external benchmarks, and then leaders are forced to draw red Xs on organization charts. The logic to determine where the Xs are placed is often quite simplistic: consolidate or split teams; eliminate functional support for some business nodes; reduce the highest paid, least tenured, or those managing too few direct reports. More recently, employees who predominately work virtually are also more likely to be targeted.[1]

Downsizing remains the most highly visible way to demonstrate to the investor community that leaders are serious about cost and productivity. Look no further than the 7.5 percent boost to Spotify's share price in December 2023 on its announcement of a 17 percent reduction to its global workforce[2] or FedEx's three-year stock price high after announcing its plan to cut costs.[3] Such stock boosts are often fleeting, however, when it becomes clear that the underlying cost drivers haven't changed. If the work and ways of working are not redesigned while the organization is downsized, costs tend to creep back in. In fact, research indicates that most companies witness little to no sustained financial return following a reduction in workforce.[4]

A modern approach to reducing labor costs and complexity can change the way an organization performs work. It aligns core business strategy with labor allocation, and it is clear-headed about the impact of two types of decisions: big, strategic choices that fundamentally shift how the company does business; and operational choices that enable greater productivity.

Complexity is a determining contributor of a company's cost structure. But, when we untangle organizational complexity, design the right work that maps to a lean workforce, and align to an intentionally designed company culture, we accelerate productivity and business performance. This modern approach is made possible by:

- New methodologies and technologies to analyze and diagnose business operations including products, services, geographies, and the broader operating model construct
- The power of new technology to decipher work routines
- The promise of artificial intelligence and automation to eliminate work in previously unthinkable ways, and scale businesses at a much lower marginal cost.

Over the course of this chapter, we will discuss several ways to take a modern approach to labor cost and complexity management by:

- Aligning your labor strategy with your business strategy
- Shifting your foundational cost structure
- Optimizing ways of working to increase productivity.

Align labor strategy with business strategy

The approach starts with understanding how to orient your labor allocation strategy around the drivers of growth and market differentiation unique to your business. Knowing what you need to preserve and protect and where you need to invest is the first step in shaping an optimized and sustainable cost structure. Michael Porter's economic theory of competitive differentiation[5] provides a framework to prioritize all business units, geographies, and functions in the context of *growth potential* and *desired differentiation*. This creates clarity in investment priorities and serves as a tool to align leaders around where to invest and where to optimize.

Figure 2.1 Prioritization framework: growth and differentiation ambition

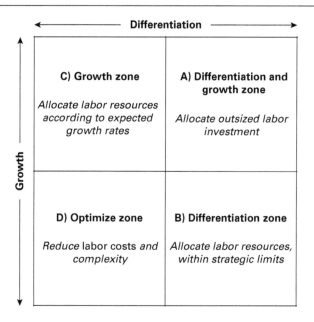

Zone A in Figure 2.1 represents areas where a company should allocate outsized investment. Zone A should drive 60–80 percent of expected growth and differentiation and therefore requires prioritization and protection. In high-growth companies, this zone is frequently the home for the latest product and service innovations that drive leading price-to-earnings ratios in the market. This zone can also include emerging products or services, countries with attractive demographics, or perhaps data and analytic capabilities that the business needs to grow. A recent example is Nvidia's big push into AI hardware and software during the heightened demand for generative AI.[6]

Zone B represents areas where a company should allocate labor resources but within limits and in a carefully monitored way. Zone B often contains "horizon 3" business areas, with products and services that create significant differentiation within the market but are not necessarily proven core revenue growth drivers today. Examples include Meta's metaverse investment or Apple's virtual reality headset investment.[7] Zone B could also represent an investment in internal operations, such as an employee learning program that the company believes allows it to attract, develop, and retain talent, which will eventually contribute to the creation of market differentiating products and services. The Zone B segmentation is important because, although the company should allocate more than a "baseline" level of labor, the company must resist temptation to over-allocate when the proven ROI is less than other zones.

Zone C represents areas where the company should allocate labor resources relative to expected growth rates. These are business areas that are expected to drive growth but do not necessarily create meaningful market differentiation. Often, the company is executing on an expansion plan into adjacent areas or following others in innovation. An example is the expansion of an existing, commoditized product into a hypergrowth geography, such as Starbucks rapidly expanding in India.[8] Or, it could simply allow a company to catch a market trend, like J.P. Morgan launching JPM Coin.[9] In these instances, the company should look to support anticipated growth by allocating precisely the right level of resources aligned with these growth rates. The goal of this zone for most companies is cost-effective growth with a lens on margin, not just revenue.

This brings us to Zone D, where companies should focus their attention on reducing resource allocation. In our experience, at least 50 percent of business operations fall into this zone. To be clear, optimize does not mean eliminate; nor does it mean low revenue, low value, or low risk work. It simply means that the company should pursue all available options to reduce complexity and lower cost structures, while continuing to deliver minimum viable business outcomes. In our experience, larger and more mature areas of the business are often the best candidates for optimization. This can be true in the core business, such as when Comcast's Sky laid off 1,000 engineering workers in their slowing cable business.[10] It is also true in more traditional support functions, such as when Nike announced the reduction of 1,500 back-office jobs.[11]

All work is valuable and should be valued, including work in the optimize zone, but the executive team members need to be honest with themselves and the enterprise about where investments will be made and the rationale behind those decisions. It is also important to note that the traditional definition of "resource allocation" is rapidly evolving. Advancements in data, AI, and collaboration technology create a new definition. Traditionally, growth meant adding capacity through labor. Today, resource allocation encompasses human and machine workforces, internal and external ecosystems, and non-traditional workforces such as gig workers and outsourced labor.

Shift your foundational cost structure

Any company looking to reduce costs significantly and sustainably should first consider big choices, as they often have the largest impact on a company's cost structure and complexity. Big strategic choices take significant leadership commitment as they may fundamentally change *who* a company is or *how* it operates. It requires significant stakeholder buy-in from investors, the board, and senior leadership. For these reasons, there is often a reluctance to entertain big shifts, opting instead for incremental improvements. However, it is important for leaders to understand that incremental improvement produces incremental value. Most forms of incremental standalone optimization, such as co-location and process standardization, yield 5–10 percent financial value.

To achieve material results, companies need to look first at big, strategic choices. To get big, you need to go big.

The first big choice is to understand the company's power relationship across business units and between the business units and corporate center, and then to align power relationships to the right organization strategy. The second choice is to consider if there are other ways to group and manage the middle of the business portfolio.

Business configuration and cost

A significant driver of cost comes from the misalignment of strategy and business unit portfolio power and decision-making with regard to the role of the center—what we call "business configuration". In *Networked, Scaled and Agile*,[12] Kates, Kesler, and DiMartino defined the operating framework continuum. It summarizes the amount of autonomy given to business units, the role of the center, the implications to management processes, and ways of working. In Table 2.1, we add the drivers of cost for each choice, and considerations for cost reduction approaches.

Fully integrated single business

Companies using a fully integrated single business configuration have a single strategy and culture, and nearly all processes and practices are common. They have found a business model that can sustain growth around a tightly related set of products, services, or experiences. Growth comes from innovation within the portfolio of offerings or expansion geographically. The center drives functional policy, staffing, and standards to build a consistent global way of working. Because of this underlying commonality, the single business model creates the greatest opportunities for shared services, standardized processes and enterprise-wide technology and automation at scale. Complexity and cost are usually the result of geographic diversity where local regulations or commercial practices require some differentiation.

Table 2.1 Business configuration framework with cost drivers

	1. Fully integrated single business	2. Closely related portfolio	3. Loosely related portfolio	4. Holding company or conglomerate
Strategy & customer value	Single strategy guides all P&L units with minor variations	Complementary business portfolio and core strategies with synergies	Diverse, relatively autonomous businesses set strategies, with limited synergies across units	Structure varies by operating company, enabling buying and selling of separate assets
Governance	Strategy and execution oversight comes from organizational center All process and practices are common Single culture	Business units drive strategy and execution, often with shared resources in a matrix Benefits of scale sought in core technologies, product and commercial platforms, and back-end operations	Business units drive nearly full execution of results with limited matrix Cross-business unit scale is selective (e.g., government relations, technology transfer, back-end shared services) Some effort to harmonize culture	Focused on appointing leaders Business units return financials to parent No common processes Multiple cultures
Role of the center	Drives functional policy, staffing and standards to build a consistent global function presence across the company Functional costs are managed centrally	Orchestrates and owns a common strategic agenda and most processes Collaborates closely with divisions to support execution Manages company-wide talent process and shared services Influences functional cost structure	Builds skills, tools, and talent practices necessary to strengthen a few functional capabilities Priorities are guided mostly in divisions May be a few selective shared services Costs managed primarily within the business units	Limited company-wide policies and practices mostly focused on risk and fiduciary matters
Cost Drivers	Greatest opportunity for shared services, standardized processes, enterprise-wide technology, and automation at scale Cost often the result of geographic diversity (local regulations or commercial practices)	Sizable opportunity for shared technology platforms, common processes, and shared services Shared services suitable for enabling and business functions, including business, customer, and supplier-facing services	Function costs typically skew higher due to a limited degree of common processes or technology within business operations Shared services can be utilized for enabling functions, typically focused on transactional processes	Independent function teams imbedded within businesses Limited standardization, shared technology, or shared services Typically has highest function cost as a % of revenue
Company examples	Apple Salesforce	P&G Medtronic	Nestle RTX Corporation	Alphabet Tencent

One practice that can be employed most easily in a fully integrated single business is that of looking at processes from an end-to-end perspective. Rather than orienting around functional silos, where many handoffs are required to complete a process, fully integrated businesses have the best conditions to work across functions in a boundaryless manner. Examples of this end-to-process approach include order-to-cash and hire-to-retire, which enable lower function costs through scale, process standardization, and enterprise technology.

Companies can take this practice one step further by considering end-to-end value streams. By connecting end-to-end processes to make end-to-end value streams, such as "plan to make" across the company, workflow can be redesigned holistically, tracking back from the customer. Value streams are a major operating model change, but, in addition to cost reduction, this approach can improve customer experience. (We discuss value streams in more detail later in the chapter.)

Closely and loosely related portfolios

The most complex cost questions arise in closely and loosely related portfolios. In these cases, business leaders want to allow some degree of business unit and market autonomy while gaining the benefits of resource leverage that come with shared functions and processes.[13]

Loosely and closely related portfolio companies require a very nuanced approach to understanding drivers of complexity and cost. A closely related portfolio provides greater opportunity for cost structure optimization.

Closely related portfolio

A closely related portfolio provides greater opportunity for cost structure optimization, given the greater possibility for shared technology platforms, common processes, and company-wide talent practices. The scope of process routines that are well-suited for consolidation and standardization expands to include all enabling functions, together with aspects of business functions, as summarized on the following pages.

Enabling functions

- **Finance:** record-to-report, invoice-to-cash, procure-to-pay, acquire-to-retire, management reporting, and aspects of planning, budgeting, and forecasting
- **Human Resources:** talent management, employee services, administration and payroll, and HR operations and support

- **IT**: end-user computing, application development and support, service desk and data center, voice and data network, and aspects of business intelligence
- **Legal**: contracting and employment law
- **Real estate**: facilities management and project management.

Business functions

- **Marketing**: consumer marketing, marketing support services, and aspects of product development
- **Sales**: sales support services, internal communications, and aspects of trade marketing and channel and customer sales
- **Supply chain**: demand planning, supply planning, and aspects of fulfillment.
- **Innovation centers**
- **Enterprise data and analytics.**

In a closely related portfolio, there are a broad range of service delivery models, including internal centers and third-party outsourcing relationships. Considerations are often about the prioritization of how to deploy internal talent and which distinctive capabilities are worth owning versus renting.

Loosely related portfolio

Too often we see companies with a very loosely related business model seek to pursue enterprise models that require a high degree of standardization and shared technology. The result can produce tension between the business unit's need for flexibility and the enterprise functions' desire to drive toward standardization and centralized service delivery.

Enabling functions, however, are where the company with a loosely related portfolio can find value from optimizing through consolidation and standardization. Some examples include:

- **Finance**: invoicing, accounts payable, accounts receivable and cash application, fixed assets, and managing master financial data
- **Human resources**: benefits administration, leave of absence administration, payroll, and HR master data
- **Procurement**: contracting, requisitions, payments, travel and expenses reimbursement, and managing supplier master data
- **IT**: data center support, infrastructure support, application support, information security operations, and help desk support.

Companies with loosely related business portfolios often take consolidation and standardization further by electing to have a lean internal team manage the relationship with an outsourcing provider.

Holding company

In a holding company or a conglomerate, each unit has a high degree of empowerment to operate the business in an autonomous manner. The concept of "enterprise" is very limited, often referring to a very small corporate center focused on high-level talent and financial decisions. As a result, corporate leaders typically have limited ability to reduce cost and complexity from the center beyond the distribution of top-down targets.

Even with these constraints, one way today's holding company leaders can generate scale and streamline cost is to make a big choice around outsourcing. This often takes the form of precision-focused infrastructure, application, or business process arrangements. A third-party provider uses their expertise to drive optimization both within a portfolio company and across the portfolio companies. The focus is on using technology to improve work orchestration, automation, and analytics to reduce the cost of delivery and improve the quality of outcomes within an operating company or portfolio-level company. Selective outsourcing or centralization, such as accounts payable and payroll, can improve control and reduce risk, while increasing consistency and optimizing the cost of the process. Outsourcing can also make the holding companies' assets more attractive as they can be sold without complex Transition Service Agreements (TSAs), simply allowing the existing outsourcer to continue providing the same services under new ownership.

It is important to note, there is no "better" or "worse" business configuration. Two companies within the same industry may conclude the key to their competitive advantage is reflected in different configuration choices. Coca-Cola, for example, is focused on beverages with a higher degree of operational similarity than PepsiCo, which includes beverages, breakfast foods, and snacks. Acknowledging that there are many dimensions to evaluating operational complexity, when it comes to the product portfolios of the two companies and the associated operational complexity, Coca-Cola is more likely to be the left side of the business configuration and PepsiCo to the right of center. Typically, we see a high correlation between operational sameness and cost to operate, but it is not always the case.

What does create cost is when leaders espouse one configuration and operate in another. We often see senior executives praising the benefits of scale, common processes, technology platforms, and shared capabilities and resources while remaining squarely committed to the philosophy of general managers having broad autonomy over investment choices and ways of work. This mixed message allows operators to "opt in to" or "opt out of" enterprise capabilities and services, leading to unproductive tension between business unit leaders and those who have been tasked with making the "stronger center" model a reality. The result, all too often, is wasted time, energy, and money.

We saw this scenario at a large healthcare conglomerate with a diverse portfolio. Senior leaders concluded that they were not taking advantage of their scale. With much fanfare, they launched a transformation initiative to drive enterprise-wide scale across the corporate functions. However, the costs were being driven by the business structure and ways of working as much as by functional bloat. As an example, finance needed thousands of people to support a complex matrix structure of brands, franchises, and multiple geographic levels (local, regional, and global). The number of intersections required to operate in this model was a significant source of function cost. The program, led by highly capable function leaders, quickly encountered resistance. While corporate leaders valiantly tried to centralize capability and create scale, the business leaders were fully committed to a loosely related business configuration, and some even believed they should move more towards a holding company construct. The CEO, fearful of the threat that too much commonality would disrupt revenue and profits, did not push for resolution. The transformation was successful in many ways, but the ambition was never fully realized. The effort also exhausted employees and created cynicism that poisoned enterprise initiatives for years to come.

Simplifying the middle to reduce unrewarded complexity

Jay Galbraith defined a construct to illustrate how work is typically grouped in large multidimensional companies that have closely or loosely related portfolios.[14] See Figure 1.2 (page 26). The "front" is the customer-facing components of the organization. These may include sales channels, customer marketing, product localization, solutions integration, and customer service. The "middle" owns the business strategy and development of the offering, whether a product, service, brand, or category. The "back" houses essential expertise that creates and delivers the offering profitably. Typical back-end groups are core engineering, operations, supply chain, manufacturing, technology platforms, research, and data and analytics. This expertise is often expensive to obtain or requires intense capital investment. The use of the term "back" pertains to the fact that it is less directly visible to customers, but by no means does this diminish its importance within the organization.

The composition of the business portfolio in the middle often drives the most complexity and the need to add resources in the front and back. So, while your business may currently have most people in the functions in the back, strategic shifts in the middle may have more impact than optimization efforts described in the Operational Choices section of this chapter.

When it comes to the "middle", many companies grow by generating new offerings and expanding into new geographies. The first question to ask is, "Are we really benefiting from the diversity of businesses that we have?" There is much to be gained by narrowing the focus of leadership and reducing the complexity of operations across diverse businesses.

A significant trend in the 2000's—and an example of a big strategic move—is the decision to divest or break up the classic conglomerate. The rationale for this is simplification and focus. Look no further than GE, Honeywell, Kellogg, Dow, and Johnson & Johnson. Take, for example, Johnson & Johnson. For over a decade, then-CEO Alex Gorsky faced pressure from the investor community to break up what was a loosely related portfolio and to separate the high-margin pharmaceutical and medical device businesses from the low-margin, low-growth consumer health business. In 2021, the break-up was announced with the separation overseen by Joaquin Duato, the incoming CEO.[15]

GE provides another example. The company's vast and complex portfolio was shaped into three distinct businesses that as standalones can operate with greater focus and preserve their market distinction. GE resisted pressure to break up at many times in its 100-year history. It took successive years of low performance and an outsider CEO to make the bold move, and it was rewarded in its move to spin off the energy and healthcare businesses. After struggling with 10-year lows, at the point of the final break up in 2024, GE's share price reflected a five-times improvement on the previous three years.[16]

This is an example of orienting toward *operational sameness*. Operational sameness can be done to create focus in standalone businesses, as well as looking across customers, channels, products, and production processes to identify the most natural connections for multiple businesses within the same enterprise. Take, for example a consumer goods company, which manages over 25 brands across multiple categories, including makeup, haircare, skincare, and fragrances, each with different revenue sizes. Historically, these brands have been managed as individual business units within a loosely held portfolio. Now, focus has shifted to finding opportunities to drive operational sameness through common clustering logic across brands to ultimately drive profitability. By aligning brands with similar business models, growth velocities, market maturities, and customer channels, teams can reap the benefits of scaled expertise.

Another effective strategy to reduce unnecessary complexity is to take a hard look at the matrix. Taking geographic structure as an example, eliminating management nodes reduces the number of intersection points and layers of functional support required. Putting this into practice, having HR or other functional groups replicated at the global, regional, cluster, and country levels often slows decisions without differentiating value. A smarter approach might be to put the business partner where the business strategy is located. Support centers can then be moved up into regional hubs, and operational local support can be shifted closer to the front line.

A company can also simplify the matrix structure by collapsing entire business units or forming clusters of countries under a single leadership structure. While you could design an organization structure that shares business unit CFOs and CHROs, simply removing the business unit inherently reduces the need for those roles and the need for sharing. Alternatively, managing similar adjoining countries together, such as Belgium, Netherlands, and Luxembourg as Benelux, allows you to pull some work out of each country and manage it at a higher cluster level with fewer people. Examples include having one sales director for the cluster as opposed to sales directors in each country, or producing one monthly management reporting pack and business review for the cluster (including country detail) as opposed to separate reports for each country.

A third consideration to reduce cost and complexity in the middle is to examine the number of products and services being offered. The more stock-keeping units (SKUs) that must be maintained, tracked, reported on, manufactured, and delivered to customers, the more complexity there is in overall business operations. The existence of an unnecessarily high SKU volume extrapolates into a multiplying effect of support required to sustain this complexity. Rationalizing the offerings can be as simple as identifying how many versions of a product are truly needed to drive value to the customer.

REAL-LIFE STORY   McDonald's

McDonald's, the global restaurant chain with an iconic brand, made several of these big strategic decisions about its business configuration, distinctive capabilities, and go-to-market strategy. The company has a single, integrated business with limited matrixed geographies. While McDonald's has restaurants in over 100 countries, it has been very selective in what is internally owned, choosing to directly operate restaurants in fewer than 20 countries, franchising over 95 percent of the global restaurants, and outsourcing the supply chain.

An example of a big choice was the decision to reduce the number of businesses and products offered to reduce the complexity required to run the business. Several years ago, McDonald's sold its controlling interest in Chipotle and other non-core businesses to focus solely on the McDonald's brand.[17] Since its founding, McDonald's has been famous for prioritizing a smaller core menu offering.[18] Every SKU comes with the need to design, manufacture, sell, deliver to customers, and support with enterprise functions, which adds cost and complexity to the business. Rationalizing the offerings can be as simple as asking how many versions of a product are truly needed to drive value to the customer—and aligning operations to exactly what is needed, nothing more.

The big choices that McDonald's made translate into fewer than 10,000 headquarters employees across all business functions. For context, we have seen other companies with similar revenues and global footprints, but different strategic choices, staff over 5,000 employees in the finance function alone.[19] While it's possible that McDonald's strategy leaves some earnings growth on the table, between 2017 and 2022, McDonald's stock price grew 65 percent while the market only grew 44 percent.[20] The McDonald's story is a powerful demonstration that, when it comes to growth, strategic simplicity and focus can prevail over additional headcount.

These examples of big choices—business configuration and go-to-market portfolio, and simplification of "middle" operations—demonstrate the ability to drive sizable reductions in complexity and cost structure. Choosing to narrow the company's focus requires consciously choosing to forgo short-term revenue opportunities or potentially losing customers that don't fit a narrower market; but it may nonetheless be the right answer. Big choices give clarity on where to focus, how best to serve the market, and how to run the business, all with a view to the complexity and cost of the enterprise.

Understanding the implications of these choices—and making them together as a leadership team—ensures that the right trade-offs can be made when balancing growth, differentiation, and cost.

Optimize for productivity: five operational choices

After considering big strategic shifts, company executives have a wide array of operational choices to address the inefficiencies that senior leaders see every day. They see analysis being done in Excel because core systems aren't adequate. They see mid-level leaders create unnecessary work by holding meetings on topics for which they don't hold decision rights, or asking for reports where their reviews add little-to-no value. They wait longer than expected to receive critical information or deal with customer escalations due to broken internal processes.

In this part of the chapter, we show how leaders can use five operational choices to address these pain points, while also freeing up time and energy to reinvest in growth, deliver cost savings objectives, and create focus by reducing overall complexity within the organization (summarized in Table 2.2).

Table 2.2   Five types of operational choice to address inefficiencies

Operational choice	Speed to value	Level of investment
1. Organizational structure	Faster	Low
2. Work elimination	Faster and/or slower	Low to medium
3. Artificial intelligence	Faster and/or slower	High
4. Automation	Slower	High
5. Cost-effective locations	Slower	Low to medium

As you read this section, keep in mind that:

- Some operational choices offer faster outcomes on a relative basis because you can simply stop work without impacting business operations.
- Some options can be activated quickly by changing human-to-human communications.

- Other choices require a more deliberate approach to allow for thoughtful redesign, or take longer to ensure compliance with local regulations such as works councils.

- Similarly, some choices require significant investment to build new technology or physical infrastructure, which also takes longer to activate.

- All operational choices require leadership commitment and organizational restructuring to realize their full value potential.

1: Optimizing the organizational structure

Speed to value: fast
Level of investment: low

Broadening spans of control while reducing layers of management is the traditional way that companies think about organization structure when they need to rapidly reduce labor costs. However, senior leaders are often disappointed in the results. Spans and layers are an important element of organizational hygiene, and provide a quick hit to labor cost, but they don't translate to lower labor costs in the long term. If jobs are eliminated but the work isn't changed, the work and cost will creep back in. Further, traditional spans-and-layers benchmark targets are quickly outdated. Leaders looking to reduce labor costs and improve productivity through structure should consider three principles:

- The work and responsibility of leaders must change.

- Modern workforce constructs increase the number of managers leading something other than company employees.

- The actual driver of labor cost is the number of people at each job level, not necessarily spans and layers.

Let's discuss each of these principles in detail, and how a modern approach to labor cost and complexity management tackles them differently.

The work and responsibility of leaders must change

A flat organization structure with a low number of layers is typically considered ideal for reducing organizational complexity. In theory, the fewer steps the final decision-maker takes, the faster the company will make decisions.

The challenge is that leaders in a removed layer were usually doing some amount of real work, even if that work was supplemented with spin. Therefore, when a company removes a layer in the organization, it must explicitly declare if the orphaned responsibilities are delegated upwards or downwards. New patterns must be overtly mapped, requiring a redesign of layers, roles, decision rights, and workflows. It may also require talent assessment and development.

If the work of the removed layer is moved up, the company must reset expectations that senior leaders will be doing more operational work and are familiar with how the deliverable comes together. This changes how senior leader time is spent. What is the cost of highly paid leaders taking on the work they had previously delegated? Can it be eliminated or done differently? What strategic work may not get done because senior time is more constrained? Or, should they not have delegated the work in the first place?

If delegated downwards, the company must empower more junior leaders to make decisions and ensure they are enabled with the right data, judgment, and skills. To get this right, a holistic design exercise is needed. This involves defining the purpose of every layer of leadership, identifying the orientation of power and how decisions are made, and being clear on the metrics that will drive behavior, all while designing new roles and responsibilities. In parallel, a thoughtful and unbiased talent assessment can help senior leadership understand if the organization has the right people in the right junior places to receive this newly delegated decision authority. The assessment outcomes will either help senior leadership trust the new model or prompt them to make talent changes.

Modern workforces have more managers leading something other than company employees

Traditionally, work was manually performed by employees of the company, which made team size a good proxy for work responsibility. However, modern workforce constructs challenge this assumption. Advancements in technology, including automation, AI, and GenAI, are eliminating the need for large numbers of employees, and the use of ecosystem partners to perform core operations and enabling services is shifting many employees outside the firm's bounds. For example, there's a good chance that pilots at the helm of the airplane you fly on are not employees of the company whose app you use to board the flight.

If you look at an organization chart, there could be a manager who has no direct reports but who is accountable for the relationship with a third-party that is delivering millions of dollars in operational services. This leader may not have to manage a large number of company employees, but they are still responsible for training, explaining, and sustaining hundreds of bots and lines of coding logic that automates 90 percent of the company's transactional purchases and payments. For reasons such as these, team size is no longer a fair proxy for work volume, and traditional spans and layers of employee targets are often obsolete.

The driver of labor cost is the number of people at each job level, not their span or layer

An employee's job band (VP, Director, Manager, Analyst, and so on) is directly correlated to a compensation range. While there can be compensation variability within a job band, one can generally say that removing a VP role saves more money than reducing an Analyst, and we can confidently quantify these savings.

In contrast, spans and layer are indirectly correlated with compensation. Certainly, there is an implicit assumption that removing a layer or increasing a management span will allow a company to eliminate leadership roles. But this assumption is flawed as the process is easy to manipulate in a way that does not generate cost savings. Examples include redistributing employees from one manager to another for the purpose of hitting a target span, or elevating a manager's team to report to the same leader as the manager to hit a target number of layers.

The only way to confidently reduce organization spending is to reduce the number of employees at each job level, relative to the work responsibility, work type, and strategic importance of the business area they lead, as discussed in more detail in the following.

Traditional spans-and-layers targets are obsolete

A modern approach to organization structure considers the number of employees at each job level relative to the strategic importance of each business area, work type, and work responsibility. Strategic importance is inherently unique to each company, so there is no one-size-fits-all framework; however, we find the following logic useful, regardless of unique company traits.

First, link back to your strategic priorities. To the extent you have areas of the business where you expect both growth and differentiation, you would expect to allocate more leaders, relative to areas of non-growth and differentiation. Next, consider work type. Work type refers to activities that are: strategic, analytic, or execution. We generally expect to see:

- A similar ratio of senior employees to non-senior employees in business areas performing strategic types of work, such as corporate strategy, and brand marketing
- Fewer senior employees to non-senior employees in business areas performing execution work, such as accounts payable, HR operations, and sales administration
- Middle ground in analytic types of work, such as application development, total rewards, and supply-chain planning.

Finally, consider work responsibility. As just described, work responsibility refers to all work that a business area is accountable for, regardless of whether it is primarily performed by internal employees, external partners, or technology. In these instances, companies should update job profiles and shift from managing *people* to managing *outcomes*, such as selecting managed service partners, overseeing technology build, managing performance, handing escalations, and strategizing future value-creation opportunities.

Table 2.3 summarizes our view of job-level allocation and target layers across several primary business functions. This insight is based on our experience across hundreds of companies, including companies who have adopted modern workforce constructions.

In reviewing the table, it is normal to expect higher proportions of VPs and Directors in the Legal function, given that, on average, the market compensation for lawyers is much higher than other function specialties. It is also normal to expect slightly higher numbers of VPs in the Finance function, given the number of finance sub-specialties that often require their own leader. Further, it is reasonable to expect lower percentages of Directors in Supply Chain and IT as these functions have large bases of intelligence and execution work that dilute the percentage of core strategic work performed by senior leaders on a ratio basis. In parallel, it is reasonable to expect similar numbers of Managers to Analysts in the Marketing and Legal functions, as these have comparatively less execution work to provide a large base of Analysts and create a true pyramid. Beyond these outliers, the overall job level allocations are relatively similar across the functions.

Table 2.3   Modern view of business-function pyramids

	VP+	Director	Manager	Analyst	Clerical
Sales	1%	9%	25%	60%	5%
Marketing	2%	13%	40%	40%	5%
Supply Chain	0.5%	4.5%	20%	50%	25%
Procurement	1%	9%	30%	55%	5%
Finance	2%	8%	25%	55%	10%
Human Resources	1%	9%	25%	50%	15%
IT	1%	4%	30%	55%	10%
Legal	3%	17%	40%	40%	0%

NOTE Legend
VP+: CEO, President, Executive Vice President, Senior Vice President, Vice President
Director: Senior Director, Director
Manager: Senior Manager, Manager
Analyst: Senior Analyst, Analyst, and other permutations of exempt entry-level jobs
Clerical: Clerical white-collar, non-exempt jobs (excludes blue-collar jobs)

Table 2.4 then shares our view of function job-level allocations and adds the dimension of work activity type. As suggested, we expect to see higher ratios of senior leadership for strategic work activities, and higher ratios of Analyst and Clerical workers for execution activities.

Note that for both tables, we expect these ranges to flex according to corporate strategic priorities, and the percentages are general guidance that will differ from company to company. In addition, we expect these percentages to evolve as execution work is increasingly impacted by automation and intelligence work increasingly impacted by AI. However, we believe these ranges are directionally correct and can serve as a valuable starting point for your own organizational design work.

Table 2.4 Modern view of business function pyramids by work type

	Strategic				Intelligence				Execution			
	VP+	Dir	Mgr	Ana	VP+	Dir	Mgr	Ana	Dir	Mgr	Ana	Cler
Sales	3%	7%	45%	45%	1%	9%	15%	75%	5%	20%	60%	15%
Marketing	4%	21%	50%	25%	3%	17%	40%	40%	10%	40%	45%	5%
Supply Chain	3%	37%	50%	10%	1%	9%	25%	65%	2%	8%	80%	15%
Procurement	2%	18%	30%	50%	1%	9%	25%	65%	2%	28%	60%	10%
Finance	4%	16%	30%	40%	2%	8%	20%	70%	3%	8%	50%	40%
Human Resources	3%	22%	40%	35%	1%	4%	20%	75%	5%	10%	60%	25%
IT	2%	8%	45%	45%	1%	4%	20%	75%	2%	8%	80%	10%
Legal	15%	30%	30%	25%	10%	20%	25%	45%	20%	40%	40%	0%

SOURCE Accenture Experience and Analysis

NOTE Legend
VP+: CEO, President, Executive Vice President, Senior Vice President, Vice President
Dir: Senior Director, Director
Mgr: Senior Manager, Manager
Ana: Senior Analyst, Analyst, and other permutations of exempt entry-level jobs
Cler: Clerical white-collar, non-exempt jobs (excludes blue-collar jobs)

2: Eliminating work from the organization

Speed to value: faster and/or slower
Level of investment: low to medium

Organizations tend to grow in organic and unwieldy ways, at least from a structural perspective. Roles may be created for individual employee-retention purposes or be maintained in a team even though the work has long been done. It is usually easy to create fast savings by eliminating these roles, but it can take time and the right skills to find these pockets. Humans are rarely more creative than when they need to invent work to preserve their employment status. Work elimination often takes three forms:

- Stopping work and not replacing it
- Changing the amount of work required
- Simplifying and standardizing processes to unlock productivity.

Stopping work is the fastest way to generate savings. For example, at Accenture—a $75 billion professional services firm that employs 740,000 people across five services groups and three geographies—our analysis of our own Marketing function showed that clients were not engaging with a significant amount of the content that we produced. As a result, we declared that we would eliminate 25 percent of content production and draw up stricter criteria for what was produced. That statement alone took significant work out of the system, immediately releasing 20 percent capacity in the Marketing function.

Another possibility is to re-evaluate service levels to reduce costs. For example, an HR operations processing team was staffed to process all requests within 24 hours. However, we could see that the team had significant hourly variation in transaction volume. By shifting the KPI from 24 hours to 48 hours, we were able to normalize work volumes and reduce the need to staff to peak volumes, while maintaining the same level of employees' satisfaction in their experience.

When considering a change to the amount of work required, we have seen companies that process manual financial journal entries for cost movements of less than $100. Moving this small level of cost from one P&L to another will barely move the needle for either P&L, with no impact at all for the enterprise. Perhaps at one point it made sense to do this. Maybe, over time, it was accepted as practice and not questioned. Alternatively, creating a new policy to block financial journal entries under $25,000 eliminates significant transaction volumes and reduces finance labor requirements, with no material change to company performance or decision-making quality. We find the same with delegation of authority to approve spending. Raising limits eliminates layers of review with little impact on risk.

Many off-the-shelf tools exist to help companies assess opportunities for simplification and standardization. Programs such as Celonis rapidly ingest source data and identify process inefficiencies. Other tools, such as Microsoft Viva Insights, identify overworked people or test for over- and under-collaboration. These tools are also useful when identifying tactical opportunities in end-to-end processes that span multiple functions.

3: Increasing productivity with artificial intelligence

Speed to value: faster and/or slower
Level of investment: high

According to the World Economic Forum, we are in the middle of the Fourth Industrial Revolution[21]—a once-in-a-generation technological advancement powered by the emergence of AI. GenAI's expansion into language mastery across context, sentiment, emotion, grammar, and syntax brings together a combinatorial effect of numbers and words with the potential for massive impact.

To be clear, GenAI is different from automation. One of the simplest distinctions we have seen is: "Rules-based automation is where output is created based on certain inputs via pre-programming. Whereas in GenAI, the technology generates novel text or images based on the data it has been trained on."[22]

Figure 2.2 provides an indication of GenAI's likely impact on different job categories, with the highest potential shown towards the top-right. As the figure depicts, while the excitement for GenAI is high, the impact that it will have on different work activities is likely to be more nuanced.

We envision that GenAI will impact cost and complexity in the following four ways.

GenAI unlocks significant savings and productivity now, without significant investment

At this point, many people have seen basic GenAI use cases in action, such as marketers using tools such as writer.com to input a simple brief, let the GenAI tool synthesize insights and produce first-draft market-ready content to reduce time and effort. The upside of an example like this is that the tools are available for purchase today and require little to no configuration

Figure 2.2 Exposure to GenAI by role

	Out-of-box GenAI	**Customized GenAI**
Cost savings	• Marketing artwork • Marketing and sales writing • Call center	• Pricing • Supply chain planning • Billing disputes • Legal contracts
Reinvest capacity	• Business leadership • HR business partners • Corporate attorneys • Strategy practitioners	• Field sales • Technology development • Financial planning and analysis • Tier 1 marketing
Limited potential	• Physical product/service front-line workers • Warehouse and transportation workers	

investment before generating value. These are good places for any business to start to build their GenAI foundation with demonstrable impact.

GenAI unlocks significant savings and productivity later, and requires time and investment to customize

Work activities such as pricing, supply-chain planning, accounts-receivable disputes, and simple legal contract reviews are primarily analytic activities that currently involve pulling data, investigating scenarios, and creating recommended actions, all of which is perfect for GenAI to assist with. However, these activities are also central to business operations, and rely on company-specific data and business strategies to properly function. For these reasons, it is reasonable to expect that use of GenAI in these areas will take longer to implement and require more investment to sufficiently train and customize the GenAI tools uniquely for each customer and activity combination.

This type of responsibility requires senior, experienced talent that understands both strategy and operational nuances. Without the right talent shaping the AI solutions, companies run the risk of GenAI producing incorrect results on a large scale, such as inaccurate pricing across an entire product portfolio or undesirable legal terms added to all contracts. Further, with limited AI talent in the market, companies must rigorously prioritize and sequence use-case development to build momentum and demonstrate value. Prioritization is always difficult, but critical here to avoid spreading resources too thinly and expending capital with limited tangible returns.

GenAI unlocks significant productivity later, with capacity repurposed to drive growth

Consider activities such as financial planning and analysis, field sales, technology development for front-office applications, and tier 1 marketing content creation. These activities have many analytic tasks that GenAI can overcome with the right time and configuration to business strategy. But these activities are also either parts of people's jobs with other strategic or customer-centric components, or performed by high-performing employees who can make value contributions in other ways.

Many companies will choose to repurpose GenAI savings to do more with the same head count, rather than reducing head count for cost savings. For example, if GenAI allows a salesperson to free up 20 percent of capacity by giving them customer information faster and automating sales data entry, this capacity is best used to serve additional customers or build deeper relationships with existing customers, rather than cut head count. Similarly, GenAI that allows a technology developer to free up 20 percent of capacity by automating testing would likely use that time to take on 20 percent new backlog. In this way, GenAI also helps companies avoid future costs by allowing them to break the model that more head count is required for more output.

Cost avoidance in this context can refer to business growth (same head count to support higher revenues) or to companies taking on more value-generating complexity in their operating model (same head count to support complex products, markets, and customers).[23] Regardless of how a company chooses to realize value, the use of GenAI in this way will require a talent evolution. Future high-performers will be skilled in asking the right prompts to GenAI that make them smarter and faster, leading to differentiated performance results.

GenAI has limited impact

We foresee areas where the impact of GenAI will be limited. These include activities that primarily require physical interaction with products, services, customers, and tasks, and deeply human-to-human interactions. Local marketing and events, transportation and manufacturing, and infrastructure maintenance are all activities that require physical interaction. Meanwhile, deep human-to-human connection includes HR business partners navigating highly complex personnel matters, and business strategy leaders running a P&L. In some ways, this second category closely resembles a bucket of capacity repurposed for growth. The difference is simply an assumption of a much higher ratio of human-to-human work versus machine work, and therefore materially less potential capacity to repurpose.

Operational choices around GenAI need to align with and directly support big strategic choices. Companies that choose a fully integrated business or a closely related portfolio will find it easier to scale the benefits of GenAI as they see more platforms and sharing across their front, middle, and back. Conversely, loosely related portfolios or holding companies should remember to exercise caution and avoid the urge to scale standard GenAI tools across non-standard businesses and functions. Regardless of portfolio configuration, significant use of GenAI requires companies to reconfigure the way work gets done to get real results. Examples include changing from call centers full of people to intelligent hubs, or exploring better management of end-to-end processes to enable the AI solutions.

GenAI, while saving on labor, generates other costs in terms of configuration investments, and ongoing data processing and energy costs. For example, the energy required for a month of all global ChatGPT use was estimated to equal the energy use of 175,000 Western households. This was in January 2023, before wide-scale adoption.[24] While many business leaders are excited for a GenAI future, there are cases where a human solution may be less expensive than a GenAI solution.

4: Automating work that requires manual effort

Speed to value: slower
Level of investment: high

If AI is one of the biggest technology trends, automation is one of the longest standing technology trends. From the dawn of the industrial age, automation has been the preferred answer any time an executive sees large numbers of employees performing seemingly repetitive tasks. However, as any manufacturer knows, automation is much easier said than done, and often more expensive than originally anticipated.

The reality is that automation is and will always be important, but it can also fall into the negative return-on-investment trap where the costs of training and sustaining the automation exceed the benefits realized.

Therefore, automation programs must be assessed and prioritized by cross-functional leadership to ensure alignment with business strategy. It is best when viewed as part of an enterprise digital core strategy. Successful automation is not a standalone IT initiative; automation also requires the redesign of business processes, and the thoughtful design and configuration of business rules. Successful automation programs require disciplined, thoughtful execution through at least eight distinct phases:

1 Identifying opportunities to leverage automation
2 Prioritizing opportunities, typically based on feasibility and potential value
3 Designing and building the high-level solution and selecting technologies to be implemented
4 Determining how the work will be delivered and putting together the right team
5 Gathering detailed business requirements and confirming solution scope
6 Implementing the solution
7 Testing and fine-tuning the automation
8 Adopting new ways of working within the organization and managing the change.

If implemented in the right way, automation will deliver work in a new way with far fewer resources, but it must be planned and managed successfully rather than viewed as a silver bullet.

5: Optimizing the locations where work gets done

Speed to value: slower
Level of investment: low to medium

Location optimization for managing labor costs is a well-established cost management strategy. It works especially well when work can be standardized, and capabilities shared across business units. For a large company in a developed market, the labor cost differences can be significant. The loaded compensation in India and similar parts of Southeast Asia, for example, currently results in savings of 50–70 percent over high-cost markets for junior to mid-level workers performing analytic activities. When companies need this work performed in a similar time zone, locations in Eastern Europe and Latin America can still result in savings of 30–50 percent over high-cost markets. Effective location optimization doesn't need to move work across country borders: ultra-high-cost locations in developed markets, such as New York, San Francisco, London, Paris, and Singapore, often cost 20 percent more than sites in other cities in the same country or region, such as Chicago, Austin, Birmingham, Amsterdam, and Kuala Lumpur.[25]

Beyond cost savings, optimizing your location strategy expands your talent pool and potentially enables 24/7 ways of working. For truly global companies, internationally distributed locations also unlock truly diverse perspectives by allocating talent to better match the customer base and revenue versus being skewed to headquarters locations in the West. An analysis of the 10 largest multinational companies in the Fortune 100 indicates that, on average, approximately 40 percent of revenues are earned outside the United States.[26] Yet, all these top 10 largest multinationals have their global headquarters in the United States, with only regional headquarters outside the country. Shifting a degree of strategy-forming and decision-making to other parts of the world infuses more globally diverse insights from the start.

As mentioned previously, companies should always anchor to their business strategy when considering location strategy, as different companies will have different perspectives regarding value potential from the same work activity. However, the location strategy guidance shown in Table 2.5 has a logic that can apply to any company.

Table 2.5   Modern approach to location strategy

Location type	Primary use	Examples
Ultra-high-cost locations (globally distributed)	Highest value core-business activities that are concentrated in specific ultra-high-cost locations	• Technology leadership and high-end developers in San Francisco • Investment bankers in New York and London • Oil executives in Houston and Dubai
High-cost locations (globally distributed)	Highest value strategic and analytic work activities	• Core business / P&L leadership • Marketing and brand strategy • R&D priority leaders • Investor relations • HR business partners

(continued)

Table 2.5   (Continued)

Location type	Primary use	Examples
Similar time-zone cost-effective locations	Repeatable work activities that require frequent virtual interaction with high-cost location stakeholders or local-language speakers	• Front-office technology development • Local language call centers
Globally cost-effective locations	Repeatable work activities that can occur without frequent stakeholder interaction	• Simple marketing production and distribution • Supply chain analytics • Payables processing • Back-office technology development
Always local, regardless of cost	Activities that require frequent in-person interaction with customers or physical products, or are required to be local by law or statute	• Field sales (local to country, not necessarily a specific city) • Core business operations (e.g., nurses, utility line repair workers, retail store assistants)

These five operational choices can unlock productivity and cost savings in nearly any organization. With new and improving tools for global collaboration, and a growing technology backbone supporting globalized ways of working, most businesses have untapped opportunities to rethink their fundamental ways of working. When linked to strategic choices and supported by the right investment of leadership time and energy to redesign the organization and work so that savings are sustained, the benefits can be broad, significant, and long-lasting.

Conclusion: Managing cost and complexity

There is a clear link between complexity and cost, and, in many cases, it's a cause-and-effect relationship. Higher complexity almost always translates to higher cost. Not all complexity is bad, however. Sometimes it serves a clear and compelling purpose to deliver distinctive value to customers. What is critical is to be able to decipher the good from the bad, and to employ the right techniques to root out *unnecessary* complexity and cost. Recent advancements in data and technology have created new ways to absorb complexity via digitization. This provides new and promising avenues for business leaders. As these avenues mature, what remains true is the thought process outlined in this chapter:

1 Align your labor strategy with your business strategy.

2 Shift the underlying foundational cost structure tied to simplifying the business model, internal operating structures, and/or ways of working.

These are the most significant and most sustainable methods for achieving the optimal cost to operate. By following this path, business leaders can make the dreaded battle of the "red pen versus the organization chart" an exercise of the past.

Key takeaways

- A modern approach for managing cost and complexity maintains a keen focus on the connection between executing business strategy, translated into the operating model and the allocation of resources.

- The biggest impact on reducing cost and complexity comes from having the clarity and courage to make big, strategic decisions.

- The first big decision involves being very deliberate in keeping customer needs at the forefront and translating this to running the business, paying special attention to avoid overcomplicating internal operations.

- The second big decision involves being crystal clear on the best-fit business configuration, the level of integration and independence in your enterprise, and the implication to the cost structure.

- Operational choices play an important role in how, where, and by whom work is performed. This can require heavy investment and leadership energy, and the ability to drive cost savings is influenced by your big, strategic choices.

Notes

1   Chen, T.-P. (2024) Remote Workers Bear the Brunt When Layoffs Hit, *The Wall Street Journal*, March 26. wsj.com/lifestyle/careers/layoffs-remote-work-data-980ed59d (archived at https://perma.cc/J52C-YD6E).

2   Schneider, M. (2023) Spotify Slashes Global Workforce by 17% in Latest Cost-Cutting Effort, *Billboard*, December 4. billboard.com/business/streaming/spotify-layoffs-2023-restructure-job-cuts-1235531731 (archived at https://perma.cc/6EN6-3HFX).

3   Assis, C. (2024) FedEx's Stock Soars Towards a 3-year High After a Profit Beat, $5 Billion Buyback, *MarketWatch*, March 22. marketwatch.com/story/fedexs-stock-jumps-10-after-logistics-company-raises-guidance-trims-spending-2b1048d6 (archived at https://perma.cc/JP8W-YG2U).

4   Sucher, S.J. and Westner, M.M. (2022) What Companies Still Get Wrong About Layoffs, *Harvard Business Review*, December 8. hbr.org/2022/12/what-companies-still-get-wrong-about-layoffs (archived at https://perma.cc/9F2A-9TUF).

5   Accenture perspective, adapted from M.E. Porter (1980) *Competitive Strategy*, New York: The Free Press.

6   Fitch, A. (2024) Nvidia's Supercharged Investment Strategy is About More Than Returns, *The Wall Street Journal*, March 10. wsj.com/tech/ai/nvidias-supercharged-investment-strategy-is-about-more-than-returns-b868e51d (archived at https://perma.cc/H4Q5-9XYL).

7   Koller, A. (2024) Initial Demand for Apple's Vision Pro Headset Could Wane, Top Analyst Cautions, CNBC, January 22. cnbc.com/2024/01/22/demand-for-apple-vision-pro-headset-could-wane-top-analyst-warns.html (archived at https://perma.cc/97JU-EW3R).

8   Starbucks Stories (2024) Tata Starbucks to Accelerate Growth in 1,000 Stores, Double Employment in India by 2028, January 8. stories.starbucks.com/press/2024/tata-starbucks-to-accelerate-growth-to-1000-stores-double-employment-in-india-by-2028 (archived at https://perma.cc/LC8D-NV7V).

9   Roberts, J. (2023) JPMorgan Chase, Siemens, and FedEx Show that Blockchain Finance is More Than a Buzzword, *Fortune*, November 16. fortune.com/crypto/2023/11/16/jp-morgan-siemens-fedex-blockchain-finance-jpm-coin (archived at https://perma.cc/AQT2-K6NS).

10 Pan, E. (2024) Comcast Layoffs 2024: What to know about the latest CMCSA job cuts, *Investor Place*, January 30. investorplace.com/2024/01/comcast-layoffs-2024-what-to-know-about-the-latest-cmcsa-job-cuts (archived at https://perma.cc/J5X5-7FRD).

11 Golden, J. (2024) Nike to Lay Off 2% of Employees, Cutting More Than 1,500 Jobs During Broad Restructuring, CNBC, February 16. cnbc.com/2024/02/16/nike-to-lay-off-2percent-of-employees-cutting-more-than-1500-jobs.html (archived at https://perma.cc/3S3A-8T7B).

12 Kates, A., Kesler, G., and DiMartino, M. (2021) *Network, Scaled, and Agile: A Design Strategy for Complex Organizations*, London: Kogan Page.

13 Kates et al. (2021).

14 Galbraith, J. (2005) The Front-Back Model: How does it work?. jaygalbraith. com/wp-content/uploads/2024/03/FrontBackHowitWorks.pdf (archived at https://perma.cc/WYZ3-XT5Z).

15 Kaplan, S. and de la Merced, M.J. (2021) Johnson & Johnson to Split into Two Public Companies, *The New York Times*, November 12. nytimes.com/2021/11/12/business/johnson-johnson-split.html (archived at https://perma.cc/3TWN-AYGY).

16 Singh, R.K. and Ganapavaram, A. (2024) GE Completes Three-Way Split, Breaking Off Its Storied Past, Reuters, April 2. reuters.com/markets/us/ge-completes-three-way-split-breaking-off-its-storied-past-2024-04-02 (archived at https://perma.cc/CAD5-4YSB).

17 Cunningham, R. and Wu, H. (2021) Why Did McDonald's Sell Chipotle?, *Rebellion Research*, August 2. rebellionresearch.com/why-did-mcdonalds-sell-chipotle (archived at https://perma.cc/2GPZ-S2BT).

18 Piehl, O. (2024) McDonald's Marketing Strategy: The rise of the golden arches (+4 key strategies), *Co-Schedule*, April 1. coschedule.com/marketing-strategy/marketing-strategy-examples/mcdonalds-marketing-strategy (archived at https://perma.cc/RP79-7DRY).

19 Accenture Experience and Analysis.

20 Yahoo Finance (2023) McDonald's (NYSE: MCD) Shareholders Have Earned a 13% CAGR Over the Last Five Years, February 10. finance.yahoo.com/news/mcdonalds-nyse-mcd-shareholders-earned-110046919.html (archived at https://perma.cc/XSP5-5EFP).

21 World Economic Forum (2024) Fourth Industrial Revolution. weforum.org/focus/fourth-industrial-revolution (archived at https://perma.cc/JH76-4PDM).

22 Chanoine, J.-M. (2023) Automation and Generative AI Within the Sales Organization: How to leverage AI with less risk, *Forbes*, December 8. forbes.com/sites/forbesbusinessdevelopmentcouncil/2023/12/08/automation-and-generative-ai-within-the-sales-organization-how-to-leverage-ai-with-less-risk/?sh=4d6d25313a5f (archived at https://perma.cc/Y8BT-3VG9).

23 Kolbjørnsrud, V. (2024) Designing the Intelligent Organization: Six principles for human-AI collaboration, *California Management Review*, February 1. cmr.berkeley.edu/2024/02/66-2-designing-the-intelligent-organization-six-principles-for-human-ai-collaboration (archived at https://perma.cc/8S5S-Z5NW).

24 Oremus, W. (2023) AI Chatbots Lose Money Every Time You Use Them. That is a Problem, *The Washington Post*, June 5. washingtonpost.com/technology/2023/06/05/chatgpt-hidden-cost-gpu-compute (archived at https://perma.cc/ZT27-UC4U).

25 Accenture Experience and Analysis.

26 Accenture external analysis of 2023 Fortune 100 list, filtered for multinational corporations.

Execute Mergers, Acquisitions, and Divestments

03

STEVE GILES, LYNN GONSOR, GREG KESLER

Contributors: J. Neely, Andrew Sinclair

In August 2005, Sprint acquired Nextel Communications in a roughly $38 billion deal, combining the third and fifth largest wireless carriers in the United States.[1] The combination of the two would increase their customer numbers close to those of the two leading competitors and create a third telecom titan. The CEO at the time was quoted as saying he was "jazzed" by the deal and "looking forward to competing... for the preeminent role in wireless and telecommunications".[2] Soon after the merger, an exodus of Nextel executives and mid-level managers began. Cultural, customer, and decision-making issues abounded. Within three years, after undertaking cost-cutting and layoffs, Sprint wrote off $30 billion in goodwill and its stock was given a junk status rating.

This high-profile story, with a calamitous outcome, is not unique. How can deals that look so good on paper go so awry so quickly? What must leaders do to deliver on deal intent?

Active portfolio management is a key lever for achieving strategy. The ability to merge, acquire, or divest enables CEOs to gain market share and refocus their portfolios, as well as add new capabilities and assets. However, many transactions do not fully deliver the value promised, particularly on profitability. Our research on large deals shows that, although 54 percent of companies improved revenue growth in the three years following a deal, only 27 percent saw improvements in both revenue growth *and* operating margin.[3]

A merger, acquisition, or even divestiture (what we will call M&A) can be an exciting time for a company—the beginning of something new and a path to growth and expanded opportunities. It can be a catalyst for reinvention. Too often, though, the deal is a drag on leadership time and energy. Cost-cutting—euphemistically called "cost synergies"—often dominates the discussion, and lack of sustained focus on finishing the play often distracts from achieving the long-term strategic intent. Up to 90 percent of deals experience delays due to insufficient focus on organizational integration and post-acquisition activities, and 67 percent of mergers are delayed in meeting financial targets due to cultural conflicts.[4]

More than ever, we believe the M&A playbook needs a vigorous organizational and operating model set of tactics for a number of reasons:

- Enhanced and new capabilities are often the purpose of an acquisition (or a merger) and the only way to integrate, expand, and fully exploit nascent capabilities is through intentional alignment of organization, ways of working, technology, and talent.

- Portfolio decision-making is an operating model challenge, and both acquisitions and divestitures tend to shift power dynamics. The decision-makers in a substantially new business portfolio will likely change. The metrics and the incentives must be reset to meet the needs of newer businesses that now make up the company.

- Integration choices often impact the "autonomy" of entrenched business units and P&Ls, as well as established leadership norms. Avoiding these hard choices is a mistake and likely to reduce the payoff from a deal.

- Today, CEOs and their teams are often engaged in enterprise transformation and utilize acquisitions as a part of that much larger ambition and strategy. The organization and its people are central to today's transformation agenda.

This chapter examines three enablers for delivering the commitments of a significant acquisition or divestiture. It will then explore four M&A transaction types, looking more deeply at specific organization implications and tactics for each. Throughout, we will make the case that substantial M&A transactions should be viewed as opportunities for transformation, and that transformative leaders succeed in these ventures by setting a clear "North Star" early in the change process that provides guidance and alignment to the organization around a clear and consistent agenda that is likely to be accomplished over an extended period of time in order to realize the full benefit of the initiative.

Set a clear M&A North Star

Three elements have proven critical to executing and fully delivering on the value case for mergers, acquisitions, and divestitures. The North Star here is comprised of a future set of commitments around three enablers:

- **Strategic choices.** Effective business strategy underpins all effective deals and provides the basis for all integration decisions and trade-offs with a bias for growth. Deal logic needs to be grounded in a granular set of long-term business outcomes and capabilities.

- **Organizational intent.** Execution of the M&A ambition requires a substantive and ongoing assessment of the organizational requirements for integration (as well as understanding the current models in each of the legacy businesses), from due diligence through implementation, proactively resolving the structural, process, metrics, and talent requirements.

- **Leadership focus and tenacity.** Top executives set the expectation for continued leadership focus and investment of time and energy for an extended period of time in order to deliver the potential value of a smart transaction.

Strategic choices

Strategy

The late renowned professor in innovation and disruption, Clayton Christensen argued more than a decade ago that the reason so many acquisitions fall short of expectations is because executives incorrectly match target companies to the strategic purpose of the deal, "failing to distinguish between deals that might improve current operations and those that could dramatically transform the company's growth prospects".[5]

Companies entering into substantial deals owe shareholders a clear set of expectations for the impact of a proposed deal, beyond vague references to "synergies". If the outcomes are essentially about the cost and efficiency benefits of scale, make the case. If the intent is to drive substantially new growth opportunities, companies can lay out the hypotheses based on specific technology synergies, new routes to market, filling gaps in lines of business, and other capabilities. These commitments must then be translated into actionable integration programs and plans.

Recent major acquisitions and mergers in the aerospace and defense industries, in advanced technology, and in healthcare underscore this need for a clear strategy, which is something more than compelling deal logic. A business strategy is anchored to the market and answers the question, "How will this combination of assets produce growth that exceeds the combined results of the two separate entities?" We have seen the problem of vague commitments to synergy without clear strategic decisions to achieve those synergies.

Consider healthcare and the many acquisitions aimed at creating more integrated health solutions and outcomes by combining risk management (insurance), care delivery, and pharmacy services. The theory of the business case is compelling, but marrying these diverse sets of capability into a new business model requires deep knowledge of targeted patient communities, clinical services, consumer-facing technology, the ability to create new and innovative products and services, and more. Hard decisions are required of the legacy businesses, and, without a clear and granular strategy, nothing magic happens when the deal closes. The work only gets harder. Driving transformation is impossible without sharp strategy choices. A similar argument can be applied to most industries.

For example, Quaker's acquisition of Snapple back in 1994 was a logical idea, extending the Snapple brand with stronger marketing and moving the brand into mass grocery chains.[6] But there was no strategy going into the integration process and the marketing objectives were wrong. Snapple's niche was convenience stores and gas stations, and the brand didn't translate to the wider trade channels. The holding company sold the failing business at less than 20 cents on the dollar.

The components of a clear strategy must include market-focused insights, clear goals and timelines, and differentiated points of view on where to play and how to win, which are then translated into distinct capabilities.

Capability

Capabilities are an extension of strategy, and can be defined as the few things an organization must do exceptionally well to differentiate against competitors. In short, what does the business need to do well in order to execute and win in its markets? In M&A strategy, capability is especially critical, and is often an explicit part of the business case. The value of a given asset may be characterized primarily as an existing capability (that the acquiring company lacks) or it may be expressed as a new muscle that must be built in order to bring the acquired business model or technology to life.

Returning to our telecom example, Sprint was challenged in customer service consistency, which overshadowed Nextel's reputation for customer responsiveness in the combined entity. A lack of focus on scaling service as a *capability* was a miss in the market and created tension and distrust between the legacy leadership teams.[7]

Every successful company has a set of distinctive capabilities that produce a competitive advantage. In a merger, the leaders of the new entity should be clear on what these capabilities are, how they are complementary, and how they need to be combined and reinvented for the future organization. It is easy to overlook capability opportunities, particularly if the deal is driven by a consolidator's mindset running a playbook focused on scale. Taking the time to look for capability opportunities can release hidden value, as seen in the cases just discussed.

Today's integrated healthcare companies also provide a good example of the need simultaneously to protect critical capabilities in acquired businesses while building new ones. As CVS Health and its competitor Cigna have acquired or partnered with care delivery businesses,[8] they recognize the major differences in running clinics versus pharmacies and healthcare insurance; leadership must now nurture care-delivery capabilities. At the same time, a set of completely new capabilities are required—many heavily rooted in digital technology and data—to build deep relationships with patients, covered by their insurance plans, as the companies aim to bring all of their assets to bear in improving health outcomes at a lower cost.

All stakeholders, including investors, benefit from a granular business case, rooted in market realities, with a long-term vision for growth and profitability. This is the foundation for a transformational North Star. To achieve this, the following set of strategy questions should be answered early in the process:

- What growth expectations do we have from this deal and what will be necessary to achieve them?

- What are the differentiating capabilities that we will protect or that we must develop to achieve value in the deal? What role do the two entities play in that regard?

- How do we measure success in a way that drives long-term economic, customer and employee value?

Organizational intent

Effective organizations are built to power the vision and strategy of a business, and at no time is that more important than in a significant M&A transaction. Everyone knows that the organization design is a critical part of integrating an acquisition or the merger of two equals. It is also intuitive that, in the case of a substantial divestiture, organizations often need to change in order to reduce fixed costs that were built for past higher revenues.

It is often the case, however, that the process of thinking about organization comes too late or is treated with a haphazard and often bottom-up approach (aligning function by function and business by business) rather than starting with enterprise architecture that is envisioned to transform the company or major businesses within. The common practice of setting up organization design teams for each major unit of the new company—with members assigned from both companies—may feel collaborative, but it nearly always produces a set of compromises that become barriers to value creation. Top leadership must set an organizational direction before delegating this task. This is another critical element of the North Star.

The track record of larger mergers and acquisitions makes it clear that culture is also a critical element in successful integration and building new capability. The intent for major deals should include explicit expectations for the future culture and leadership norms.

This work starts with an analysis of the current state in the acquired (and perhaps the acquiring) company. It is not uncommon for misunderstanding to prevail after due diligence when there is an inadequate review of the operating model of the prospective partners. Sprint was governance heavy, while Nextel was run with an entrepreneurial spirit that ultimately caused them to part ways.[9] How well were those dynamics understood before closing the deal?

With a deep understanding of the current situation, including the legacy cultures of the two entities, the future organizational intent can be assembled at a high level. In the simplest of terms, how are both companies run today, and how will the new one be run? As Watkins described in *Harvard Business Review*, the failed merger of Daimler and Chrysler was largely a matter of what Daimler perceived to be aggressive tactics in telling Chrysler executives how to run its business as integration progressed.[10] A lack of shared vision on an operating model for the new company led to a complete breakdown in the partners' ability to work together.

A cursory online search for the causes of botched acquisitions and mergers reveals numerous articles that highlight the frequent collision of cultures in newly formed companies. While it might not be wrong to say that a given failure was due to cultural differences, that diagnosis is superficial. Effective, early organizational analysis will reveal how differences in organization structures, business process, technology deployment, reward systems, people practices, and metrics shape culture. Due diligence should take these specifics into account; and before integration begins, an organizational strategy, and a shared plan between the two companies, should provide a road map for those same variables in the future state.

Structure

Laying out a road map for the future operating model can be difficult, and the instinct often descends into drawing organization charts. This is a mistake and offers little in the way of shared meaning on how the new company will be run. The top executives of the 'acquiring' and potentially 'acquired' companies should confer in detail about their current operating models, and may exchange views on a potential future operating model that combines the businesses. The business configuration framework outlined by Kates, Kesler, and DiMartino is shown in Table 2.1.[11] The framework provides a continuum of options, ranging from the fully integrated, single business to the holding company. In between sit the closely and loosely connected options. This fundamental view helps joint leadership understand where each company operates in the status quo and can lead to a clear North Star view of where the new company wishes to go.

Acquisitions and divestments often present opportunities to rethink how closely to connect businesses in the evolved portfolio, an opportunity that should not be missed. In the merger of United Technologies (UTC) and Raytheon, the strategy was heavily oriented to achieving technology synergies across its defense and aerospace portfolio, bringing together jet propulsion, missile, and AI-powered communications platforms in connected battle-space nodes. The legacy UTC operating model was a loosely connected organization of diverse commercial and defense businesses. Before the Raytheon marriage, UTC divested the Carrier and Otis companies to narrow its focus.

The strategy for the new, combined corporation—RTX—was to be heavily focused on technology-driven connectivity, and the organization model needed to power that outcome.[12] The incoming CEO, Chris Calio, set a clear North Star, aiming to move the new operating model to a closely related portfolio. Over time, a series of changes in the business unit and functional organizations were staged. The intent was to retain strong, P&L-focused business units as the center of gravity in the organization, with selected functions playing a more active, center-led role in driving key areas of integration across the businesses for both growth and cost synergies.

Once business configuration is clear, and the primary orientation is reset, the next steps are to design the combined organization architecture to create the right focus, simplicity, accountability, and points of integration. This will define accountabilities between the center and business units, particularly in areas such as research and development, product design, sales and marketing, and investment, where cross-company processes increase in impact and importance.

Business process

The operating model framework provides a foundation for effective management and business processes, from investment allocation to customer management. In the more closely connected operating model process, technology and data-enabled ways of working are perhaps the most powerful ways to create more integration across the new portfolio. The nature of capabilities to be developed will inform which processes are most critical. Process design can be a key element in enabling a more integrated operating model.

As Medtronic has acquired numerous medical device businesses, it has faced the challenge in today's connected medical care environment of needing a single, integrated approach to medical device data management.[13] Products developed by the surgical equipment businesses gather data during surgical procedures and make it available to surgeons in real time through the cloud. With more than 20 business units, it is critical for Medtronic to manage a coordinated approach to data pools and effective clinical outcomes with a governance process that assures effective and compliant commercial use of the data by the separate businesses.

Process redesign unfolds over time, and companies often struggle to finish the play given the protracted, intensive nature of the reengineering task. It is easy to lose track of the program without a clear North Star vision for the organization that keeps process redesign a priority.

Metrics and targets

Accountability is designed into the new organization through effective metrics aligned to key roles. The strategic logic behind an acquisition should be the foundation for metrics, and it makes sense to lay out early thinking in this regard before the deal closes, then refresh and bring more detail during the integration process. Keeping the integration teams focused on key metrics is critical, as metrics send powerful signals about expectations for cost and growth synergies. Targets should be ambitious and balanced and, importantly, managed over time with sustained energy for both.

Role-specific targets should reward leadership behaviors that push the organization in the desired direction, which include indicators of successful integration, as well as delivering the current business plan. As part of determining what should be measured, be prepared to discard metrics that will drive counterproductive behaviors or are not essential to performance outcomes.

A leading pharmaceutical company, for example, established an integration dashboard with metrics in three classes: financial (synergies, one-time costs, new product success), operational (integration execution), and organizational (retention, employee satisfaction). This dashboard is reviewed by the board integration committee, keeping a balanced view front of mind for the executive team, and transparent throughout levels of leadership.

The alignment of profit-and-loss accountability and budget approval levels is one of the best ways to use metrics and process to drive new decision-making. Be prepared, however, to adjust these as the organization evolves and new ways of working are embedded. For instance, if acquiring a strategic, innovative asset that relies on creative input and continuous experimentation, leadership should allocate sufficient budget and freedom for that asset to succeed.

The following is a set of foundational operating model questions to consider before the deal is closed. The answers to these questions become part of the North Star. Each question should be asked in terms of the legacy organizations as well as the future state.

- What is the basic shape and nature of the organizational model we will build? What are the basic business units and functions?
- What capabilities will be owned at the enterprise level, and which will be owned within separate business units?
- How will we run the company in the future? How independent or how integrated will the business units be? What role will the enabling functions play?
- Where will essential decision authority be placed? How center-led or distributed will it be?
- Where do we want integration, and where is separation and focus important in the organization?
- What is the greater ecosystem within which this business operates?
- How do we use this transaction to reinvent, such that the new organization is greater than the sum of the parts?

Leadership focus and tenacity

The central role of leadership during an acquisition, merger, or divestiture is to manage a complex and sometimes disruptive set of tensions among competing priorities. Perhaps what makes the challenge most difficult is the need to manage this strain over a prolonged period of time, during which competing objectives will pressure leadership to declare victory prematurely in order to get back to a steady state. This impulse must be overcome if the transaction is going to deliver the value expected. Major transactions may very well require two to three years of active integration-program management.

Courage is a critical part of the leadership formula during integration. We have discussed treating the M&A transaction as an opportunity for transformation. As for all true transformations, leadership keeps the ambition high and assures the organization it is achievable with a tangible path forward. The willingness to make hard decisions about the leadership team itself is usually among the first challenges to be met. Again, the urge to stabilize the organization must be balanced against the longer-term interests of the new company.

Leadership appointments

Mergers and acquisitions offer opportunities to carefully consider the makeup of leadership teams with an eye to the future. Typically, organization design focuses first on the organization model and then aligns leadership team roles and builds out their unit structures. In the case of mergers and acquisitions, the leadership team often needs to be designed early on to guide the integration even as the organization model is still emerging. The need to stabilize roles and membership in the new organization should be balanced with the need to have the right team in place for the future of the company. It is often most practical to set up roles for key members of both teams with an understanding that further changes are likely in the future. Perhaps the question to ask is, "What does our 'day 1' leadership structure need to be in order to have the right conversations to drive integration and value?"

In large deals, it is ideal to communicate the CEO-1 structure at the announcement of the transaction, or shortly thereafter. This cuts down on political divisions as it becomes clear who is making decisions. CEO-2 or even CEO-3 should be communicated as close approaches or shortly after, depending on the level of impact and disruption, and the role of the broad leadership team in driving integration.

Redesign of subsequent levels of the organization can be addressed layer by layer after the close, which keeps the organization connected and integrated laterally. In parallel is the work of harmonization by creating consistency in levels, pay grades, titles, and job descriptions. Without a logic for leadership roles and accountabilities, decision rights, processes, performance management, and budget and funding approvals become harder to manage.

Leadership forums

The CEO will likely want to reconsider the executive committee structure in the new entity. What voices need to be heard in order to execute the strategy? The integration period is a time of uncertainty for broad swaths of the organization, especially in the case of divestiture. The top team will be wise to consider a forum staffed with a broad cross-section of business, geographic, and functional leaders that can help to carry messages out into the organization and bring effective feedback to the top of the business.

The roles that these forums play should be clearly defined to distinguish decision-making responsibilities from teams that provide input and serve as eyes and ears in the broader organization. During the integration process, these groups can be set up as transition structures that are part of the greater program management effort; they may be dissolved later or may morph into broad-based management committees.

Leadership work during integration

To get the most out of a deal, planning and activation for the long term must start in the short term, commonly characterized as "day 1", and carry through to completion. Short-term plans should set out enough of the guardrails that long-term activities can emerge without relitigating decisions already made, and getting the balance of effort right is needed so the workload is manageable and sustainable for the team.

Organizations often spend a lot of energy in the short term. Teams devoted to customer impact, legal, operational, financial, and organization readiness are formed. Teams work long hours to design and execute on what will be needed to integrate and operate from day 1. These activities often take people out of substantive roles and put them into a big program condensed into a short period, with a lot of intense decision-making.

By the time day 1 is reached, the teams are exhausted. They are more than ready to hand off to the leaders to pick up ongoing operations. While celebrations at this milestone are warranted, it is too often confused with the finish line. Design and activation are often handed off to change management teams and the focus turns to realizing cost synergies. This delegation is often insufficient to maintain the required focus on the strategic intent of the deal and the leadership needed to deliver. Focus and tenacity are capital leadership virtues in this space.

Aligned, frequent, and repetitive communication to employees needs to be the norm as day-1 changes are announced, and as people leave the business and new leaders are appointed. We notice, however, that cross-business communication tends to reduce as leaders shift focus to their own units. But true integration is a long game. Reinforce the model and expectations through consistent, transparent communication. Celebrate wins and positive indicators. This will help counter the natural drift that can occur over the years that true integration can take. Attention to the future culture that leadership seeks to create must remain in the foreground as day-1 plans evolve to longer-term organizational change strategies.

Talent practices

Developing new talent process often requires at least two annual cycles to work through the best practices that reinforce critical behaviors. The goal is to get management KPIs to align horizontally and vertically with qualitative measures that support both strategic intent and the values of the new company. Align performance cycle timing and unify the policies, principles, and practices that make this possible. Accenture has had positive experiences with its "shared success" approach to focusing the top 700 leaders on shared outcomes, all aligned around five performance metric categories, which include explicit leadership behaviors, as well as financial, client, thought leadership, and sustainability measures.

The following questions can guide conversations around selection, onboarding, and engaging the senior leadership teams:

- How different are the management and decision styles across the two entities, and what do we need from this for the future?

- What other elements of culture are critical for our leaders to embrace, and what can they do specifically to help drive new norms?

- What are the critical leadership forums we need to establish to assure we are driving clear direction across the organization and to assure we are getting candid feedback?

- What are the leader profiles required of the new and transformed business, once the integration is complete?

- What leadership behaviors and norms should we adopt (and make part of the North Star)?

- What individual performance targets will we set for key leadership roles to assure we are achieving both short- and longer-term results?

- What are some of the hard decisions that lie ahead that we will need to lean into with courage and tenacity?

Realize value: Four archetypes

While the three sets of enablers we have discussed are widely applicable, specifics will vary depending on the nature of the transaction. We will examine four common archetypes, each with different organizational implications:

- Expansion into a new market or geography

- Acquisition of a strategic asset, intended to build specific capabilities

- A novel combination of companies adjacent in the value chain, enabling more integrated solutions and/or business models

- Divestitures and spin-offs.

The following sections illustrate how the three enablers of strategic choices, organizational intent, and focus and tenacity can play out in specific contexts to accelerate growth and profit objectives.

1: Expansion into a new market or geography

When a company has reached saturation in its current markets, it is not unusual to seek expansion into adjacent markets or geographies. A quick way to enter the market is to combine with a similar company that can provide complementary product lines or access to new distributions and customers. For example, global consumer goods companies will often build a portfolio of brands. Some originate in the home market but are distributed globally; others are acquired brands, specific to local markets. The challenge, in this case, is to grow revenue while maintaining or leveraging scale, and while not eroding margin.

A new market or target company may have a high degree of similarity to your own, but do not assume there are not small but impactful differences in regulations, customer preferences, culture, and ways of working that can destroy value. Making the effort to understand these early and being intentional in uncovering and responding to them will strengthen the veracity of your business case and affirm deal intention. Some common organizational challenges include the following.

National cultures

Regardless of how much positive intent is displayed by the principal players negotiating a deal, differences in country cultures will manifest as the people in two organizations figure out how to work together. In 1984, renowned researcher Geert Hofstede published *Culture's Consequences*,[14] a look at international differences in workplace values based on decades of survey data gathered through his work at IBM. This research has since been extended in numerous studies, and the six dimensions of culture he identified are now well established and understood as a framework for how people of different cultures behave in an organizational setting. However, this is often overlooked in cross-border M&A, and contributes to a lower success rate for these deals.

Cultural differences often show up in regard to decision-making and the impact on autonomy and outcomes. Consider an acquired firm from a culture where decisions are made quickly, individual accountability is high, and performance is put above workplace community considerations. Were this company acquired by an overseas competitor with a culture of respecting hierarchy, and consensus-driven decisions based on broad consultation, tension becomes inevitable. In fact, in cases like this, we have seen the acquired managers quickly frustrated as decision-making slowed, resources became constrained, autonomy was impinged, and the performance of their business declined. This can lead to the departure of key leaders, and the loss of important relationships and a deep working knowledge of the organization and local industry. Some forethought about relationship management and delegation of authority in the context of cultural differences can help avoid significant and sustained losses. Incorporating consideration of national culture, values, and behavior in the workplace into your integration planning will improve the likelihood of success.

Customer preferences and expectations

Customer behavior can vary greatly from region to region. During the first decades of the 21st century, a large consumer products company with a portfolio of brands made a number of acquisitions of competing brands. Initially, these brands remained very locally managed in terms of product design and development as well as go-to-market practices. When growth waned, however, and profit margins shrunk, top leadership shifted the operating model to a more global approach to product and brand management. Inspired by others' success in globalizing the management of categories, the model was implemented across brands with the most worldwide reach. Some were more effective than others. While design trends may move fluidly across the United States, Europe, and Asia, brand stories often do not translate as well. Few brands have sufficient brand power to leverage in this way successfully.

When geographic expansion elicits fundamental change in the detail of an operating model, ask:

- What will be centrally controlled and consistent across the new entity, creating economies of scale and realizing cost synergies?
- Which elements require localization and local control in order to respond to the voice of the customer and market?
- If product design is to align to local trends, how will the product life cycle and design approvals be managed, and what is the implication for manufacturing and supply-chain logistics?
- What must be organized by category, brand, or product in order to provide business and product or service line leadership?
- Will advertising be the same everywhere with only language translation, or is it necessary to have in-market teams to make this relevant to the local market?
- What marketing spending limits will be put in place?

You can also apply this logic to enabling functions in order to determine centers of expertise, global business service centers, regional or geographic hubs, and what must sit locally or in lines of business.

Channels

Marketing, purchasing, and distribution channels can all impact the economics of getting products to customers, and can vary greatly from country to country. Additionally, the channel mix may also be very different between the companies coming together in terms of traditional or modern trade, and direct or indirect channels. When the Mars Wrigley confectionary business, part of Mars Inc, acquired the Kind brand for healthier snacking bars it gained a transnational brand. Leadership knew that this brand would need to be kept largely separate from the core candy business in order to protect the special value of Kind in the market. There would be benefits of scale in integrating it into the mass grocery channel in the United States and Europe, but differences in consumer taste were a factor in the decision to move very slowly in integrating the Kind products into core channels.[15]

In some countries, e-commerce is not well developed, while, in others, it is a significant part of most businesses. With the globalization of content and supply chains, the opportunities for creating economies of scale and delivering direct to consumers are greater than ever. However, if you are entering a market that has a distribution model more reliant on agents, entrenched sales networks, or established infrastructure such as retail aggregators, resolving relationships and contractual agreements in the short term may be unfeasible. The short-term organization design will need to align to this, including acceptance of any embedded costs, but long-term plans should include a transformed operating model with improved channel management and reduced costs.

2: Acquisition of a strategic asset for specific capabilities

Companies may acquire a smaller company to secure a strategic asset—a technology platform, product, or service capability that is the result of specialized knowledge and innovation. In 2020, Neste, a leading Finnish provider of diesel and aviation biofuel, invested in Sunfire, based in Germany, a maker of electrolyzers (which produce renewable hydrogen and syngas—a mixture of hydrogen and carbon monoxide—from renewable electricity, steam and captured carbon dioxide). The deal—and the technology that came as part of it—is helping Neste as it reinvents itself as a supplier of renewable energy.

IBM's $34 billion deal for the open-source software leader, Red Hat, was intended to be an acquisition of an adjacent capability to the core business.[16] The deal came as a surprise to investors and the business press, given the small revenue stream from Red Hat's Linux-based products. The bet was that Red Hat know-how would be IBM's path to hybrid cloud computing. It was agreed by many that the value of the deal would ultimately come down to the approach IBM would take in integrating—or not—this very interesting company into its core. IBM remained true to its strategy and maintained the platform neutrality it promised for Red Hat's role in the market, and, six years after the deal, IBM's growth increased (to 8 percent in 2022) after years of no growth. Observers largely agree that Red Hat is a significant element of IBM's growth strategy.

So, when the acquisition is a smaller, innovative, nimble company, the acquirer faces a challenge in how to integrate the new asset in a way that sustains its inherent value. Carefully considering function integration is as important as business capability. HR policies will influence how individuals are compensated and what behaviors that drives. If the acquisition were to acquire teams that innovate product or service offerings, that capability could be diminished by the wrong HR practices. Done poorly, the acquiring company can suffocate the ways of working that made the asset successful, followed by an exodus of talent, customers, and the degeneration of strategic value. There are three clear moves that can be made to preserve value.

Provide balanced autonomy

Placing leadership of the acquired entity under layers of leadership in the acquiring organization can confuse decision rights, cause tension, and generally slow down the decision style and pace that have contributed to prior success. For leaders who are founders that built the acquired entity, or an executive team who are used to calling the shots, this loss of power can be frustrating and demoralizing. Focus is diffused and integration falters. Conversely, fully preserving autonomy can create confusion internally and for customers and diminish the benefits of connecting new capabilities to the acquiring company. Therefore, a balance of freedom within the framework of broader organizational governance is required. This works well when:

- Integration is staged over an extended period of 12–36 months to allow for client transition, pricing harmonization, rebranding, and the gradual transition of ways of working.

- Acquired leaders are given recognition and a voice to influence the broader organizational agenda. In short, take advantage of the capability they bring to get the most out of the acquisition.

- Budget is agreed ahead of time for a period and then left alone. There should be no take-backs due to broader company economics and no layers of post-approval renegotiations that distract from the core mission and hinder productivity. This should be subject to meeting performance expectations, of course, but not at the expense of pace and agility.

Quarantine culture and identity

Culture is often a defining characteristic of companies that have developed a new technology, product, or service. It is embedded in policy, employee experience, and ways of working such that it attracts and inspires the type of leaders and teams who have driven the innovation. They have a strong affiliation to the brand and the internal community. Preserving this sense of belonging, identity and pride, and factoring it into deal assumptions is critical. It is likely to add some additional management cost in the short term, but this will be repaid in retaining the people and capability that developed the strategic asset in the first place.

Unfortunately, significant culture clash is something that often occurs when "big buys small". The hope for these deals is that a large company can offer many opportunities to a high-flying, rapidly growing business in terms of distribution reach, a strong balance sheet for investment, complementary products and services, and other scale advantages. In return, the large company gets access to new growth avenues or a scalable platform for growth, such as a digital-native brand or technology platform that is disrupting part or all of the value chain. All too often, however, what happens next is the larger organization in one way or another alienates the employees, creates P&L pressure through cost allocation, and strangles nimbleness with large company processes and reporting. Comparatively simple things become flash points: leaders of a company who have also just experienced a major liquidity event are rebadged with titles that firmly signal middle-management; or right after close a huge burden of compliance and other training is piled onto employees at all levels; or a small brand is put on large-scale technology infrastructure, drowning it in overhead costs. Talent bleed ensues and, sooner or later, the high-flying growth business is shuttered, written-off or sold—in some cases just so that someone can repurpose the assets rather than sustain the business. Quarantining culture by preserving ways of working will protect value as the strategic asset is scaled.

Measure what matters

It is wise to avoid moving people onto a corporate performance management program that does not relate to how they achieve business outcomes, or how they have developed as professionals. Ensure the right metrics and rewards for leaders and employees are in place to retain talent, promote the right outcomes, and encourage personal and professional growth. Geoffrey Moore argues in his book *Zone to Win* that startups, including small, innovative acquisitions, should be measured on qualitative disruptive innovation factors, venture-funding milestones such as minimal viable product, market definition, and customer uptake, avoiding profit-and-loss and return-on-asset metrics entirely.[17] As the business matures, there can be a shift in metrics and degrees of integration into the core.

Serial acquisition of strategic assets can be a competitive advantage, replacing internal innovation, but doing it well takes practice. Accenture acquired over 160 companies between 2018 and 2023 and developed well-honed skills to determine where and when to fully integrate, and when to leave degrees of autonomy and independence. Leading serial acquirers reap total shareholder returns between 91 and 129 percent depending on region.[18]

Strategic acquisitions can be a catalyst for growth in isolation or as a repeatable mechanism. Either way, be cautious to preserve the uniqueness and value of the acquisition, and to use the process to build and extend internal capability.

3: A novel mix of companies adjacent in the value chain

Establishing a new combination of companies that are adjacent in the value chain creates a platform to serve the same or overlapping customer segments with a more connected offering. The opportunity is to create much more integrated solutions. These new combinations bring special organizational challenges, however, when business models, distribution models, and company cultures are vastly different, making them especially challenging to integrate.

Global health company Cigna Group has launched Evernorth, a subsidiary company that provides integrated health services by combining Cigna's 2018 pharmacy benefits manager acquisition (Express Scripts) with its medical insurance, behavioral benefits management, and provider networks to create a comprehensive and personalized care experience for patients living with high-cost health conditions. The Evernorth branded business was viewed as the most practical way to build a new business model with its own distinct organizational focus, capabilities, and culture. This relative independence is also important to establish "neutrality" of its services when it markets its solutions to other insurance companies and large employers that do not use Cigna medical insurance.

Despite being in the same industry and providing adjacent services or products, the capabilities required to serve employer health plans and patients are very different indeed. For example, health insurance is a premium product designed and managed by actuaries who measure long-term risk and reward with a large business-to-business component. Pharmacies are largely retail outlets, where low-cost and competitive pricing determine success. The people working in these two sides of the company will work in fundamentally different ways, measure success differently, and think differently about how to operate. Combining these cultures and ways of working within a large corporation is a daunting task. Carving out a subsidiary to build something entirely new rather than trying to embed it into the core business, in the manner Cigna has done, can make a lot of sense.

4: Divestitures and spin-offs

We have focused mainly on mergers and acquisitions, but divestitures are another mechanism to optimize the business portfolio when strategy changes. A divestiture is the sale or spin-off of part of the business. A spin-off is a specific type of divestiture that stands up a public company. Such moves are used to raise capital, narrow strategic focus, reduce management complexity, or simply to exit a non-performing business.

During the last 10 years, there has been a clear trend towards rethinking the conglomerate business model. In the United States, General Electric, United Technologies, DuPont, Danaher and others have split up and refocused. In Germany, companies such as Siemens, Bayer, Fresenius and Thyssenkrupp have seen demands to break up their diverse business portfolio to release value. In Japan, Toshiba is now a smaller, more focused company. This trend is likely to continue in parallel with mergers and acquisitions, requiring expertise in the organizational implications of divestitures for the business leader and organization designer.

If we once again consider the business configuration framework (see Table 2.1)—the continuum that represents degrees of integration across major business units—it will be evident that the more the legacy operating model resembles a conglomerate or holding company, the simpler the divestiture will be. When divesting an organization that operates mostly independently, the task is largely focused on legal, contractual, and financial activity. The complexity of divestment becomes more complicated the more integrated into the core of the company the asset is.

So, while the playbook is consistent across divestitures, the extent of design effort will differ according to the legacy business configuration and the nature of the transaction. When a business is sold to an acquiring company, the organizational challenges for the seller are largely about managing the impact on the retained organization, not the divested asset. In the case of a spin-off, the "seller" carries the burden to organize all elements of the new company to make it viable and attractive in public capital markets; that responsibility is part of the existing commitment to shareholders who will now own shares in this NewCo. The NewCo now must have a robust strategy and an operating model that incorporates all functions necessary for running a public company versus only those functions that were necessary to support the business as a division of a larger parent.[19] It must also be staffed with the right talent.

The spin-off

Divestitures are predicated on the notion that the separate parts are greater than the sum of the two. Transformation opportunities are abound in the spin-off. United Technologies' spin-off of the Carrier climate-control business was an outstanding example of value creation.[20] Placing one of the best executives UTC had on its leadership bench into the CEO role at Carrier was a major win. The strategy was completely reconsidered, focused on digitally powered, intelligent building services. A more center-led operating model was defined as part of the North Star. Among the first moves was consolidating a shared engineering group with greater emphasis on scalable, digital innovation and centralized approaches to developing control systems and other platforms that worked across its commercial and residential lines of business, and a centralized supply chain enabled more productive utilization of capacity. These changes occurred over a roughly two-year period following the spin-off from UTC. The former parent assured that all the essentials were in place prior to the NewCo shares coming to market, but the new leadership team assembled its own North Star after the spin was complete. Carrier continues to be an innovator in rethinking technology and data-powered ways of working as it reshapes its own portfolio.

The retained business

This is an opportunity to take a comprehensive approach to the future needs of the business, removing costs with the view to building something new. Support functions need to be rebuilt for purpose, sized for the retained organization, and should be candidates for reinvention as the organization transitions to generative AI and digital workflows. Layers of support can be simplified and realigned against the revised portfolio of businesses and geographies, or simply removed.

Labcorp, a US-based diagnostic testing company, chose to spin off its clinical development contract business in 2023, standing up Fortrea as a publicly traded company.[21] Labcorp CEO, Adam Schechter, chose the opportunity to double down on capital allocation strategies to drive innovation and growth in its core business, strengthening the innovation teams and resources. Each of the functional groups were tasked with right-sizing to fit the smaller and more focused company. The effect of a narrower focus meant that more functional activity could be moved to the center. Separately, the decision was made to give Fortrea access to Labcorp's vast health and clinical dataset through an arrangement which enables Fortrea to provide enhanced trial execution and a differentiated value proposition.

Similarly, when the RTX business structure was reset following the spin-off of Carrier and Otis, there was a focus on moving work from the business units to more centralized centers of expertise within the HR, finance, and supply chain functions. This is a common opportunity taken by many companies after divestiture.

These considerations by archetype have been summarized into Table 3.1. As you apply these recommendations, use transactions to learn and grow. As leaders cycle through transactions, they use each to extend and improve their framework and tools, to make tighter connections between strategy and execution, and as a means to attract, develop, and retain top talent. In summary, they get better with every acquisition.

Table 3.1   M&A archetype considerations

Archetype	New market or geography	Strategic asset	Novel combination	Divestiture/ spin-off
Considerations	• Plan for national and cultural differences in decision-making • Understand differences in customer preferences and buying habits • Assess expectations and costs around channels to market	• Maintain acquired leadership autonomy and give authority in the hierarchy • Quarantine culture and identity • Align KPIs for sustained performance of the new capability	• Proactively and intentionally manage operating model differences, not only complementary areas	• Design the NewCo for independence, and with a greenfield mindset • Use the spin-off to reinvent the retained organization

Conclusion: Executing mergers, acquisitions, and divestures

Mergers, acquisitions and divestments are essential as levers for growth or to refocus a portfolio, but history shows us that the long-term promise of transaction value is hard to achieve. Companies that succeed take three actions on a future set of commitments:

- Make strategic choices for all integration decisions and trade-offs with a bias for growth, grounded in the deal logic on long-term business outcomes and capabilities.
- Run a substantive and ongoing assessment of the organizational requirements for integration, from due diligence through implementation, proactively meeting the requirements for structure, process, metrics, and talent.
- Set the expectation for continued leadership focus and investment of time and energy for an extended period of time.

While these three actions are universal to all transactions, the four archetypal transactions highlight the specific elements with the power to make or break a deal. Make the extra effort to tailor implementation to your situation to preserve deal intent and value.

Key takeaways

- Mergers, acquisitions, and substantial divestitures should be rooted in decisive and granular business strategy that is the foundation of a North Star set of outcomes for the transaction.
- Focus on what will be different, what to exploit, what new capabilities make the deal attractive, and what must be translated into organization and operating model designs. Identify which culture or elements of culture are critical to success.
- Define your business configuration and primary operating model orientation around the growth and profit strategy, while shaping your day 1 design to create the foundations and deliver on the deal thesis. Align metrics and people practices to elicit the behaviors that shape your desired culture at the outset.

- Leadership is a critical component of the mergers, acquisitions, and divestment transformation process. Put the right leadership team in place early and create clear and visible accountability for long- and short-term results.

- Be aware of your deal archetype: new market or geography; strategic asset; novel combination; divestiture/spin-off; and plan accordingly to avoid common pitfalls and errors.

Notes

1 Kumar, V. and Sharma, P. (2019) Why Mergers and Acquisitions Fail? in *An Insight into Mergers and Acquisitions*, Singapore: Palgrave Macmillan. https://doi.org/10.1007/978-981-13-5829-6_10 (archived at https://perma.cc/N84Q-J2FD).

2 Kane, M. (2005) Sprint, Nextel Agree to $35 Billion Merger, CNET, February 14. cnet.com/tech/mobile/sprint-nextel-agree-to-35-billion-merger (archived at https://perma.cc/79BF-DYFX).

3 Accenture (2021) Making M&A Pay, July.

4 Kenny, G. (2020) Don't Make This Common M&A Mistake, *Harvard Business Review*, March 16.

5 Christensen, C. (2011) The New M&A Playbook, *Harvard Business Review*, March.

6 Deighton, J. (2002) How Snapple Got Its Juice Back, *Harvard Business Review*, January.

7 Lev-Ram, M. (2008) Sprint Tries to Clean Up Customer Service Mess, *Fortune*, June 3.

8 Poulin, J.N. and Johnson, D.W. (2019) *After the Breakups: Big payers find vertical love in new faces*, Innosight.

9 Kumar and Sharma (2019).

10 Watkins, M.D. (2007) Why DaimlerChrysler Never Got Into Gear, *Harvard Business Review*, May.

11 Kates, A., Kesler, G., and DiMartino, M. (2021) *Networked, Scaled, and Agile: A Design Strategy for Complex Organizations*, London: Kogan Page.

12 Brumpton, H. and Duguid, K. (2019) United Technologies, Raytheon to Create $120 BLN Aerospace and Defense Giant, Reuters. reuters.com/article/idUSKC-N1TA01T (archived at https://perma.cc/3Q27-99T3).

13 CBInsights (2022), Analyzing Medtronic's Growth Strategy: How the medical device giant is expanding its portfolio, December; Yahoo Finance (2024) *Medtronic Digital Transformation Strategy Report 2024: Accelerators, Incubators, and Other Innovation Programs*.

14 Hofstede, G. (1984) *Culture's Consequences: International Differences in Work-Related Values*, 2nd edn, Beverly Hills: Sage.

15 Accenture (2024) Interview. Unpublished.

16 Miller, R. (2022) How Red Hat Became the Tip of the Spear for IBM's Rejuvenation Strategy, TechCrunch, May.

17 More, G.A. (2015) *Zone to Win: Organizing to compete in an age of disruption*, New York: Diversion Publishing.

18 Accenture Research (2021) Building M&A Strength, September.

19 Often, TSAs (transitional service agreements) are written where the former parent company provides legal, information technology, and other services to the newly spun company until these activities can be fully embedded in the new entity. The sooner these agreements can be eliminated, the better, but, in the spin, management time and attention is spread thinly and these agreements are a powerful benefit to the team for a period of time.

20 Cornell, J. (2020) Raytheon Technologies, Otis and Carrier Begin Regular Way Trading, *Forbes*, April.

21 PRNewswire (2023) Labcorp Completes Spin-off of Fortrea, July.

Reinvent with Data and Technology   04

**TOM FALKOWSKI, KENT MCMILLAN,
GERD SAALFRANK**

Contributors: Ashwin Acharya, Adam Burden

For many years, pundits have espoused the potential to use data and technology to fundamentally change the way we work. Recently, that hype has reached a crescendo. One life-science executive we work with stated:[1]

> We need digital officers that wake up every morning thinking of how we drive towards what I call the self-driving enterprise. We have self-driving cars that benefit from technologies like sensors, cameras, LiDAR, radar, GPS/navigation systems, inertia measurement units that feed machine learning and artificial intelligence algorithms. Why should a company be any different?

In this chapter, we look at the potential of data- and technology-powered organizations and what they need to do to realize this potential. We begin with a perspective on the emergence of a new age of management that is characterized by collaboration between human and machine intelligence. We discuss the organizational implications of this collaboration and the impact that data and technology can have on decreasing the cost of managing complexity and diminishing the traditional organization trade-offs that companies needed to make. We then stress the importance of being clear on the organization's ambition relative to data and technology, building the right foundation, and shaping the organization to achieve that ambition. The chapter closes with a summary of how to leverage data and technology to build new organization capabilities.

REAL-WORLD EXAMPLE A look into the future

Here is a vision of how the future might look when we fully harness the power of data and technology. Like great science fiction, it may soon become reality!

In the heart of Silicon Valley, Maria Regent, CEO of Adicaeilum, a high-growth industrial company, sat in her office, reflecting on the seismic shifts her company had undergone. Adicaeilum had transformed under Maria's leadership into a beacon of innovation, a change driven by data and artificial intelligence.

Maria remembered her initial skepticism about the data-driven approach. The old ways of intuition-led decisions had served her well, but the competitive market and a few missed opportunities convinced her to explore new frontiers. The integration of AI, robotic process automation, and enterprise resource planning systems marked the beginning of a new era for Adicaeilum.

The first major change made was in individual roles. Employees who once performed routine tasks were now collaborators with sophisticated AI systems. For instance, Theresa, a long-time employee, shifted from manual data entry to managing a team that trained AI algorithms. Her work became more strategic, a shift that echoed across the company.

Team dynamics underwent a radical transformation. Adicaeilum's system evolved from rigid, hierarchical structures to fluid empowered teams. Team composition varied depending on the remit.

Innovation teams were responsible for the entire life cycle of products, from innovation through to end of life. They were comprised of R&D product managers, marketing specialists, customer success managers, business analysts, data scientists, data engineers, AI/ML engineers, UX/UI designers, software developers, QA engineers and AI agents. The AI agent would serve as a central hub, providing real-time data-driven insights and automating processes to enhance productivity and innovation across the team.

Commercial teams were responsible for driving revenue and ensuring customer satisfaction throughout the customer journey. These teams included sales representatives, AI agents, customer service representatives, data analysts, marketing specialists, customer success managers, and technical support engineers. They drove all aspects of sales, including lead generation and qualification, customer outreach, sales pitching, negotiation and closing, onboarding, account management, upselling and cross-selling, collecting customer feedback, performance monitoring, and collaboration with marketing and product teams, all enhanced by AI-driven insights and automation.

Product supply teams were responsible for sensing demand signals and managing the entire supply chain. They were made up of supply chain managers, AI agents, demand planners, procurement specialists, logistics coordinators, inventory managers, quality control analysts, and data analysts, and their accountabilities included demand forecasting, supplier selection and procurement, production planning, inventory management, logistics and distribution, quality assurance, risk management, performance monitoring, and collaboration with sales and product teams, again, all enhanced by AI-driven insights and automation to ensure efficiency and responsiveness throughout the supply chain.

Automated customer service systems reduced the need for large customer service departments. The role of traditional support functions was also transformed. Functions were compressed and redefined. Resource planning and management was seamless across strategy, finance, HR, IT, and operations. Most functional services were replaced with AI-enabled engines that performed back-office work with little to no human intervention. Business partner roles were replaced with intelligent bots that monitored business performance and served up functional advice in the context of market opportunities and headwinds. The functional experts who remained were sharply focused on deep functional expertise, innovation, and those cases that required human interaction.

Ad hoc teams were stood up and disbanded based on project needs, a far cry from the static teams of the past. The common thread across all these teams were the AI agents that operated as team members.

Adicaeilum could now rapidly form incubators and business units without needing to build commensurate support functions. When a new market opportunity arose in renewable energy, Maria was able to quickly assemble a team combining internal AI experts, external consultants, and strategic ecosystem partners.

These ecosystem partners became integral to Adicaeilum's operations. Collaborations with startups, academic institutions, and even competitors led to breakthrough innovations. Maria realized that, in this new business landscape, collaboration and knowledge-sharing were critical to competing.

Amid these changes, Maria's role as CEO evolved dramatically. Maria now spent much of her time fostering a culture of innovation, encouraging experimentation, and ensuring that her team was equipped to make data-driven decisions. Trust, relationships, and teamwork became more important than ever. It wasn't easy. While some colleagues embraced AI, others worried for their jobs, and still others distrusted AI. Maria spent less time on near-term decisions; she became a leader focused on the future, guiding her team through uncharted waters.

The impact on company culture was profound. Risk-taking was encouraged, and failures were seen as learning opportunities. Employees were empowered to take the initiative, leading to a more engaged workforce.

As Adicaeilum grew, so did its influence. The company not only adapted to market changes, it often anticipated or even created them. As she reflected in her quiet office, Maria realized that the journey of transformation was never really about technology. It was about people—empowering them, leading them, and creating an environment where they could thrive. She pondered the future; a future where data and AI continued to evolve, and with that, the ways of leading and growing a business.

Looking out of her office window, Maria felt a sense of pride and excitement. Adicaeilum, once a traditional industrial company, was now at the forefront of a data-driven revolution, a testament to the power of embracing change and leading with vision in the age of data and AI.

The age of collaborative intelligence

The futurist from the 1980s Alvin Toffler, in his trilogy of books (*Future Shock, The Third Wave*, and *Powershift*), and management guru from the 1990s Michael Hammer, in his book *Reengineering the Corporation*, anticipated the current focus on data, AI, and GenAI.[2] These works share a common theme: the transformative impact of technological evolution on society, economies, and organizations.

The industrial age was characterized by the assembly lines and economies of scale that produced efficiency, hierarchical organization structures, and centralized decision-making. Then, mechanical engineer, Frederick Winslow Taylor introduced the era of scientific management in the early 20th century.[3] Scientific management was focused on optimizing labor productivity through time-and-motion studies and standardized practices, laying the groundwork for mass production.

The information age, heralded by the advent of computers and the internet, shifted the focus towards knowledge and information as the primary sources of value creation. This period saw the rise of networked computers, digital communication, and the democratization of information.

Today, the emergence of advanced forms of artificial intelligence, fueled by vast amounts of data and leaps in computing power, marks another pivotal evolution. AI and generative AI are not merely tools for automating tasks; they are already becoming integral to decision-making, strategic planning, and innovation. These technologies are enabling organizations to uncover insights, predict trends, generate novel ideas and concepts, and, perhaps more importantly, enable personalization at scale. As this next age of management emerges, companies will use data and technology to scale, leading to a decoupling of head count (number of people required) from output.

The age of collaborative intelligence will be characterized by a partnership between human and machine intelligence that will foster a hybrid decision-making environment where strategic and operational decisions are made through a blend of AI insights and human judgment. Tom Malone, in his book *Superminds*,[4] explains how teams can make better decisions when AI agents are included. He coined the phrase "from humans in the loop, to computers in the group". This can be seen in, for example, the collaboration between Accenture, Meta, and Nvidia to develop an AI refinery that, among other things, will create an agentic architecture that enables AI systems to act autonomously—to reason, plan, and propose tasks that can be executed responsibly with minimal human oversight.[5]

Several years ago, Scott Brinker, a marketing technologist, introduced the notion that technology is changing exponentially, yet organizations change logarithmically.[6] This failure of organization design to keep pace with advances in data and technology results in a reinvention gap (see Figure 4.1). Organizations must close that gap if they are to reap the full benefits of data and technology. Closing the gap will require organizations to rethink their operating models and the frequency with which they adapt them.

Figure 4.1   The organization/data and technology reinvention gap

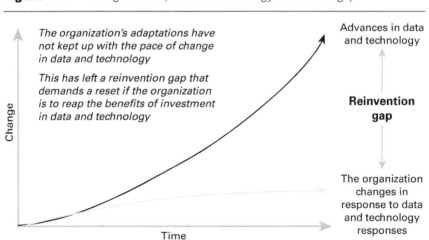

The organization's adaptations have not kept up with the pace of change in data and technology

This has left a reinvention gap that demands a reset if the organization is to reap the benefits of investment in data and technology

Advances in data and technology

Reinvention gap

The organization changes in response to data and technology responses

Change

Time

SOURCE Adapted from Brinkler (2016)

Sources of value

In the recent past, data-driven insights provided a competitive advantage. Today, not using data creates a significant disadvantage. As a result, power dynamics within and between organizations shift as access to and control of data and AI capabilities become critical differentiators.

Research and innovation will be further accelerated by data, AI, and GenAI. Manufacturing and operations will become "touchless" and more informed by data and AI-driven demand signals. Marketing, sales, and service roles will shift as the nature of interactions of consumers with products and services changes. Data and technology will act as a multiplier to human intervention. Consider how Moderna uses AI to optimize the design of mRNA sequences, which allows for the faster development of vaccines and therapies; also how they use AI predictive models to help anticipate call center volumes and allocate staff.[7]

Processes that cut across multiple functions, such as sales and operations planning and new product innovation will be compressed, with AI eliminating the need for handoffs. For example, Coca-Cola completed a data harmonization journey with Fractal that standardized disparate data sources to support cross-functional teams.[8]

Enabling and support functions will be reconfigured to provide a cross-functional view of business support needs. Many functional services will be replaced with AI-enabled engines that perform back-office work with little to no human intervention. AI agents that continuously monitor business performance and serve up functional advice in the context of market opportunities or headwinds will replace strategic business partners. The functional experts who remain will be focused on deep functional expertise and are likely to be deployed into value-stream teams.

Traditional methods of driving cost efficiencies may also change. We have seen two trends emerging. First, labor arbitrage is becoming less of the equation for shared services, with data and technology increasingly being the key differentiator to manage operations and to transform them, bringing data, hyper-automation, and GenAI to the table for lower cost and greater flexibility. Second is the rise of global capability centers in taking on higher-value work using the company's own people in locations with rich talent pools in the prime value chain, such as engineering and innovation. The success of these teams would not be measured in cost savings but in the value created by outputs like intellectual property.

The very shape of organizations will also change. AI can help to both flatten organizations and manage communications and complexity across organization layers. The traditional pyramid may diminish and be replaced with organizational shapes such as diamond or pentagon, with work being eaten by algorithms. AI and GenAI provide a greater breadth of information to senior levels of the organization, enabling broader spans of control and the breaking down of silos. Different parts of the organization will merge and have end-to-end accountabilities, with AI eliminating the need for hand-offs from one department to the next. The middle level of the organization will be composed of multidisciplinary teams integrating technical, analytical, and domain-specific skills. Even how spans of control are calculated will change as AI bots and AI agents become part of the calculus in determining spans of control.

Changing roles

We can expect to see an acceleration towards a skills-based workforce as the increased use of multidisciplinary teams require T-shaped skills—a combination of technical expertise with strong relationship, trust, critical thinking, judgment, and decision-making abilities. New skills, such as skepticism and discernment, will be required for knowing when data- and AI-generated solutions are valid. New roles and algorithms to ensure responsible use of AI will also be critical.

All of this will result in career paths that are more fluid and personalized and a greater focus on a skills-based workforce. GenAI will accelerate the creation and delivery of targeted, personalized training that aligns with career paths and is delivered when and where the learner needs it, decreasing the importance of experience in entry-level roles. The importance of coaching and apprenticeships may increase, however, as a way to develop the soft skills that can't be replaced by AI. There may be a challenge in developing future leaders and deep functional experts when traditional junior development roles are eliminated through automation. Organizations will need to augment their traditional experience-based development programs with a combination of AI-driven scenario training and deliberate coaching programs.

GenAI will be responsible for providing content and insights. Humans will be responsible for applying human considerations in order to achieve the best outcomes. Future roles will be geared around what remains distinctively human. There will be an increase in professional roles and a decrease in administrative, analysis, and basic creative content-generation roles. Agentic AI will become a digital intermediary that assists professionals in administrative tasks and making decisions. Some roles will be eliminated, and others will be created. Some of these roles will be in the realm of data and technology; others, however, will combine various disciplines to oversee complete values streams, disrupting the way we think about education and talent development. Some work will be "outsourced" to the consumer, who uses GenAI agents to replace the role of sales and service people. The net impact is yet to be determined, but will not likely be evenly distributed by industry or geography.

New employee experiences

Individuals will need to adapt to a world where AI augments their human capabilities, necessitating lifelong learning and adaptability as the technology continues to learn and adapt. Career paths will be more ambiguous as the shape of the organization evolves and roles shift. AI will hyper-personalize the employee experience based on the individual's wants, needs, and expectations. Learning and communications will be tailored to employee requirements and can support engagement. Companies will be able to tune in better to employee perceptions. AI provides a means to hear employees better and more frequently and to gather insights in a more dynamic, "always on" way rather than through intermittent surveys and focus groups.

As AI takes over routine tasks, GenAI offers the opportunity to decrease administrative work and increase the focus on the work employees enjoy, generating more opportunity for innovation and creativity. We can expect new opportunities to elevate human creativity, problem-solving, and emotional intelligence to emerge.

However, AI will also present threats. Establishing trust within the organization around how GenAI is utilized will be essential. For example, those in creative fields who depend upon intellectual property protection are in the midst of figuring out how GenAI fits with their work, as seen during the 2023 Hollywood writers' strike. Where AI will replace and where it will augment human ingenuity is still to be seen.

Heightened importance of leadership and culture

Changes must be driven by the C-suite. Leaders will be more important than ever in building trust and relationships. They will need to be more transparent with employees about how they plan to use GenAI as they adapt to new employee, organizational, and customer environments and expectations.

The responsible use of AI in terms of privacy, security, verity, bias, and intellectual property will create new reputational and ethical considerations.

CEOs and their teams, augmented and assisted by data and AI, will need to push to challenge current paradigms and ways of thinking. The convergence of advanced algorithms, vast amounts of data, and incredible computational power (yes, quantum is coming too) is enabling the visionary insights of Toffler and Hammer. As organizations navigate the age of collaborative intelligence, the ability of leaders to help individuals, teams, and organizations adapt, innovate, and ethically leverage these technologies will determine success in this transformative landscape.

While the picture of the future is compelling, what will it take to get there? How do organizations close the reinvention gap?

Human resources evolution

With the changes to roles, employee experience, and leadership and culture, HR must evolve and play a critical leadership role. Like all functions, HR will need to employ new service delivery models that use AI to support the employees, create signature experiences, and transform their back-end HR operations. These models will free up time and enable HR to drive reinvention. HR will need to promote new thinking on how organizations are designed and how the best talent is attracted. As AI enables new structures at the enterprise, business, function, and team levels, HR will play a central role in designing and activating new operating models and organizations. With these new operating models, traditional strategic workforce planning approaches will be disrupted as AI and AI agents are used to scale organizations.

Go beyond design trade-offs

Organization leaders have always had to make trade-offs. How do we simultaneously grow new businesses while sustaining our core? Where do we drive scale, and where do we want to drive agility? Should we be more global or local? Often, trying to solve these organization design trade-offs lead to complexity and added cost to manage that very complexity. Making effective use of data and technology has the potential to reduce the cost of complexity and diminish the traditional organization trade-offs that need to be made. Table 4.1 provides examples of where infusing technologies and making associated organizational shifts can push the boundaries of these trade-offs.

Table 4.1 Diminishing organizational trade-offs

	1. Core and new	2. Sale and agility	3. Global and local	4. Fixed and flexible	5. Inside and outside
Description	Grow the existing business while driving innovation	Respond quickly to customer needs while delivering efficiently at scale	Make big bets while empowering local decision-making	Maintain a strong core organization that can flex with market changes	Design around critical capabilities, enhanced by ecosystem partners
Infusing technology	• Shared data and technology platforms across the value chain • Metaverse and digital-twin-enabled experimentation • Data- and technology-driven product and business innovation	• Digitization of customer offer and core value chain work • Real-time data-driven insights and decision-making • Adaptive self-service functional service models, powered by data and technology	• AI-driven mass personalization of customer offer and experience • Data transparency enabling decision-making closer to the customer • Data and technology used to identify opportunities and make enterprise-level bets	• Repository of data and tech components used to rapidly configure new solutions • Standard integrated systems, with ability to quickly recut performance data • Collaborative technology enables cross-functional and multi-location working	• Developer platforms with repository of digital components open to external parties • Blockchain-enabled authentication and trust between parties • Shared data-sets to enhance customer offers

(continued)

Table 4.1 (Continued)

	1. Core and new	2. Sale and agility	3. Global and local	4. Fixed and flexible	5. Inside and outside
Aligning organization	• Build differentiated teams focused on breakthrough innovation and new sources of value • Simplify the core for clear accountability with the ability to share insights and know-how across businesses and functions • Increase data transparency across businesses and community governance of data	• Provide freedom within a framework of common processes, data, and technology • Design customer-centric teams that are able to work across P&Ls and other boundaries to deliver complex customer solutions	• Create complementary P&Ls for global and local teams, with shared accountabilities and common data • Build shared, horizontal ways of working, including simplified decision rights that empower local teams	• Develop mechanisms to quickly create, deploy and redeploy teams • Cultivate a culture where requirements continuously evolve and experimentation is encouraged	• Tap into the ecosystem to rapidly infuse innovative technology and other talent • Evolve relationships with third parties (from vendors to partners) and seek ways to share in risks and rewards

SOURCE Adapted from Falkowski, T., McMillan, K., and Jeruchimowitz, P. (2023) *The Tech Powered Operating Model*, Accenture

So, how do organizations begin to close the reinvention gap, minimize organization trade-offs, and reduce the cost of complexity?

As GenAI first hit the radar for many companies, they began by setting up GenAI centers of excellence (COEs) to drive experimentation and build data and technology expertise in leveraging AI to drive growth and productivity, and change ways of working. However, leaders have become impatient. They want results and they want them quickly, and narrowly focused GenAI COEs won't get them the results they are looking for in the near term.

The initial focus for many AI COEs has been on technology. However, we have found that the solution comes at the intersection of strategy, data and technology, and organization. Enterprise value is created by fusing the three. Organizations must address each of these elements.

Set the ambition and direction

The first step in any journey involves setting a clear direction. For many organizations, the journey begins with the objective to *optimize* the current ways of working by modernizing platforms and developing a strategy to better leverage the cloud. Others have moved beyond basic digital modernization and are using data and technology to *transform* the way they work. Many organizations aspire to *reinvent* themselves by using technology, data, and AI to fundamentally change how they develop products and service, and how they make money, but only a select few have effectively fused strategy, data and technology, and organization to enable their journey.

Not every company needs to reinvent. It is nearly impossible, however, to leverage data and technology to reinvent your organization without first laying the data and technology foundation needed to optimize and transform. Having a clear road map allows a leadership team to understand the destination, to make smart, sequenced investments, and ultimately accelerate impact.

Optimize

Information technology (IT) infrastructure modernization and transitioning to the cloud have become foundational strategies for businesses aiming to stay competitive and efficient in a digital-first world and for those considering AI and GenAI initiatives. Today, optimization, in many ways, means using cloud partners, and many established companies are still on this part of their journey.

Cloud platforms enable rapid application development and deployment, enhancing collaboration across a company's workforce by allowing employees to access data and applications from anywhere, at any time on any device. They provide businesses with scalable IT resources, including high-performance computing essential for AI and GenAI technologies. The cloud facilitates the aggregation, storage, and management of vast datasets necessary for AI, while reducing IT complexity by abstracting infrastructure management. Modern cloud services enhance security and compliance through advanced security measures and regulatory tools, ensuring business continuity with reliable disaster recovery and back-up solutions. Additionally, cloud computing offers cost efficiency through a pay-as-you-go model, reducing capital expenditure on hardware and maintenance.

Overall, IT modernization through cloud transition enables organizations to be more agile, secure, and focused on delivering value rather than maintaining infrastructure. This transition is fundamental to digital transformation strategies that seek to harness the power of modern technologies and AI solutions to drive business success.

The immediate organizational impact is generally confined to changes in the IT and data organizations as they adopt a combination of cloud and on-premises services. These organizational changes free up time that was spent maintaining infrastructure, and they enable IT and data organizations to get closer to the business and focus on performance enablement.

Transform

Transformation uses the power of the cloud to leverage data to build new capabilities. The next step is the use of enterprise platforms such as enterprise resource planning (ERP) or customer relationship management (CRM) systems that integrate business functions across the organization, facilitating improved efficiency, data accuracy, and strategic planning. Now the core work and decision-making of the business can be transformed in a variety of ways.

Advanced analytics enhance demand forecasting by analyzing historical sales data, market trends, and seasonal variations, allowing companies to predict demand and adjust production schedules. Enterprise systems optimize production planning, ensure quality management, and reduce waste. Automated order processing streamlines the order-to-cash cycle, improving accuracy and customer satisfaction through integrated CRM functionalities. Supply chain and distribution efficiency is boosted by route optimization, warehouse management, and automated procurement, reducing delivery times and costs. Customer engagement is enhanced with targeted marketing campaigns and quick access to customer information. Enterprise systems also facilitate compliance and sustainability by maintaining traceability and automating reporting processes to monitor environmental impacts.

For example, most companies utilize some form of ERP system to manage their core business processes. As they consider upgrading and integrating their ERPs, they face a generational opportunity to leverage this investment to transform their ways of working. Modern, cloud-based ERPs offer advanced capabilities such as automation, data analytics, GenAI, and cloud integration, enabling businesses to streamline operations, improve decision-making, and enhance collaboration across departments. The capabilities are being extended with every new release of software and are increasingly accessible for companies of different businesses and sizes. By adopting these innovations, companies can achieve greater efficiency and drive strategic growth and competitive advantage in an increasingly digital marketplace, setting the foundation for reinvention.

Organizations must challenge themselves in how they use enterprise platforms. The tendency in many organizations is to leverage platforms to optimize, standardize and codify processes and value streams. Transformation is about leveraging the data and platforms to rethink and reengineer traditional ways of working. This is best done during the design of the platforms and sets the foundation for reinvention.

Reinvent

Once cloud and enterprise platforms are set up to optimize infrastructure and transform core processes, a company has the foundations in place to truly reinvent. By leveraging data and AI, companies can significantly improve their internal operations. Enhanced data analytics and AI-driven insights enable businesses to streamline processes, increase efficiency, and ensure more informed decision-making. These improvements help them to fix the basics, creating a solid foundation for further reinvention. Simultaneously, these technologies enhance the external lens by revolutionizing customer engagement. Companies can better understand customer needs, personalize experiences, and elevate customer service. This customer-centric approach not only strengthens relationships and drives loyalty but also fosters growth.

With these fundamental improvements in place, companies can push forwards to disrupt their current capabilities, re-imagine their core value chain, and drive innovation. Advanced technologies allow them to uncover new insights, automate complex processes, and innovate at a rapid pace. This leads to the development of new business models, enabling them to transition to fully digital businesses. Organizations that reinvent themselves set new industry standards and achieve sustained competitive advantage by actively driving and embracing change rather than merely adapting to it. Figure 4.2 shows how the scope and focus change as organizations progress along their journey.

Figure 4.2 Journey of data and technology operating model reinvention

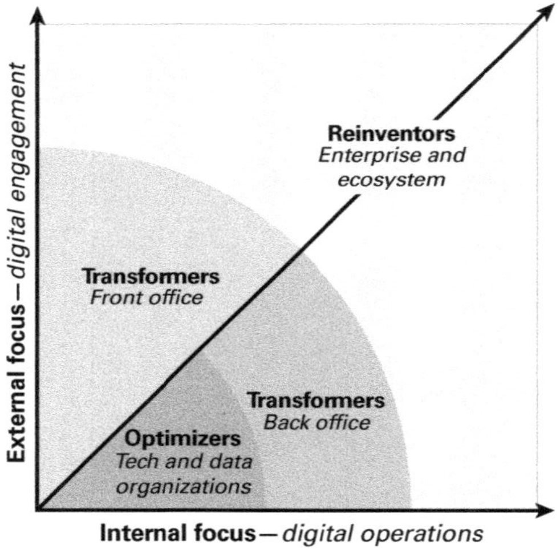

Transformers
Focus
- Data platforms (ERP, CRM, etc.)
Value play
- Efficiency/productivity
- Experience
Main organization impact
- Corporate functions (HR, finance, operations)
- Front-office functions (marketing, sales)

Optimizers
Focus
- Cloud transformation
- Infrastructure optimization
Value play
- Efficiency
Main organization impact
- Technology and data organizations

Reinventors
Focus
- Breakthrough disruption
- Sustainable competitive advantage
Value play
- Efficiency/productivity
- Experience
- Growth and innovation
Main organization impact
- Core value streams
- Business units
- Enterprise
- Ecosystem

External focus — *digital engagement*

Internal focus — *digital operations*

Reinventors
Enterprise and ecosystem

Transformers
Front office

Transformers
Back office

Optimizers
Tech and data organizations

Data and technology, especially AI and GenAI, enable new business models, innovation, and customer engagement that go far beyond what traditional ERP systems, no matter how robust, can do. They can also impact the work of traditional functions and diminish their impact over time as the work is augmented and automated by AI.

Determining where the value is for a company and then guiding management focus and investment become the leaders' strategic work. We are observing a number of emerging opportunities that will require new organizational constructs to support them.

Customer engagement

The integration of AI and GenAI into consumer engagement creates the most visible impact:

- **Personalized experiences and loyalty programs.** The number of tools becoming available for text-to-image creation, such as Midjourney, DALL-E, and many more throughout the entire spectrum of formats like presentations, videos, and ads, is increasing every day. A huge step forward has also been made on localization and customization of existing content to specific customer groups, for example the different nuances needed for age groups, regions, and so on. The advantage is that this can reduce external agency cost and increase speed as iterations can be done just by trying a different prompt. Organizationally, these tools allow content creation and localization to happen anywhere, diminishing the global/local trade-offs and requiring fewer resources, which are augmented with AI tools to generate content.

- **Customer service automation.** This is seen in the evolution of chatbots that become more sophisticated (such as Intercom) and virtual assistants becoming more and more realistic, flexible, and powerful. A large consumer company, for example, found a solution that helped to simulate different scenarios, with the AI acting as different types of customer (happy, rude, dissatisfied, aggressive, shy, and so on) to help staff be better prepared. Today, organizations are thinking about how to improve their call centers; tomorrow, they need to be asking whether they need call centers at all.

- **Social listening and sentiment analysis.** In an era of more and more digitally held conversations, there are several ways to understand the word-of-mouth of potential customers. While building these skills is time consuming and therefore expensive, there are several companies, such as Brandwatch, that analyze libraries of trillions of online conversations and give relevant insights on the voice of the customer. AI-powered tools can understand slang and track expressed emotions.[9] As a result of these changes, organizations must rethink the human–machine balance as more work is automated and human agents are augmented by AI.

Product innovation

GenAI has already become a transformative force across various industries, fostering new product innovations and reshaping existing markets.

- **Healthcare**: GenAI models are revolutionizing drug discovery by predicting molecular structures that can lead to new medications. By simulating and predicting the effectiveness of new drug compounds, the research and development phase of drug discovery can be reduced.

- **Automotive**: AI is being used in the automotive industry to simulate and analyze thousands of design iterations to optimize the aerodynamics, safety features, and aesthetics of vehicles more efficiently than traditional methods.

- **Consumer products and fashion**: Companies are using GenAI to design personalized products based on customer preferences and body measurements, resulting in bespoke items that meet individual styles and fit. For example, the ability to analyze skin types to formulate personalized skincare and beauty products not only enhances product effectiveness but also opens a new category in personalized health and wellness.

- **Architecture**: AI can generate thousands of architectural designs based on criteria such as space utilization, energy efficiency, and aesthetic preferences, revolutionizing how buildings are designed and constructed.

Ultimately, these changes will impact new product development processes and the structure of new expanded product development teams that have broader end-to-end accountability.

New business models

With data and AI, companies can deliver more as-a-service business models, including software-as-a-service and platform-as-a-service, which provide recurring revenues and closer customer relationships. Additionally, AI allows for dynamic pricing, where prices adjust in real-time based on demand and competition. The following examples illustrate how these technologies are being harnessed:

- **Subscription models.** Utilizing AI, companies can offer tailored subscription services that adapt to user preferences, enhancing customer retention and opening new revenue channels. For example, media services such as Netflix adjust their content offerings and subscription plans based on user viewing habits and preferences, ensuring a continuous engagement and revenue flow through personalized subscriptions.[10]

- **Multisided platforms.** A multisided platform is a business model that facilitates interactions between two or more distinct but interdependent groups, such as Uber connecting drivers and riders, Airbnb linking hosts and guests, and eBay bringing together buyers and sellers.

- **Dynamic pricing.** AI enables subscription-based services to optimize their pricing models in real time based on market demand, user engagement, and inventory levels. Ride-sharing apps such as Uber and Lyft use dynamic pricing algorithms that consider time of day, weather, and traffic conditions to adjust fares, maximizing profitability and managing supply and demand.

- **Freemium to premium upselling.** AI algorithms analyze user behavior in freemium apps to identify the particular moments and features that encourage users to upgrade to paid versions. Apps such as Duolingo use AI to offer personalized language-learning experiences and strategically prompt users with premium features that enhance their experience, with the aim of converting them into paying customers.

- **Financial services innovation.** AI helps in identifying investment opportunities by analyzing market data trends, providing personalized financial advice to customers, and better credit scoring and fraud detection.

- **Health and wellness.** AI enables companies to offer personalized health and wellness coaching services, creating new revenue streams in the health tech sector. Apps such as Noom use AI to provide customized diet and exercise plans, leveraging personal data to offer paid health coaching tailored to individual needs.

Business and technology strategies go together. What is possible—along with competitors and customer expectations—often drives strategic ambition. Without clear choices and an uncluttered road map, however, investments and energy will be scattershot and diluted.

Build the data and technology foundation

We know two things about data and technology: both continue to advance at a breakneck pace, and the interdependence between the two continues to grow.

Data and technology organizations

From an organization perspective, this means rethinking how data and technology organizations are designed.

Stewardship of data is at the heart of realizing the ambition to transform or reinvent. It starts at the optimizing phase of the data strategy journey. We are seeing a move away from centralized, monolithic data organizations to more domain-oriented, federated management and governance, where data and AI is *democratized* with transparency and access across the enterprise. Figure 4.3 shows the evolution of how sophisticated companies are thinking about their data to support the democratization of data and AI.

The democratization of data is enabled by organization design and the data architecture. Data mesh is a decentralized approach to data architecture that treats data as a product and emphasizes domain-oriented ownership. Unlike traditional centralized data platforms, data mesh empowers different business domains (such as marketing, finance, and sales) to manage their own data pipelines, ensuring data ownership and accountability within the specific domain. The key principles of data mesh are:

- **Domain ownership:** each domain manages its own data, leading to increased autonomy and better alignment with business goals.
- **Data as a product:** treats data as a product, focusing on usability, discoverability, and quality.
- **Self-service data platform:** provides the necessary infrastructure and tools to enable domain teams to manage and serve data independently.
- **Federated computational governance:** ensures standardized practices and compliance across domains while allowing for domain-specific customizations.

A semantic layer bridges raw data and end users, providing a business-friendly view of data by translating complex structures and technical jargon into understandable terms. It offers a consistent and standardized view of data from different systems, encapsulates business rules and logic, enhances data accessibility through intuitive interfaces, and facilitates better data governance by ensuring consistent definitions and calculations across the organization.

Figure 4.3   Organizing for data and AI (D&A)

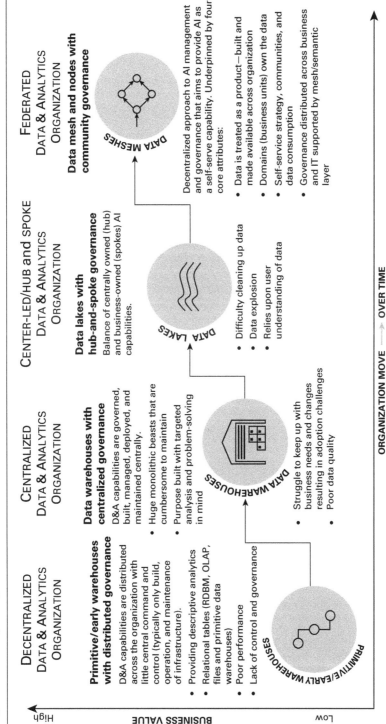

DECENTRALIZED DATA & ANALYTICS ORGANIZATION

Primitive/early warehouses with distributed governance

D&A capabilities are distributed across the organization with little central command and control (typically only build, operation, and maintenance of infrastructure).

- Providing descriptive analytics
- Relational tables (RDBM, OLAP, files and primitive data warehouses)
- Poor performance
- Lack of control and governance

CENTRALIZED DATA & ANALYTICS ORGANIZATION

Data warehouses with centralized governance

D&A capabilities are governed, built, managed, deployed, and maintained centrally.

- Huge monolithic beasts that are cumbersome to maintain
- Purpose built with targeted analysis and problem-solving in mind
- Struggle to keep up with business needs and changes resulting in adoption challenges
- Poor data quality

CENTER-LED/HUB and SPOKE DATA & ANALYTICS ORGANIZATION

Data lakes with hub-and-spoke governance

Balance of centrally owned (hub) and business-owned (spokes) AI capabilities.

- Difficulty cleaning up data
- Data explosion
- Relies upon user understanding of data

FEDERATED DATA & ANALYTICS ORGANIZATION

Data mesh and nodes with community governance

Decentralized approach to AI management and governance that aims to provide AI as a self-serve capability. Underpinned by four core attributes:

- Data is treated as a product—built and made available across organization
- Domains (business units) own the data
- Self-service strategy, communities, and data consumption
- Governance distributed across business and IT supported by mesh/semantic layer

PRIMITIVE/EARLY WAREHOUSES

DATA WAREHOUSES

DATA LAKES

DATA MESHES

High · BUSINESS VALUE · Low

ORGANIZATION MOVE — — → OVER TIME

Both data mesh and semantic layers play crucial roles in modern data management, promoting agility, scalability, and improved data governance within organizations. Implementing a data mesh and a semantic layer involves significant organizational design challenges and decisions about what aspects of data management should be centralized and what should be federated.

Organizations that reinvent are making data available across the organization, with self-service, and governance distributed across business and IT, supported by a mesh and semantic layer. Organizationally, those who reinvent are moving from centralized data management to a federated model in which data and AI experts sit with the business. Governance is distributed across business, data, and IT.

Data and technology leadership

The rethinking of how data is used in the organization has prompted a shift in technology roles. Companies have proliferated technology leadership roles as they try to provide the right focus on infrastructure, data management, and applications, and distinguish between employee and customer needs. These roles include:

- **Chief information officer (CIO).** While traditionally focused on IT management and infrastructure, the CIO role has evolved to encompass broader business strategy integration, focusing on the how technology underpins business operations.

- **Chief technology officer (CTO).** Previously this role would lead new technological development and deployment. Now the CTO's role has expanded into a strategic visionary position that aligns cutting-edge technology initiatives with long-term business goals.

- **Chief data officer (CDO).** Initially created to focus on data governance and compliance, the CDO now typically plays a role in strategic decision-making, data analytics, and information asset monetization, often driving data-centric business models.

- **Chief AI officer (CAIO).** This is an emerging role to organize data and AI strategies to drive value and growth. A 2023 CIO magazine survey showed 11 percent of mid-to-large companies had hired a CAIO and another 21 percent were seeking to hire one.[11]

The challenge is the overlap between these roles. CEOs need to determine whether they need all of these roles or if they are creating duplication and confusion. We are seeing merged roles to reap the benefits of combined leadership in technology and data management in an effort to create more cohesive and agile decision-making processes where technology and data strategies are seamlessly integrated:

- **CIO and CDO.** As data becomes a critical asset for decision-making, digitization, and operational efficiency, the CIO role is often expanded to include responsibilities typical of the CDO. This can include oversight of data analytics, data governance, and information policy, positioning the CIO as both a technology and data leader. Sometimes this is visible in the job title, for example by establishing a chief digital and information officer in the way that audio-products company Harman has done.[12]

- **CTO and CDO.** In tech-driven firms, especially where the product heavily relies on data, such as AI-native or Internet of Things companies, the roles of CTO and CDO might converge. The combined role focuses on leveraging technology and data for product innovation and competitive advantage. Walmart merged its CTO and CDO roles to increase the pace and magnitude of change.[13]

- **CIO and CTO.** In some companies, the CIO and CTO roles have merged into a single position overseeing both internal IT operations and the development of customer-facing technologies. This is common in businesses where internal IT capabilities are closely tied to the product or service being offered.

In organizations where these roles remain distinct, there is, nonetheless, often a strong emphasis on collaboration. This ensures that the IT infrastructure supports data initiatives and that technological innovations leverage data insights effectively. When designing closely related leadership roles, several key considerations must be addressed. The roles should align with the company's strategic objectives without compromising IT security, data privacy, or technological innovation. Leaders must possess a blend of technical, strategic, and managerial skills, with clearly defined scopes for CIO, CDO, and CTO responsibilities to prevent overlap. The roles should be scalable and flexible enough to adapt to growth and changing market conditions, with external partners such as contractors aiding flexibility. Organizational structure must support effective communication and decision-making, fostering collaboration among teams.

In addition to the convergence of traditional information technology, operational technology, and data and analytics work, the use of low-code/no-code tools powered by GenAI is pushing much of the work to business users. Data and technology leaders need to enable the business use of these tools while, at the same time, maintaining the enterprise architecture standards and governance. Effective change management strategies are essential to ensure smooth transitions and maintain operational continuity when integrating or redefining these roles.

Ecosystem partners

Regardless of technical organization, it is impossible today to do everything on your own. In recent years, companies have increasingly embraced the strategy of expanding beyond their organizational boundaries to form partnerships with other firms. This trend of interorganizational collaboration involves companies joining forces to innovate and deliver goods and services more efficiently and effectively. By leveraging the strengths and capabilities of multiple organizations, businesses can achieve outcomes that would be difficult or impossible to accomplish independently.

Modern businesses generate vast amounts of data, and the ability to analyze and act on this data is crucial for maintaining a competitive edge. However, developing the necessary AI capabilities in-house can be prohibitively expensive and time-consuming. By partnering with specialized firms, companies can access cutting-edge technologies and expertise without the need for substantial internal investment. These collaborations enable businesses to harness the full potential of data and AI, driving innovation and efficiency across their operations. To accelerate their reinvention, companies are expanding their ecosystem partners beyond traditional boundaries, focusing on the right combination of hyper-scalers and cloud providers, selecting the right foundation models, and collaborating with the right application partners.

Hyper-scalers are essentially the giants of the cloud computing world. Think of them as the backbone that allows businesses to expand their digital operations swiftly and efficiently without needing to invest heavily in physical infrastructure. These companies own and operate enormous data centers across the globe, ensuring on-demand access to computing power, storage, and various other IT resources. The major players in this space include Amazon Web Services (AWS), Microsoft Azure, Google Cloud Platform (GCP), IBM Cloud, Alibaba Cloud, and Oracle Cloud.

This ecosystem approach involves forming alliances with a diverse array of partners, including technology providers, startups, academic institutions, and even competitors in some cases. These partnerships provide tools and insights that reduce risk while the company determines the optimal business and technology strategy combination. Leadership plays a crucial role in strategically selecting partners who not only bring technological capabilities but also align with the firm's vision and values. This expanded ecosystem approach fosters a culture of continuous learning and adaptation, essential for thriving in today's fast-paced business environment.

There are also growing numbers of companies that provide foundation models. Foundation models are powerful, large-scale AI models that form the basis for various applications across different industries. These models are trained on vast amounts of data and can be fine-tuned for specific tasks such as natural language processing, image recognition, and more. They offer a robust starting point for developing sophisticated AI applications, saving time and resources by providing a pre-built, highly capable foundation. Prompt engineering—a technique used to tailor the input prompts given to these models—allows developers to guide the model's outputs more effectively, ensuring that the AI meets precise requirements and performs optimally for designated tasks. Additionally, many companies are developing GenAI applications built on top of foundation models to create sophisticated tools and solutions that transform various industries. These applications include content creation, design, programming assistance, and more.

The shift towards an expanded ecosystem of partners has significant implications for organizational governance and integration mechanisms. Traditional hierarchical governance structures are often ill-suited to managing complex, interorganizational relationships. Companies need to develop more agile and responsive governance frameworks that facilitate seamless collaboration and decision-making across organizational boundaries. This includes establishing clear roles and responsibilities, robust communication channels, and effective conflict-resolution mechanisms.

Additionally, integration mechanisms must be rethought to ensure smooth and efficient collaboration. This involves investing in advanced digital platforms that enable real-time data sharing, joint project management tools, and collaborative innovation processes. Companies also need to foster a culture of openness and trust, encouraging employees to embrace external partnerships and actively contribute to collaborative efforts.

With such expanded partnerships come increased concerns around intellectual property (IP) rights, data rights, and data privacy. Clear agreements and contracts must be established to define ownership and usage rights of jointly developed IP and data. Companies must ensure that data shared with partners complies with the rapidly expanding data privacy regulations, safeguarding customer information and maintaining trust. Effective data governance practices are essential to manage these aspects, ensuring that data is used ethically and legally within the ecosystem.

The trend of expanding beyond organizational boundaries to partner with other companies is reshaping how businesses innovate and deliver goods and services. By leveraging data and AI through an expanded ecosystem of partners, companies can accelerate their reinvention and stay ahead of the competition. However, this requires a fundamental rethink of governance and integration mechanisms, ensuring that organizations are well-equipped to manage and thrive within a complex network of collaborators while addressing critical IP, data rights, and privacy concerns.

Revisit the Star Model

Jay Galbraith, a renowned organizational theorist and consultant developed influential frameworks and models that have been in use for nearly 50 years to help design organizations that achieve their strategic goals more effectively. Most prominent among these is the Star Model, which illustrates the system of strategy, structure, processes, rewards, and people practices behind every organization.

In 2014, Galbraith wrote an article on Big Data and the impact of organization design, anticipating the importance of technology and data to organization form.[14] Building on this and how we see organizations today and in the future, we have now included data and technology at the heart of the Star Model.

The elements of Jay Galbraith's Star Model are still critical, but each needs to be considered through the lens of data and technology (see Figure 4.4). It requires a different set of questions and new paradigms in how we see each of the elements of the Star Model.

Figure 4.4 The Star Model with data and technology

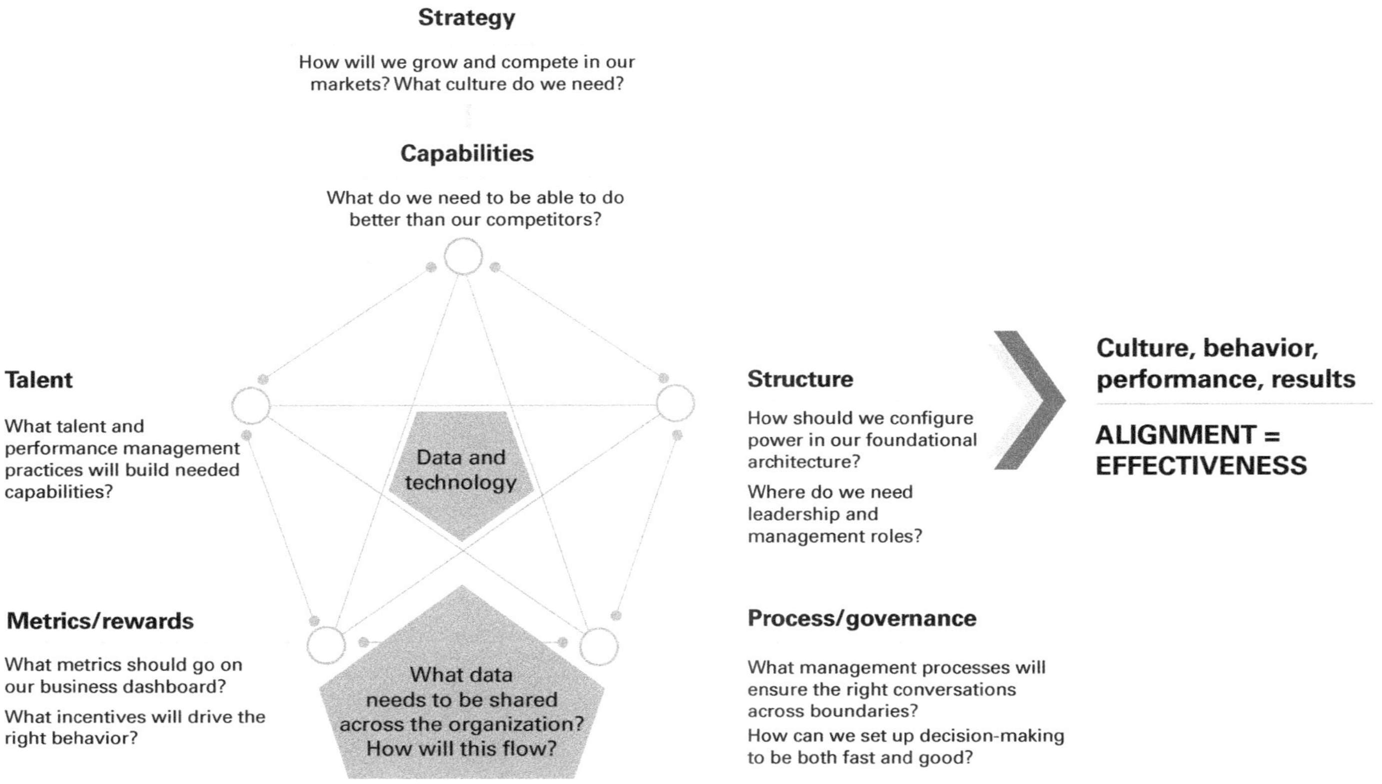

Strategy

How will we grow and compete in our markets? What culture do we need?

Capabilities

What do we need to be able to do better than our competitors?

Talent

What talent and performance management practices will build needed capabilities?

Metrics/rewards

What metrics should go on our business dashboard?

What incentives will drive the right behavior?

Data and technology

What data needs to be shared across the organization? How will this flow?

Structure

How should we configure power in our foundational architecture?

Where do we need leadership and management roles?

Process/governance

What management processes will ensure the right conversations across boundaries?

How can we set up decision-making to be both fast and good?

Culture, behavior, performance, results

ALIGNMENT = EFFECTIVENESS

SOURCE Adapted from Jay Galbraith

Strategy

The foundation of any organization is its strategy, which defines its direction and goals. Traditionally, leaders leveraged historical data and intuition to form strategy. AI-driven analytics enable companies to uncover patterns and correlations in data, offering a competitive edge by predicting market demands, analyzing customer sentiment, and identifying operational inefficiencies answering the age-old questions of where to play and how to win.

Today, AI is both an enabler and agitator of strategy. It has sparked new businesses and business models such as data monetization and expanded the playing field beyond near adjacencies. Demanding a broader view of interorganizational collaboration. This enhanced understanding allows companies to continually refine their strategies and expand their ambition, ensuring alignment with dynamic market conditions and consumer preferences.

New paradigms

- How can we use data and technology to broaden the scope of our strategy?
- What new strategies does our data enable?
- What new capabilities can we build using data and technology that we couldn't before?

Strategy drives data and technology solutions and organization design	⇒	Value is found at the intersection of strategy, data and technology, and organization design

Organizational capabilities

Expanded ambitions require the development of new organization capabilities. Data and AI enable the development of these capabilities and the rethinking of how organizations build these capabilities. By digitizing and transforming core value streams, companies can unlock unprecedented efficiency and innovation. Examples of key business capabilities enhanced by data and AI include:

- **Product and service innovation.** Data and AI drive product and service innovation by providing insights into customer needs, market trends, and technological possibilities. GenAI tools can rapidly create multiple iterations of product designs based on specific parameters, significantly reducing the time and cost of development. Predictive analytics help in identifying emerging trends and consumer preferences, allowing companies to stay ahead of the curve and introduce products that meet evolving market demands. These capabilities accelerate the innovation cycle and ensure that offerings are always relevant and competitive.

- **Lifetime customer engagement.** AI-powered analytics enable companies to understand and engage with customers on a deeper level throughout their life cycle with the company. By analyzing customer data, organizations can deliver personalized experiences, from tailored marketing campaigns driven by AI-developed content to personalized and curated product recommendations. AI-driven chatbots and virtual assistants provide 24/7 support, enhancing customer satisfaction and loyalty. Sentiment analysis helps in gauging customer satisfaction and anticipating potential issues, allowing for proactive engagement strategies. This continuous, personalized engagement builds stronger customer relationships and enhances lifetime value.

- **Building broad ecosystem partnerships.** Data and AI both demand and facilitate the creation and management of broad ecosystem partnerships by providing real-time insights and enhancing collaboration. AI-driven platforms can integrate data from multiple partners, offering a unified view of the ecosystem and enabling better decision-making. Predictive analytics help in identifying potential partners and assessing the value of partnerships. AI tools can also streamline communication and coordination among partners, ensuring smooth collaboration and maximizing the benefits of the ecosystem. This enables organizations to leverage external expertise and resources, driving innovation and growth.

- **Developing new business models.** Data and AI enable the exploration and development of new business models by providing insights into market opportunities and operational efficiencies. Machine learning algorithms can analyze market data to identify gaps and opportunities for new business ventures. AI-driven simulations help in testing different business models and predicting their outcomes. This allows organizations to experiment with innovative approaches, such as subscription-based models, platform-based ecosystems, and data-driven services, ensuring they remain agile and adaptable in a rapidly changing business environment.

New paradigms

- How can we use data and technology to broaden the scope of our capabilities?

- What capabilities can be combined?
- What new capabilities can we build using data and technology that we couldn't before?

Narrowly focused capabilities $\Rightarrow$ Expansive capabilities cutting
across entire value streams

Processes

Data, AI, and robotic process automation (RPA) have revolutionized how organizations design and manage their processes. AI tools enable processes to be transformed with less human intervention.

Different types of process will leverage data and technology in various ways. AI will enhance processes that provide services requiring human intervention, such as medical diagnosis, legal research, and customer support, by offering advanced support tools, data-driven insights, and automation of routine tasks. This allows professionals to focus on complex and creative aspects of their work, ultimately improving efficiency and service quality. Examples include AI-driven decision support systems that provide recommendations based on data analysis and intelligent customer engagement through chatbots and virtual assistants, which handle customer enquiries and provide personalized responses.

AI and RPA will transform processes that create physical products by enhancing precision, reducing production time, minimizing errors, and optimizing resource allocation, leading to increased efficiency and cost-effectiveness in manufacturing and on assembly lines. These technologies will also enable real-time monitoring and predictive maintenance of processes, such as robotic welding in automotive manufacturing, ensuring consistent quality and timely intervention to prevent downtime. An example is process automation, where RPA automates repetitive tasks such as data entry, invoice processing, and compliance reporting.

AI will dramatically change information processes by automating data analysis, enhancing decision-making, and generating detailed outputs, such as financial reports, market research insights, strategic business plans, logistics optimization plans, and application programs, with unprecedented speed and accuracy. Examples include AI-powered route planning for logistics optimization and AI-assisted coding and debugging for application program design, delivering detailed and accurate outputs efficiently.

In product and service development, AI-powered tools such as generative design algorithms can create multiple iterations of a product design based on specific parameters, significantly reducing development time and costs for both off-the-shelf and personalized products at scale.

New paradigms

- Which processes and/or value streams are needed to build capabilities?
- Using data and technology, which processes can be compressed, combined, eliminated?
- Which processes can be completely automated?

Discrete, complementary processes	$\Rightarrow$	Merged, compressed, and automated
Sequential, step-by-step process	$\Rightarrow$	Simultaneous and instantaneous process steps
Required **human-generated** input	$\Rightarrow$	Leveraged **AI agent-developed** inputs

Structure

Organizational structure determines how tasks and responsibilities are distributed. Data and AI facilitate more flexible and responsive organizational structures. With AI and RPA handling routine and repetitive tasks, organizations can adopt flatter structures with fewer hierarchical levels. This speeds up decision-making and enhances communication and collaboration across the organization. Key structural considerations include:

- **Autonomous cross-functional teams.** Data and AI enable the creation of more autonomous cross-functional teams with end-to-end accountability for results. These teams can be assembled quickly to address specific market and customer opportunities, leveraging a robust knowledge foundation provided by AI. AI agents embedded within these teams can provide real-time insights, automate routine tasks, and support decision-making, enhancing team efficiency and effectiveness.

- **Organizational structures and layers.** AI and GenAI are set to revolutionize traditional pyramid-based organizational structures, ushering in an era of flatter organizations. In a pyramid structure, decision-making authority is concentrated at the top, leading to slower response times and less agility. AI and GenAI enable real-time data analysis and decision support, empowering employees at all levels with the information they need to make informed decisions quickly. This democratization of information-provision and decision-making flattens the hierarchy, reducing the number of management layers and fostering a more collaborative and responsive environment. Moreover, AI-driven automation of routine tasks allows for a more strategic focus among remaining roles, creating potentially a diamond or pentagon organizational structure in which the bulk of the workforce is composed of highly skilled professionals supported by AI agents. These structures promote agility, innovation, and swift adaptability to changing market conditions, positioning organizations to better meet contemporary business challenges.

- **Transforming functional support.** The support for these teams will be transformed as AI agents become integral parts of the team. Corporate functions such as finance, HR, and operations will shift from traditional siloed structures to more integrated support models. For example, resource planning can cut across finance and HR, while sales and operations planning can integrate sales, operations, and finance, supported by AI-driven analytics and forecasting tools.

New paradigms

- What groups are involved building critical capabilities today?
- Can we merge them into a cross-functional team?
- How do we merge business, data, and technology people?
- What data and technology resources should be in a team?
- Which AI agents/bots should be part of a team?

Simple two-dimensional matrix teams organized around outputs	⇒	Multidimensional matrix teams around customer outcomes
Narrowly focused, human-based teams	⇒	**Teams of human and AI agents that cut across and eliminate organization silos**
Corporate functions organized around **centers of excellence, shared services, and business partners**	⇒	New service delivery models and personalized support driven by AI agents and AI-enabled engines

Metrics and rewards

The rewards system aligns employee incentives with organizational goals. Data and AI enable more sophisticated and personalized reward systems that can concentrate on business outcomes and reinforce team dynamics. AI-driven analytics can assess employee performance more accurately by tracking real-time data on productivity, collaboration, and customer feedback. This allows organizations to design reward systems that are more closely aligned with individual contributions and overall business objectives. For example, performance-based bonuses can be tied to specific metrics tracked by AI systems, ensuring that rewards are based on measurable outcomes. Additionally, AI can help identify skill gaps and recommend personalized training programs, further enhancing employees' development and aligning their growth with organizational goals.

New paradigms

- What end-to-end metrics should we be tracking (leading and lagging)?
- What behaviors are required for success?
- How are we going to reward the team?

Discrete component metrics	⇒	Integrated outcome metrics
Leading and lagging metrics	⇒	Real-time and predictive metrics
Rewarded for quantifiable outcomes	⇒	Rewarded for innovation, teamwork, experimentation, disruption

Talent

People are the core of any organization, and data and AI are transforming how companies manage their human resources. AI-driven HR systems streamline recruitment processes by screening résumés, scheduling interviews, and conducting initial assessments through AI-powered chatbots. This increases the efficiency of the hiring process and ensures that candidates are evaluated consistently and fairly. For example:

- **Task augmentation.** The automation of routine tasks (a process change) shifts the focus to roles that require strategic thinking, creativity, and complex problem-solving. Jobs will be augmented by AI, enabling employees to leverage data and insights to enhance their work. This shift will also make roles more human, emphasizing softer skills and relationships. Employees will need to develop skills in data analysis, AI, and machine learning to remain up to date, and organizations must invest in continuous learning and development programs to equip their workforce with these new capabilities.

- **Time to performance.** AI and GenAI can significantly accelerate learning and time to performance. AI-driven learning platforms can provide personalized training programs tailored to individual learning styles and needs. These can quickly identify skills gaps and deliver targeted content, ensuring that employees acquire the necessary competencies efficiently. GenAI can create interactive simulations and virtual environments where employees can practice and hone their skills in real-time scenarios. This enhances the learning experience and reduces the time it takes for employees to reach full performance, ultimately boosting organizational productivity and effectiveness.

- **New roles.** The use of AI will create jobs that do not exist today. Roles such as AI ethics officer or AI compliance specialist will emerge to ensure that AI systems are developed and used responsibly and ethically. These professionals will establish guidelines, monitor AI activities, and address ethical concerns, ensuring that AI technologies align with organizational values and regulatory standards. In addition, roles such as AI-powered customer experience manager will arise, focusing on leveraging AI to enhance customer interactions and satisfaction. These managers will work with AI tools to analyze customer data, develop personalized engagement strategies, and optimize the overall customer journey, ensuring that AI technologies are used to deliver exceptional customer experiences.

New paradigms

- How will roles be augmented?
- What new roles are required?
- How can we accelerate learning for the team?
- What AI agents need to be included?

Human-centric	⇒	Human and machines
Static skills paths	⇒	Personalized skills paths that incorporate matching AI agents to different skills and roles
Point-in-time skill building	⇒	Continuous and instantaneous advancement of skills

The questions and new paradigms are critical to how we think about data and technology at the center of the Star Model.

Conclusion: Reinventing with data and technology

As the power of AI, GenAI and technology continues to increase, there are still many things we don't yet know and can only speculate about. However, there are things we do know today:

- Companies that effectively leverage data and technology will outperform those that do not. Accenture's 2022 research on tech-powered operating models showed leading companies that have infused data and technology in their operating model significantly outperform their competitors in areas liked efficiency (2.8x), customer intimacy (2.8x), scale (2.5x), and innovation (2.4x).

- Many companies do not have the data foundation required to match their ambition, so they need to begin or continue to build it now. That may require a change in how data and technology groups are organized and the digitization of core processes and value streams.

- The power of data and AI will be unleashed when AI agents are embedded into teams.

- Regardless of a company's ambition around the use of data and technology, employees are already using GenAI to augment their work. Employees who are enabled to effectively leverage GenAI in their day-to-day work will outperform those who are not.

Companies cannot afford to wait to see what happens. While the destination may not be clear, there are no-regret moves that every organization should be making right now:

- Becoming clear on their ambition.
- Designing their data and technical organizations to support the ambition.
- Building the necessary data foundation.
- Enabling employees to fully leverage the power of GenAI.
- Preparing leaders for a new future.
- Relentlessly driving innovation and continuing to embrace new paradigms.

While we may not get to the "self-driving enterprise" described at the beginning of the chapter tomorrow, those companies that combine human ingenuity with AI-powered agents and data- and tech-driven processes will usher in the promises of the age of collaborative intelligence.

Key takeaways

- We are at the dawn of the age of collaborative intelligence that is best characterized by the partnership of human and machine intelligence.

- Most companies are experiencing a reinvention gap, where their organization is not designed to take full advantage of data and technology or realize the promise of the age of collaborative intelligence.

- Value is found at the intersection of strategy, data and technology, and organization design. Reinvention is a journey that requires a clear ambition, a strong data and technology foundation, and the right organization design to unlock the value.

- Data and technology can radically reduce the cost of complexity and diminish the traditional organization trade-offs that companies need to make, for example global versus local and scale versus agility.

- Organizations must rethink how they build capabilities by asking new questions and challenging traditional paradigms with data and technology at the heart of the Star Model, ensuring that an integrated system is created within the organization and across ecosystem partners.

Notes

1 Gianluca Pettiti, Executive Vice President, Thermo Fisher Scientific.

2 Toffler, A. (1970) *Future Shock*, New York: Random House; Toffler, A. (1980) *The Third Wave*, New York: Bantam Books; Toffler, A. (1990) *Powershift: Knowledge, wealth, and violence at the edge of the 21st century*, New York: Bantam Books; Hammer, M. (1993) *Reengineering the Corporation: A manifesto for business revolution*, New York: Harper Business.

3 Taylor, F.W. (1911) *The Principles of Scientific Management*, New York: Harper.

4 Malone, T.W. (2018) *Superminds: The surprising power of people and computers thinking together*, New York: Little Brown Spark.

Reinvent with data and technology   131

5 Accenture (2024) Accenture Pioneers Custom Llama LLM Models with NVIDIA AI Foundry, July 23.

6 Brinker, S. (2016) Martec's Law: The greatest management challenge of our time. Chiefmartec.com.

7 *MIT Sloan Management Review* (2019) AI and the COVID-19 Vaccine: Moderna's Dave Johnson, *Me, Myself, and AI podcast episode 209, July 13.*

8 Fractal (n.d.) The Coca-Cola Company Harmonized Disparate Data. fractal.ai/ casestudies/coca-cola-company-harmonizes-disparate-data (archived at https:// perma.cc/X7CH-JGRL).

9 Dixit N. and Bai, A. (2023) How GenAI Can Help Companies Go Beyond Social Listening, *Harvard Business Review*. hbr.org/2023/11/how-genai-can-boost-social-listening (archived at https://perma.cc/25YE-B7HN).

10 Netflix (2024) Figuring Out How to Bring Unique Joy to Each Member. research.netflix.com/research-area/recommendations (archived at https:// perma.cc/G6KE-7NJ2).

11 Foundry (2023) *AI Priorities Study*, quoted in S. Carter (2024) The C-suite's Hottest New Job – The Chief AI Officer, *Forbes*, April 17.

12 Parrotta, N. (2022) Leading Digital Transformation, Harman. news.harman. com/blog/nick-parrotta-leading-digital-transformation-solutions-business (archived at https://perma.cc/C8RN-EELW).

13 Hensal, A. (2019) How Walmart is Building Out Its Tech Team to Take on Amazon, *Digiday*, May 30. digiday.com/marketing/walmart-building-tech-team-take-amazon (archived at https://perma.cc/48BW-QS2G).

14 Galbraith, J.R. (2014) Organizational Design Challenges Resulting from Big Data, *Journal of Organization Design*, 3 (1), 2.

Achieve Enterprise Agility

05

WILLIAM CARBERRY, KENT MCMILLAN

Contributors: Neetu Mishra, Kestas Sereiva, Megan Tyler

Perhaps no term in organization design has become more misunderstood than "agility". Over the past 10 years, most large companies have gained some experience with implementing Agile—an umbrella term for a set of frameworks and disciplined practices, born from the world of software development and applied predominantly at the team-level of an organization.[1] While Agile and enterprise agility share many principles—most notably the importance of cross-functional teams, close collaboration between business and technology, and iterative value delivery for customers—they are not the same.

For large, complex organizations trying to rapidly pivot strategies, drive speed to value, and ensure long-term enterprise resilience, team-level impacts alone are not enough. Efforts to scale Agile principles and practices across the whole organization (beyond teams and technology) are sensible, but many leaders tell us that these investments have not always delivered the desired results. It is our experience that, when the goal is building capabilities that deliver *enterprise agility* as the outcome, we must go beyond merely ways of working. We cannot conflate Agile with robust organization and operating model design. These efforts must go together and reinforce each other, but often they do not.

While enterprise agility is a complex topic, we hope readers of this chapter take away four key ideas:

- *Enterprise agility requires a sophisticated and aligned system that works top to bottom.* We will address it at three distinct levels—portfolio, organization, and team.

- *Models that promote agility are no longer something that a company can choose to adopt or not.* It is now an imperative for *all* organizations to be able to continuously sense, adapt, and respond to change.

- *Enterprise agility cannot be installed or copied from somewhere else.* It requires a fit-for-purpose approach, highly specific to the company strategy and business context.

- *Agile on its own rarely equates to agility.* The gap is often caused by locally optimized, unclear, or misaligned organizational structures and legacy power dynamics that don't reinforce the business strategy and agile ways of working. Addressing these issues also requires robust *organization design*.

This chapter puts forward a practical definition and clear set of design principles for *enterprise agility*. Using the three layers—portfolio, organization, and team—as the lens, we explain the few design enablers that we believe can have the most impact. Our objective is to create a practical path for leadership to bring more agility into their business no matter their industry or starting point.

Why agility matters and what it really means

The origins of organization adaptability

Although nearly 25 years have passed since Jay Galbraith, creator of the Star Model, published *Designing Organizations*, his chapter on the "Reconfigurable Functional Organization" has become a prescient description of what so many company leaders are trying to achieve today when they speak of the desire for enterprise agility. He writes:

> The challenge is to design organizations to execute strategies when there are no sustainable competitive advantages. When product advantages are not sustainable over time, the winners will be those who create a series of short-term, temporary advantages... stringing together a series of moves and countermoves in a game of chess.[2]

The reconfigurable organization, as Galbraith describes, is built from a sophisticated combination of Star Model points that allow cross-functional teams (Agile or not) to be formed from a stable structure, creating "miniature businesses around products, segments, channels, or customers"[3] (Figure 5.1). These teams can be banded or disbanded rapidly around strategic opportunities without large-scale disruption or reorganization. "If change is constant, why not design organizations to be constantly and quickly changeable?"[4]

Figure 5.1   Basic reconfigurable organization

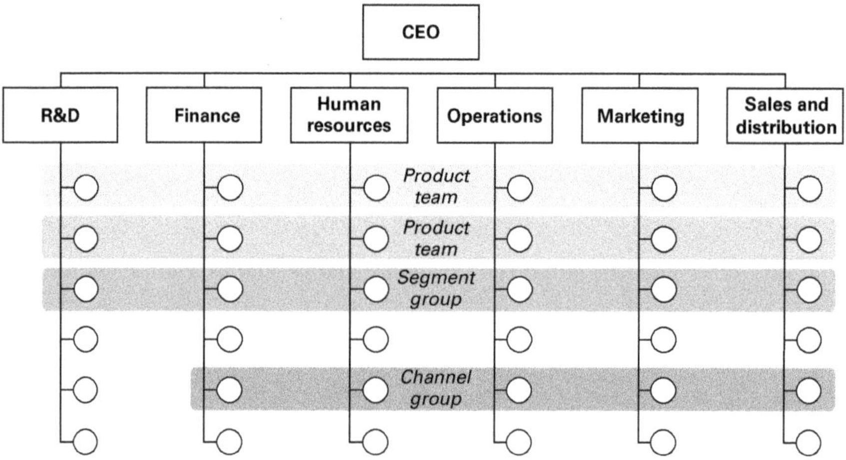

SOURCE Galbraith (2014), p. 141

While teams are the mechanism by which most high-value work gets done in a reconfigurable organization, coordinating and aligning all the moving pieces requires significant investment in fit-for-purpose technologies, tooling, systems and processes. Additionally, senior leadership must be deeply committed to managing the complexity of many semi-autonomous teams and the interdependence that is created across organization units. Despite its potential as an operating model option for delivering agility, reconfigurability still comes with significant hard and soft costs.

What has changed since the publication of *Designing Organizations* are the types of companies for which advanced models like reconfigurability are an essential fit. Formerly, reconfigurability and the extensive use of teams was best suited to companies that had technology as a significant component of their core business and were operating in industries with high amounts of disruption, consolidation, and competition. Today, not only has the advancement of data, technology, and AI greatly lowered the costs of collaboration, it has also sped up the pace of disruption in almost every corner of business, including in old-economy and highly physical industries.

Most leaders we work with are fully aware of the fundamental tension in today's operating models—the need to capture the efficiencies of more centralization, digitalization, and global scale while also preserving the speed and agility that comes from empowering smaller, distributed units and teams. Leaders understand the imperative to break down silos and work horizontally across businesses. Yet, success in achieving true speed has remained elusive and it is often unclear, amid so much new terminology, how all the necessary pieces fit together to create true enterprise agility.

The case for enterprise agility

Many executives we speak with believe their current operating model is unable to adapt quickly enough to changing market conditions, customer preferences, or technology trends. A conversation with C-suite members of a large automotive company illustrated this concern clearly:

> We face tough competition from new, nimbler players in the electric vehicle space. The future of our company will depend on our ability to innovate and meet customer's needs, but we're not built to transform ourselves. We have a legacy functional organization with strong silos, poor data and information flow, and ineffective systems for collaboration. We have rigid hierarchies and struggle with transparency. Our regional businesses have a lot of autonomy and P&L power by design, but, as a result, we have become unable to mobilize around the big-bet strategic decisions the times require. We will always be extremely focused on process, quality, and safety – that must be our DNA – but our product development and innovation cycles are among the slowest in the industry. It has become unsustainable.

Columbia University professor Rita McGrath, in her book *The End of Competitive Advantage*, explains that, over the last century, companies have passed through three distinct management phases:[5] the "execution era" with its focus on scale and efficiency, the "expertise era" with the rise of knowledge work and functional specialization, arriving today in a third era. Now, the purpose of the organization has shifted towards creating complete and meaningful experiences for customers. We have been here for some time, one could argue, but many companies are still working in a system configured to deliver outcomes meant for a previous era of management.

This new era demands that we rethink how our operating models are designed to deliver against ever-changing customer expectations. "Customers don't shop our org chart," one executive said to us during a client interview. "We need to organize more to reflect the experience they have with us, that is, across boundaries. That means we're shouldering our own complexity, so customers don't have to."

Most companies do not start from zero. They have already taken bold steps to break down silos and drive company-wide transformation efforts. In the process, many have adopted Agile or similar methodologies and have found that leveraging empowered teams to create more customer intimacy and speed has led to positive impacts but not always added up to true enterprise-level outcomes. A transformation leader from a large telecommunications company described their initial disappointment after the first phase of company-wide Agile transformation:

> We launched our scaled Agile journey to solve a cost and productivity problem in the organization and to ward off a major competitive threat posed by a new alternative in the market. While immensely challenging at first, we saw some very encouraging data at the two-year mark. We had established over a thousand Agile teams. We had flattened the organization by three to four layers to empower those close to the customers, resulting in considerable structural cost savings. Our metrics around customer satisfaction, employee engagement, and agile maturity were at or above target. People were more engaged than ever. But our leadership realized the most important needle wasn't moving. We weren't yet seeing an improvement in our *speed to market*, which was one of the key reasons for our transition to Agile.
>
> The problems became clearer once we began changing what we measured. We saw that individual teams were working more effectively, but then spent a significant time waiting – waiting for decisions around priorities, waiting for funding, waiting for other teams, waiting for data, waiting for "the vital few" with relevant expertise. We had introduced a bunch of new complexities we couldn't easily resolve, and as a result we were no faster overall.

These examples illustrate two companies in traditional industries—automotive and telecommunications—that have found their entrenched market position suddenly under threat. Not even the telecommunications company, however, two years into their transformation and with hundreds of Agile teams, had managed to achieve faster and better end-to-end outcomes. What piece of the puzzle was missing?

A definition of enterprise agility

Apple is a great example to illustrate what agility can look and feel like. Apple has continued to leverage its massive ecosystem of products and customers to bet big on new ideas. The company has expanded far beyond the Mac computer and iPhone, moving boldly now into new markets such as wearables and health, digital content, and payment services.[6] Meanwhile, deep within the halls of the company, semi-autonomous cross-functional teams of experts deliver the goods, so to speak, keeping its famed products relevant and growing. These established product platforms, enabled by common operating systems, are refreshed to the market at blistering speeds as innovations for cameras, batteries, displays, and other core technologies emerge. Apple demonstrates how a company can make decisive decisions to safeguard its financial future and then put the full weight of the organization behind new efforts, creating alignment from top to bottom.

This is the central idea behind *enterprise agility*. From this point we define the concept as:

> The ability to deliver on today's business commitments while simultaneously building the business of the future – continuously *sensing, adapting, and responding* to changing markets, customer needs, and operating environments.

This definition helps to elevate our thinking, focusing on the real goal of enterprise agility, which goes well beyond the technology function, Agile methodologies, and changes at the team level of the organization. Now we have a bolder outcome that will require not only the speed, responsiveness, and customer intimacy of empowered teams at the front line, but also significant, coordinated effort at all levels of the organization. Companies that pursue these ideals are willing to take transformative action to reinvent themselves.

Not all of Apple's "mega bets" have paid off, however. As reported in *The Wall Street Journal*, in 2024, Apple officially scrapped "Project Titan"—its quest to build a car and transform yet another industry.[7] Thinking that its technology, engineering prowess and experience with user design would enable it to overcome the incredible challenge of building cars, Apple poured billions of dollars into the bet over ten years of development work. And although not a success, Apple's decision to attempt to build an electric, autonomous-driving vehicle is still a bold example of enterprise agility. The company rallied resources against a new ambition, but also had the fortitude to decisively stop Titan when conditions changed, redeploying resources to Apple's more immediately pressing AI strategy.

Companies that intentionally invest in building enterprise agility as a capability are likely to benefit from its long-term, cumulative impacts, including customer satisfaction, employee engagement, speed to value, return on investment, and resilience.

Achieve agility: Introducing the three layers

Enterprise agility is not just one thing but, rather, the result of three distinct types of agility working together inside an organization. Again, Apple is a good illustration of this idea in practice. Despite the company's past and present successes, Tim Cook, Apple's CEO, and his team of executives keep strategic reinvention top of mind. As a team, they are willing to make big, decisive, and long-term bets, such as with Titan, ensuring Apple doesn't follow a similar fate as past Silicon Valley stalwarts that couldn't pivot and maintain their positions at the top. In this sense, Apple has tremendous *portfolio agility.*

At the same time, Apple also demonstrates excellent *team agility.* The company's ability to refresh new versions of the iPhone every year with many new advanced technologies and features is the result of effective cross-functional ways of working much lower in the organization. Empowered teams and networks of teams work together in a masterful orchestration to achieve product development cycle times that many would consider to be impossible in any other context.

However, we believe the real key to agility lies in the middle layers of leadership—two to four levels below the CEO. The leaders in this layer are responsible not only for delivering business outcomes for their own unit but also mobilizing and managing a global network of teams and assets. These leaders require a highly effective organization system to enable and incentivize working effectively across boundaries and making decisions that optimize the enterprise as a whole. This is the piece that is most likely to be missing. And it's arguably the hardest to achieve—organization agility.

This middle layer is where the translation happens from *strategy to execution,* from global to local. It is where the most critical connections are made, the trade-offs are reconciled, and the complexity is resolved in a way that unlocks the potential of teams. Leaders in these layers are close enough to the work to identify and address bottlenecks and other blockers to team progress and *flow,* or the ability to produce value continuously.[8] Organization agility, when designed intentionally and executed well, creates the enabling management system necessary for teams to deliver with few dependencies or handoffs required.

A common mistake is to focus only on one type of agility. Each is a unique concept and a unique design task, but they are most powerful when addressed together and brought into alignment. Organization agility is the connector of portfolio agility (great strategy) and team agility (great execution).

To summarize, enterprise agility is the culmination of three types of agility working together in a system (Figure 5.2). It is also appropriate to think of these three types as distinct *layers of agility* given that that the leaders accountable for activating each type map well to executive leadership, middle management, and leaders of front-line teams.

- **Portfolio agility** is the ability to make decisive bets as opportunities arise or conditions change, while still ensuring strategic clarity and alignment of priorities from top to bottom. It requires leaders be

Figure 5.2   Primary capabilities and layers of enterprise agility

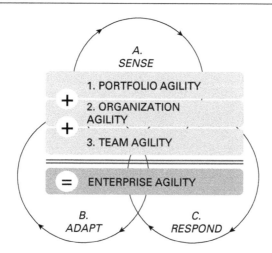

constantly monitoring for signals across time horizons that could trigger a strategic response. The response could include buying or selling businesses, entering new markets, expanding product lines, or scaling innovation.

- **Organization agility** is the ability to mobilize and manage a network of small teams and other resources, quickly and easily, to execute complex strategies or reconfigure around changes to the strategy. This requires providing clear direction to teams and working effectively across a matrix design to resolve interdependencies, trade-offs, and other blockers to team progress and speed.

- **Team agility** is the ability to treat small teams—often multidisciplinary— as the fundamental unit of work capacity and value creation in the organization. Well-designed, autonomous teams reduce expensive handoffs by keeping the majority of collaboration and capabilities required to achieve their goals within the team, thereby increasing the speed and frequency at which new ideas can be tested with customers and brought to market, reducing overall risk.

As we talk about layers in the organization, some may equate this to hierarchy. In fact, we are strong believers in the need for a healthy vertical organization design. Kates, Kesler, and DiMartino, in *Networked, Scaled, and Agile*, help us to reframe our thinking around the word *hierarchy* and the value it brings. "The idea of a hierarchy of thought and focus, and of differential velocity at

Table 5.1 The three layers of agility and their design enablers

Layer	Definition	What Does it Look Like?	Organization Design Enablers
1 Portfolio agility *Work of the board, CEO, and strategic layer of leadership*	The ability to make decisive bets as opportunities arise or conditions change, while still ensuring strategic clarity and alignment of priorities, from top to bottom	*Portfolio bets that have 2-to 5-year impact:* • Optimise portfolio through M&A • Move innovation across operating units • Incubate and scale new businesses • Drive technology synergies across units • Align portfolio initiatives across horizons	• Protect the time for executive leaders to do the work of shaping and clarifying the strategy • Create and communicate a clear strategic vision, including the top priorities for the organization • Implement new, dynamic governance models for managing the portfolios and allocating funding
2 Organization agility *Work of business unit leaders, product category leaders, functions, etc.— the integrative layer of leadership*	The ability to mobilize and manage a network of small teams and other resources, quickly and easily, to execute complex strategies or reconfigure around changes to the strategy	*Business unit strategies, product strategies, and organization decisions that have 0-to-2-year impact:* • Adjust quickly to new market entrants • Configure complex, integrated solutions for customers • Embed customer insight everywhere • Integrate data and technology platforms • Drive supply chain resilience	• Ensure the underlying organization design supports effective horizontal ways of working and scaled cross-functional teaming • Enable leaders to work with and through others to align teams, make trade-off decisions, and enable flow through a predictable pattern of operating forums and routines • Cultivate the right talent and servant leadership mindsets to fill the extremely challenging roles in the matrix • Leverage a single source of truth for executional data to make fast and informed decisions
3 Team agility *Work of front-line leadership and teams*	The propensity to treat small teams—often multidisciplinary—as the fundamental unit of work capacity and value creation in	*Incremental bets over next months:* • Move quickly from idea to launch • Innovate against customer needs and design the experience • Experiment frequently • Drive continuous process improvement	• Put high performing, autonomous teams at the center of the organization and ensure they are set up for success • Leverage modular product and technology architectures to facilitate team design decisions • Match team type to the need (product,

various layers of leadership, ensure that each layer makes a unique contribution to the work of the organization."[9] The three layers of agility shown in Figure 5.2 are built on the original layers of leadership model in Kates et al.

The use of small teams and the push for more distributed power in large organizations is a welcome trend. Research supports the use of small teams working as autonomously as possible, especially in disruptive contexts.[10] We know when teams meet certain enabling criteria (discussed further in the following pages), they become highly valuable assets to the organization, and teams match our human desires to work closely with those we can build relationships with and trust deeply.

However, autonomy and empowerment without coordination is a recipe for chaos. There is a critical distinction to be made between excess layers of management and decisions based on status or title (the dark sides of hierarchy) versus a coordinated system that unleashes energy through focus and efficient connections. We believe this means "slowing down at the top" to create real strategic clarity, enabling intentional integration and flow in the middle, and ensuring more alignment and autonomy for those teams delivering value close to the customer. Enterprise agility, therefore, requires that we design and build a system in which all three layers work together.

What "good" looks like

It is probably easiest to understand enterprise agility by describing some of the supporting capabilities required to achieve it. While our intent is not to create an exhaustive or prescriptive list, we do believe it is important to have a clear understanding of what muscles need to be built for agility to become a reality. What must the organization be able to do *really well*? In the following pages, we put forward a point of view based on our experience working with clients. Leaders can customize and prioritize this list of capabilities to fit their needs and context.

Enterprise agility is such a broad topic that we must break it down into lower-level capabilities that are specific enough to understand and action. Taking our enterprise agility definition, we can use *sense, adapt, and respond* to provide a frame for the capabilities in a way that is specific enough to guide organization design decisions. These capabilities are then built through various Star Model levers (organization structure, processes, decision-making, metrics, people practices) across all three layers of agility— portfolio, organization, and team.

The capabilities that support enterprise agility

Sensing   Aim to be **insight rich** and able to quickly recognize opportunities to increase value for customers and other stakeholders, quickly:

- **Customer intimacy**: Spend significant time with customers—internal or external—seeking to understand what they value and to anticipate their needs. Incorporate voice of the customer (and data) into all core business processes and design activities.

- **Market intelligence**: Create and protect the time and space for senior leadership to continuously survey the broader market for threats and opportunities, leveraging competitive intelligence and other mechanisms for market sensing.

- **Business and operational insight**: Leverage operational and performance data, along with internal expertise, to identify opportunities to drive continuous improvement and inform strategic direction from within.

- **Comfort with experimentation**: Treat experimentation as a value-creator and risk-reducer and be willing to constantly source new and innovative ideas from all parts of the partner ecosystem.

Adapting   Be willing and able to persevere, pivot quickly, or stop work, all without disruptive reorganization and expensive transformation programs:

- **Planning and prioritization**: Establish common processes (e.g. quarterly business reviews) to enable active and transparent business planning, allowing for frequent and timely adjustments to priorities, funding, and decisions around resource allocation.

- **Business and technology platforms**: Scan the organization constantly for opportunities to consolidate work and create common, consistent, and easy-to-use assets, tooling, infrastructure, for internal customers to use.

- **Modularity for reconfigurability**: Organize in a way that reflects the product, technology, and process architecture. Deconstruct the work into smaller discrete components that each deliver value, to enable scale, reuse, and rapid reconfiguration.

- **Leveraging partner capabilities for scale**: Earn and maintain effective partnerships and external networks that can enable ready access to capabilities and/or capacity the company does not possess for itself.

Responding   Align teams to the strategy and empower them with the distributed authority and support they need to respond quickly to changing customer needs and market conditions.

- **Strategic alignment**: Develop and maintain effective mechanisms (e.g. metrics) for driving complete alignment to the enterprise strategy from the C-suite to front-line teams.

- **Empowered and autonomous teams**: Empower teams with the context they need—clear priorities, metrics, guardrails, decision criteria, and so on—to move fast within a global framework, and grant them the autonomy to deliver increments of value to the customer.

- **Audit and risk-based governance**: Adopt a trust-but-verify approach so that teams can go until told to stop. Pivot away from traditional project management stage-gate approvals, relying more on risk visualization, transparency, and sampling.

- **A focus on continuous improvement and flow**: Track and monitor productive time and speed to value across the whole system and work relentlessly to remove systemic blockers.

Finally, we would be remiss if we did not highlight the critical role that data plays in enabling all the capabilities within sensing, adapting, and responding. Data must be foundational. Companies that seek to build the capabilities just listed will also need to invest in developing the necessary data sources, tooling, and analytics. However, advancements in generative AI are significantly lowering the cost to achieve what has historically been a monumental effort inside organizations to structure data. Going forward, having this single "source of truth" and effective tools for making data transparent and visual will be a far more achievable goal. Leaders stand to benefit greatly as they manage the many moving parts required when pursuing agility.

While we believe all the capabilities we have defined here are foundational for a company pursuing enterprise agility, the form they take and the relative priority will vary from organization to organization. It is therefore important that each leadership team takes the time to define what this all means in the context of their strategy, business model, and current state of organizational maturity. Leaders should work together to customize this list and set out clear measures of agility that will define success.

We will now discuss the three layers of agility in more detail. For each layer, we will share a set of organization design enablers for leaders to focus on. While our list of enablers is not exhaustive, we do believe it will cover the design principles that can best support development of the necessary capabilities.

Design for portfolio agility

From 2019 to 2024, the United Technologies Corporation (UTC) underwent significant reinvention. As one of the remaining industrial conglomerates, UTC was managed as a loosely related portfolio of four major businesses: Pratt & Whitney Jet Engines, UTC Aerospace Systems, Otis Elevators, and Carrier (heating and cooling solutions). In a strategic bid to double down on the aerospace and defense market, UTC divested Otis and Carrier, acquired Rockwell Collins and completed a merger of equals with Raytheon Corporation, ultimately changing the company name to RTX. The rationale of this major portfolio adjustment made sense as it allowed the new company to build greater leverage in its supply chain, to cope better with the up-and-down cycles of aerospace and defense markets, and to share core technologies across businesses. Nonetheless, some investors opposed the deal. One analyst was quoted as saying, "It looks a lot like a reconglomeration that adds complexity to a story that was getting simpler".[11] Time will tell if such portfolio agility pays off for RTX, but it is an excellent illustration of the concept in practice—the willingness of a leadership team to take transformative action to reinvent the company.

Protect the time for executive leaders to do the work of shaping and clarifying the strategy

One of the biggest shifts for executive teams building portfolio agility is reallocation of time. Building portfolio agility requires leaders to spend the majority of their time working together in a "heads-up configuration", sensing for opportunities and threats across a multi-year horizon. They need to take time to ask themselves questions such as: "What markets or businesses do we think we'll be in five years from now? Do we have the right business units and value streams? Is our innovation pipeline healthy?" While market sensing can happen at every level, only the strategic layer of leadership[12] can fundamentally redefine a company's direction by making major portfolio adjustments or scaling innovation. Leaders at this layer need dedicated time and space to do their work.

Leaders, however, do not always have a good way of assessing how they are spending their time. A calendar audit is a useful tool to show where opportunities exist to adjust forums, cadences, audiences, and agendas to ensure that senior leaders are having the right conversations, with the right participants, at the right cadence. The example shown in Figure 5.3, which uses the layers of leadership model as defined by Kates et al., describes how we used a highly visual approach to help a client correct significant gaps in

Figure 5.3 Calendar audit used to identify gaps in agendas and routines

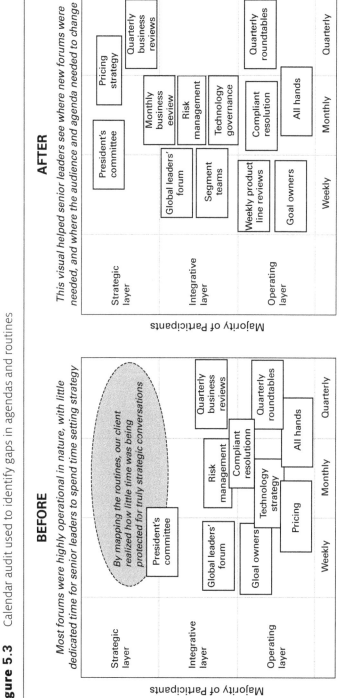

BEFORE

Most forums were highly operational in nature, with little dedicated time for senior leaders to spend time setting strategy

By mapping the routines, our client realized how little time was being protected for truly strategic conversations

Strategic layer
Integrative layer
Operating layer

Weekly | Monthly | Quarterly

Frequency

Majority of Participants

President's committee
Quarterly business reviews
Global leaders' forum
Risk management
Compliant resolutionn
Quarterly roundtables
Gloal owners
Technology strategy
Pricing
All hands

AFTER

This visual helped senior leaders see where new forums were needed, and where the audience and agenda needed to change

Strategic layer
Integrative layer
Operating layer

Weekly | Monthly | Quarterly

Frequency

Majority of Participants

President's committee
Pricing strategy
Quarterly business reviews
Global leaders' forum
Monthly business eeview
Risk management
Technology governance
Segment teams
Weekly product line reviews
Compliant resolution
Quarterly roundtables
Goal owners
All hands

strategic conversations. This simple visualization led to significant changes in routines and agendas.

Making time for these conversations and decisions might be easy if it were not for an overpowering incentive to manage business performance in the short to medium term. Across dozens of assessments we have done, it is a frequent complaint of C-suite leaders that they are not able to spend enough time together talking about the strategy and direction of the business. Their time becomes consumed with managing to short-term financial results and stepping into tactical firefights. While the firefighting is often the result of not having a high-performing and empowered integrative layer of leadership directly below the C-suite,[13] this can become a self-perpetuating cycle. C-suite leaders focused exclusively on the here and now neglect the longer-term horizons and disempower middle and senior management, forcing them to find other (often more dysfunctional) ways to establish their power and add value. The issue of constantly sacrificing the long-term for the short-term is a timeless trade-off and often tortuous to correct.

The late Clayton Christensen, a renowned professor at Harvard Business School, argued in his research article, "The Capitalist's Dilemma",[14] that the rise of efficiency metrics such as ROIC (return on invested capital) and IRR (internal rate of return) have fundamentally altered investor behaviors and leadership actions. These metrics, Clayton argues, make short-term investments that drive efficiency look deceptively better than innovative investments that drive long-term value and growth. The research article then goes on to outline several practical solutions to the issue, including using more realistic (and optimistic) cost of capital assumptions in business-case calculations and having greater insight into the true growth potential inherent in a company's innovation pipeline. If enterprise agility is the goal, leadership teams must have the courage to put the customer and long-term relevancy on the executive agenda more often.

The design of top-line management structure (typically the CEO and the two reporting layers below) can be a lever to shape the conversations and time allocation of the most senior leadership team. For companies pursuing portfolio agility, we tend to see a few common features. First is the presence of roles that consolidate end-to-end accountability for customer and business results, such as chief operating officers, heads of global business services, and leaders of major business units. These represent the businesses on the executive team, but also serve as the point of integration and accountability for most of the day-to-day execution of the operating plan, thus protecting the time of the CEO and other executives.

Another feature we see is the presence of cross-cutting integrator roles, such as chiefs of customer experience, digital strategy, business transformation, and major enterprise value streams. These leaders are accountable for driving a common strategy across the organization or executing end-to-end enterprise processes. The trend toward creating these roles reflects a growing emphasis on cross-functional ways of working and end-to-end customer value-creation in companies pursuing more agility. Giving these leaders visibility signals to stakeholders what is important, elevates their voice in decision-making, and allows leaders the necessary influence to work effectively across the organization's vertical reporting structures.

This doesn't mean that the number of direct reports to the CEO is necessarily increasing. To the contrary—we see a trend towards a smaller and more focused team at the top layer with clearly differentiated leadership layers below.

Create and communicate a clear strategic vision, including the top priorities for the organization

Our very first task when we begin our work with a new client is to understand the company strategy and gauge how far that strategic vision is shared across the executive team. Rarely do we work with a client where those are clear and aligned. We find leaders still struggle to articulate three fundamental decisions, even immediately following a strategic planning cycle:

1 Along what dimensions of our offering are we choosing to differentiate?

2 How can we map our strategy across time horizons? Who do we want to be in two, five, ten years?

3 What are the very few priorities (at most five to seven) that are *most* important we achieve this year? How would we rank these if we had to?

These questions are extremely difficult for most leadership teams to answer clearly and consistently. This is partly because many strategic planning processes don't force this level of clarity and focus, but also because enterprise strategy is often still a roll-up of business unit and market plans rather than a two-way effort and a process completed together.

If the executive team struggles to articulate the strategic choices made, imagine how hard it would be for hundreds of teams and their leaders to understand how to make good decisions. Companies that get enterprise agility right are more willing to focus their attention and commit to the vital few. They understand that a portfolio of 50 or 500 enterprise priorities will result in enormous levels of multitasking and misalignment, and will be highly unlikely to create much value or speed.

Alignment to the strategy from the top to the bottom is a critical enabler of creating speed to value and enterprise agility. Ideally, every team member should be able to clearly and specifically articulate how their work contributes to the enterprise priorities. Let's take a hypothetical example of what this can look like based on our experience. Consider a company's digital products team working on a new mobile experience for customers. At any given moment, we would want to make sure each developer on the team could clearly connect their work to the strategy: "My team and I are working on the AI-based software engine that serves relevant product offers to individual users in order to generate a 2-times higher chance of the offer being accepted while delivering 5 percent incremental revenue." Note the anatomy behind such clear statement: "I am working on X so that we can achieve a strategic goal Y as measured by Z."

Companies are increasingly leveraging objectives and key results (OKRs) as the goal-setting framework to communicate what is most important clearly and effectively. In this model, portfolio-level metrics are decomposed into business value drivers, which in turn are further decomposed into specific team-level metrics. Creating a business value tree is a useful tool to organize and document this logical decomposition and connect metrics to business priorities. OKRs can be further developed by teams from here. Figure 5.4 shows an example of a business value tree for a manufacturing company, and reflects decisions made by company leadership. Business value trees must remain living documents, continuously updated as the company strategy and portfolio priorities change.

Implement new, dynamic governance models for managing the portfolios and allocating funding

Funding business priorities and other ongoing operational activities is the ultimate expression of a company's strategic goals. As such, the processes that govern the setting and funding of strategic priorities need to be robust to create clarity of direction and preserve the organization's ability to keep moving. Two core governance concepts can make this process work effectively: funding teams as a unit of work capacity (versus individual projects

Figure 5.4 Example of a manufacturer's business value tree

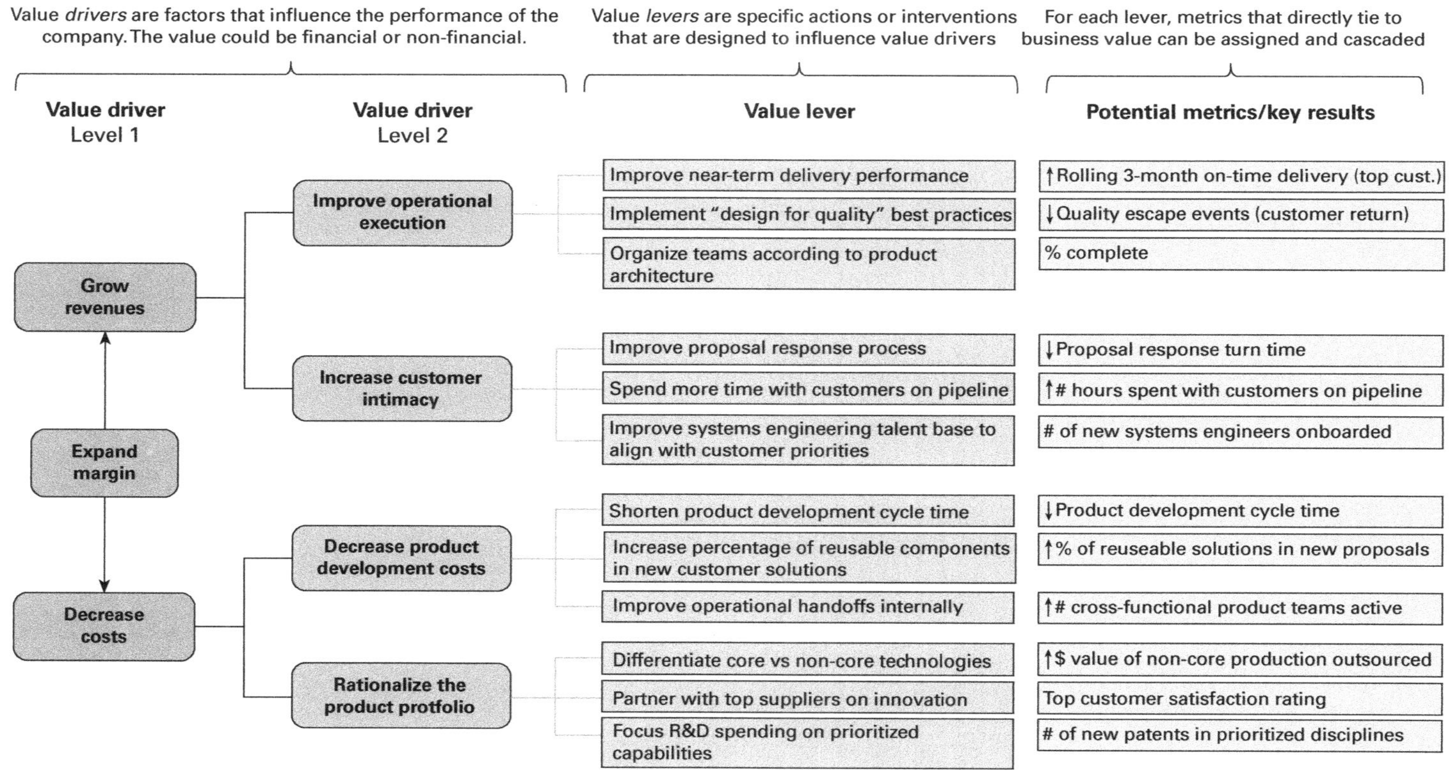

Value *drivers* are factors that influence the performance of the company. The value could be financial or non-financial.

Value *levers* are specific actions or interventions that are designed to influence value drivers

For each lever, metrics that directly tie to business value can be assigned and cascaded

Value driver Level 1	Value driver Level 2	Value lever	Potential metrics/key results
Grow revenues	Improve operational execution	Improve near-term delivery performance	↑ Rolling 3-month on-time delivery (top cust.)
		Implement "design for quality" best practices	↓ Quality escape events (customer return)
		Organize teams according to product architecture	% complete
	Increase customer intimacy	Improve proposal response process	↓ Proposal response turn time
		Spend more time with customers on pipeline	↑ # hours spent with customers on pipeline
		Improve systems engineering talent base to align with customer priorities	# of new systems engineers onboarded
Decrease costs	Decrease product development costs	Shorten product development cycle time	↓ Product development cycle time
		Increase percentage of reusable components in new customer solutions	↑ % of reuseable solutions in new proposals
		Improve operational handoffs internally	↑ # cross-functional product teams active
	Rationalize the product portfolio	Differentiate core vs non-core technologies	↑ $ value of non-core production outsourced
		Partner with top suppliers on innovation	Top customer satisfaction rating
		Focus R&D spending on prioritized capabilities	# of new patents in prioritized disciplines

Expand margin (connecting Grow revenues and Decrease costs)

and initiatives) and creating continuous alignment through the portfolio management process.

Funding *teams* is a significant yet important shift for organizations pursuing enterprise agility. Once a small cross-functional team (typically 8 to 12 individuals) has been set up and has matured, it becomes an asset to the organization with a more-or-less fixed capacity to execute work. The aggregation of teams, as units of capacity, sets the total fixed capacity of the organization to be funded. To adjust capacity of the system, funding for an entire team(s) should be allocated or removed. The aggregate capacity then determines how much work can be done and, therefore, drives prioritization of the portfolio. Funding teams contrasts to the typical approach of funding individual projects and activities without knowing how much the organization can take on. The typical approach often results in two negative outcomes. First, it becomes easy to overburden the organization by committing to more projects that can possibly be executed—remember that *projects* do not give visibility to capacity, rather, well-functioning and stable teams do. Second, overall budgets tend to spiral upwards as everyone tries to squeeze projects into the portfolio. Managing to a fixed capacity, on the other hand, clearly and transparently caps the budgets.

It takes a predictable pattern of portfolio management and governance processes to keep teams aligned to the business priorities—especially as those priorities change—and ensuring that team capacity is efficiently utilized. Organizations will typically adopt at least three portfolio committees: annual, quarterly, and monthly business reviews (often abbreviated to ABR, QBR, and MBR). While not prescriptive, these each have their typical scope (cascaded from above) with typical participants.

- An ABR is where top company leadership sets and adjusts the broad strategic priorities for the business and establishes clear expectations for portfolio-level spend and profitability.

- A QBR is where the strategy is converted to a set of portfolio priorities and OKRs. QBR meetings are owned by the top leaders in their capacity as business unit leads, general managers, and leaders of major functions along with key members of their management team. A key work output of QBRs is the business value tree mentioned earlier.

- MBRs are used to check in on the progress of ongoing work, kick off new initiatives, or stop initiatives that have ended or been deprioritized. MBRs can also be used to ingest new ideas and rapidly approve small-spend initiatives to promote experimentation. It is also common for MBRs to extend further into other weekly routines for reviewing progress towards critical priorities, ensuring a nearly continuous process to support ongoing sensing, adapting, and responding.

Most importantly, the processes that govern initiative prioritization and funding must be lightweight, fast, and free from the usual bureaucracy if agility is the objective. This requires tremendous discipline, high-quality data, and synthesis of inputs, along with a culture of preparation to drive effective decision-making. We will not go into the details of how to set up such processes as there is ample literature available on these topics.

Design for organization agility

Many of today's imperatives—innovation, customer experience, integrated solutions, process excellence, and so on—are delivered across multiple disciplines. Therefore, most of the value in large organizations is created via horizontal, cross-boundary teams and global networks. Almost all large businesses (with closely and loosely related portfolios) are now working in some form of matrix where individual and team accountabilities reflect vertical and horizontal components. When designed well, the matrix makes it easier to mobilize teams, allocate resources and resolve problems day to day.

Organization agility sits at the intersection of top-down strategies and team-level execution. It is how organizations execute complex strategies across empowered teams, functions, and other organization units at a point in time, as well as reconfigure around changes in strategic direction with minimal disruption.

Accountability for building and maintaining organization agility sits with leaders who are typically two to four levels below the CEO, in the integrative layer of leadership. These leaders have big roles. They are VPs, general managers and managing directors. They lead functions, product categories, and geographic units. They are accountable for delivering results in their own area and for working with and through others to deliver end-to-end business outcomes.

At this level, good and fast decisions are the goal. For the enterprise to achieve agility and speed to value, the working unit of the organization—each individual team—must be allowed to work as autonomously as possible with limited or no interdependencies or handoffs required. This is not easy. Even organizations that adopt advanced cross-functional teaming models will encounter bottlenecks and blockers when it comes to aligning priorities, tapping into talent, accessing funding, and sequencing work. All leaders of teams, or teams of teams, need the relationships and methods to work effectively in the matrix, resolving these roadblocks to generate alignment, flow, and speed.

The design objective at this layer is to ensure the underlying organization architecture supports effective, structured collaboration among leaders where there is significant interdependence between units and reliance on shared resources. The matrix design must promote agility, not hinder it. To do this requires a reduction of the predictable sources of conflict and friction that prevent more sophisticated ways of working from taking hold, thereby creating effective mechanisms for resolving conflicts that cannot be predicted.

Leadership teams can build organization agility through three design enablers.

Ensure the underlying organization design supports effective horizontal ways of working and scaled cross-functional teaming

No two companies will leverage networks of horizontal teams in the same way to deliver strategic outcomes. Enterprise agility does not require every organization to adopt a methodology for scaling hundreds of cross-functional teams. (Note that we use "cross-functional" as many organizations are organized by function, but this is not the case for all. It would be equally appropriate to call these teams "cross-boundary" or "multidisciplinary" teams.) These choices must be fit for purpose—highly dependent on the strategy, the nature of the business, and the problems to solve. However, we believe the more that agility and speed are critical to long-term financial performance and enterprise resilience, the more horizontal—or cross boundary—the orientation of the company will become.

It is useful to employ a continuum of options to help leaders understand where they are on the journey and the size of the gap, so to speak, to the next logical step. Figure 5.5 describes an evolution in cross-functional ways of working. As we move from left to right on the continuum, the more the work (and accountability for end-to-end outcomes) moves from traditional vertical reporting silos towards horizontal teams and teams of teams.

We suggest an approach of intentional, but incremental progress during this transition. These changes can't be merely announced and installed, and no amount of design work or formal training can substitute for the organizational DNA created through practice, reflection, and adjustment in ways of working.

Temporary and persistent cross-functional teams

Most of us have had experience of working in a temporary cross-functional team. Often, the objective is to complete a project or a small program. The

Figure 5.5 Journey to horizontal ways of working and agility

Chart the journey

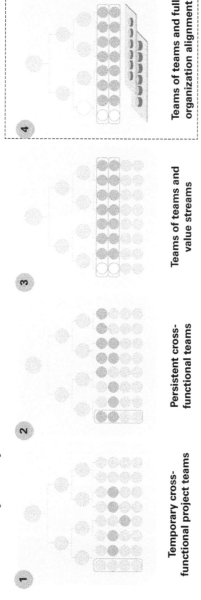

1

Temporary cross-functional project teams

Simple teams overlaid on an existing organization structure

Good for smaller projects and programs

2

Persistent cross-functional teams

Emergence of an informal matrix with dedicated leaders and accountabilities in two directions

Good for testing, learning, experimentation and iteration

Often Agile practices are adopted here

3

Teams of teams and value streams

Matrix is formalized with much more high-value work moved into the horizontals

Good for organizing around key sources of value (products, experiences, etc.)

4

- Reporting units shift to focus more on skills, talent, capability
- Cross-functional value stream leader roles are elevated
- End-to-end value streams around products, customer experiences, etc.
- Expansion of enterprise platforms for scale, commonality, and reuse

Teams of teams and full organization alignment

Underlying organization design (all Star Model levers) configured to fully enable horizontal teams and alignment to enterprise outcomes

Good for accelerating end-to-end flow and speed-to-value—enterprise agility!

INCREASED SPEED TO VALUE

GREATER COMPLEXITY AND DEGREE OF CHANGE

project is likely to be time-bound with fixed deliverables. The teams are formed from the existing organization structure, and the team members are most likely doing the work on a part-time basis, while focused on another "primary" job. While these teams can work well to solve straightforward tasks, we have all had some poor experiences on teams like this. Stable membership, availability, and accountability for the results can all be difficult issues to manage.

As the work of the team increases in strategic importance and impact, we expect to see horizontal ways of working formalize into more persistent cross-functional teams (column 2 in Figure 5.5). The work of the team will be the primary focus of its members and the team will stay intact for an extended period, perhaps one year or longer. More functions will be represented on the team, and an informal matrix will emerge, with each team member having accountability, either formally or informally, to more than one leader, although the dominant axis of the matrix remains the vertical reporting structure.

Persistent cross-functional teams can look quite different depending on the company or part of the organization involved. For three months, we worked with a dedicated group of leaders at a large credit union. The challenge was to evolve the organization such that more decisions tipped towards what was right for the customer and the customer experience rather than what was right for a single, siloed product area. This was how the credit unit assessed the gap to its intensely customer-centric strategy. The design solution created three persistent teams (column 2 in Figure 5.5) overlaid on the credit union's existing organization structure. Each team was aligned to a strategic segment of the customer base. The teams were composed of representatives from products (such as mortgages and auto lending), and from channels (mobile banking and branches), and other enabling functions. One leader from each team was selected to play the role of "captain".

The purpose of these teams was to deliver a robust segment strategy, bringing data and topic experts together to create clear customer personas and coordinate priorities through the verticals. Executive leaders made sure the work of these teams was highly visible in the organization and staffed by high-potential talent. The teams received significant management attention.

In this example, the horizontal-segment teams were not developing products. They were, however, an internal mechanism for strategic ideation, coordination of work, and alignment to the customer-first strategy. Customers would now benefit from a much more curated portfolio of products and enjoy a more seamless personal banking experience. Although this design decision required adjustments to how leaders would collaborate, it was, overall, a minimally disruptive step towards horizontal ways of working for an organization that had less experience of working in teams. In other words, it was the right design intervention. The changes were still able to address the CEO's most pressing problems around siloed decision-making and misaligned priorities. Additionally, these three teams started to build the credit union's new muscle around collaboration. This incremental learning and progress could be leveraged to take more transformative action later—action which could include breaking down the product structures to organize more formally around end-to-end customer experiences (often called "journeys"), for example.

Column 2 in Figure 5.5 is where many, but not all, companies will begin to adopt a methodology such as Agile and begin gaining experience with new ways of working. This is especially true when many teams are involved, as is often the case when developing technology-driven products and services. The issue, from our perspective, is that organizations with high requirements for speed and agility choose to stop here. At this point, investments in Agile typically remain relatively grassroots, bottom-up, and layered on top of the organization's current state. It is at this stage that, after some time, many leaders begin to realize that Agile on its own often does not equate to *agility*.

Teams of teams and broader organization alignment

Many companies, recognizing the need to connect teams and drive more end-to-end ownership, will move towards creating teams of teams and value streams (column 3 in Figure 5.5). Here, the matrix design—especially the role of the horizontals—will become more formalized. Much of the important work in the organization will shift into the horizontals with dedicated leaders responsible for developing products, services, experiences, and more. While this is a necessary step in the evolution, it can be a difficult transition. The complexity in the matrix has increased significantly. There is less certainty about how power and decision authority is allocated—either in the functional verticals or in the horizontal value streams. This stage might include end-to-end process owners or product portfolio leads who have significant accountabilities to deliver, but it is likely that the power in the organization is still retained in the verticals, or, at the very least, the roles have become unclear.

In column 3, although the use of teams has been scaled and teams have been linked, the underlying organization has not, so far, been reconfigured to make working cross-functionally as frictionless as possible. Team design and organization design have not yet converged.

This became readily apparent to a telecom company, for example, that had started operating in column 3. Roles, decision rights, key processes, and technology had to evolve significantly if the company were to achieve true agility and speed to value over the next phase of their transformation program. For this company, the shift towards column 4 meant formalizing the role of the value stream leader (the product director). In this example, he or she would own products end to end. The role was elevated too—no longer just a coordinator of project management activities, but a key leader in a prominent position. The product director role now had clear accountability for both customer and business outcomes and had the requisite control and decision authority to support these accountabilities.

The functions (the 'vertical' reporting structure in this specific example) would remain, but, the focus would shift to managing talent, skills, and domain expertise. These functions would also serve as the "homerooms" for the resources that were deployed to teams. This rebalancing of power and authority was an extremely challenging shift for many in the company, but it proved necessary to reduce unproductive tension caused by conflicting role design and unclear decision rights in the matrix.

At this end of the continuum, we would expect the use of cross-functional teams at scale to be a prominent design feature. These horizontal teams would be delivering products, services, and experiences for customers, both internal and external. To support these teams and preserve their ability to work as autonomously as possible and stay in flow, we would also expect to see other types of teams emerge, including platform and enabling teams (which will be discussed more in the section "Design for team agility").

Evolving to column 4 of Figure 5.5 typically requires significant organizational transformation involving nearly all points of the Star Model. Here, the underlying organization design (structure, roles, processes, decision authority, talent) will have been fully reconfigured in an intentional effort to facilitate effective cross-functional teaming. Further, power (often in the form of decision rights) will have been decisively allocated across the axes of the matrix in a way that clarifies accountabilities, reduces unproductive friction, and optimizes for enterprise outcomes above all else. Healthy tension will be built into the model to ensure that the best thinking and ideas from diverse voices are considered, while at the same time not forcing the organization into consensus-driven gridlock.

The key difference in column 4 is that horizontal ways of working are no longer being forced upon a legacy design meant for a previous era. Rather, everything about the matrix will have been recalibrated to wire effective connections, reduce friction, and incentivize collaborative outcomes. Given how challenging it is for companies to overcome the complexities of their own ill-defined matrix systems, spending time and attention on this organizational realignment can create a powerful source of competitive advantage. Designing to support cross-functional teams and ways of working is an extensive topic and one that we cannot fully cover here. However, we will share more principles and options in the next section, "Design for team agility."

While there are several ways of getting there, transitioning through the four columns in Figure 5.5 does often require significant organizational change, especially if the company did not grow up around technology and retains legacy silos. This is a highly sophisticated model of managing an organization and few are able to do all of it well.

There is no virtue or imperative to shift fully to column 4. Most important is to determine the level of horizontal focus required by the strategy, and a pause at column 2 may be sufficient to address today's problem statements. Then, the attention can turn to making the shift in a thoughtful and well-designed way.

Allocating power across the vertical and horizontal dimensions of the matrix

The terms "verticals" and "horizontals" tend to create a lot of confusion. In *Designing Organizations*, Jay Galbraith described one archetype—the reconfigurable *functional* organization—in which horizontal teams are formed around products and customers across a stable functional "vertical" core.[15] While common, function is not the only choice of primary organizing logic. No two companies are organized the same way. A company that organizes primarily by geography, for example, will use teams to solve different cross-boundary integration challenges. Figure 5.6 shows some of these other typical options.

Leaders will face the same cross-boundary challenges regardless of how the structural building blocks are configured. Historically, the vertical dimension has had most of the power in an organization—the power to set strategy, allocate resources, and make decisions. The verticals and their leaders had accountability for delivering all the classic business metrics, such as P&L, return on investment, growth, and capability. Horizontals were focused more narrowly, if they existed at all.

The traditional role of the vertical reporting structure will be challenged as more impactful and differentiating work shifts to the horizontals. As the organization shifts its focus to end-to-end *outcomes*, such as customer satisfaction, end-to-end product development cycle time, and speed to value, it becomes less likely that any single function or organization unit will be able to own the whole thing.

The mistake is to move more work and accountability into the horizontal organizations without addressing how the underlying matrix is designed and how power is allocated. If organization agility is really the goal, it is not

Figure 5.6 Horizontals and verticals: No two organizations will look the same

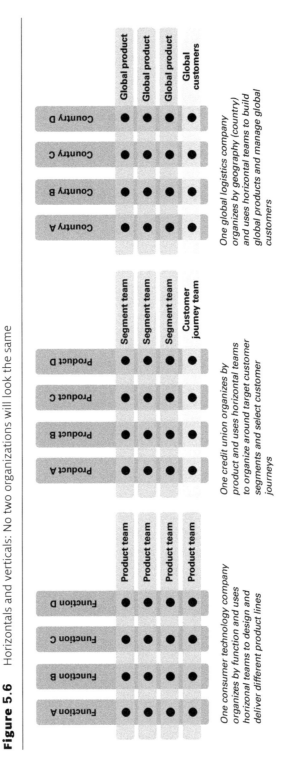

One consumer technology company organizes by function and uses horizonal teams to design and deliver different product lines

One credit union organizes by product and uses horizontal teams to organize around target customer segments and select customer journeys

One global logistics company organizes by geography (country) and uses horizontal teams to build global products and manage global customers

usually enough to layer cross-functional ways of working on top of a legacy structure without consideration for how roles, decision rights, and governance processes will need to change.

There are several organization design levers available to allocate power across the matrix to ensure the underlying organization structure supports agility and cross-functional ways of working. It is *not* common for organization design decisions—such as those that follow—to happen concurrently with decisions around team design and horizontal ways of working. These conversations often happen at different levels of leadership and at different times. However, there is the potential to create real efficiencies, value, and agility when effective organization design and team design happen together—when a top-down approach meets bottom-up in an intentional and thoughtful way.

Power levers available when designing matrix organizations for agility include:

- **Organization structure.** What's the dominant logic? What groupings are most visible higher up?
- **Metrics.** What are we measuring and talking about together? What are we reinforcing?
- **Leadership roles.** Which roles have accountability for business and customer outcomes? Where are they placed?
- **Decision rights.** Where do these tip when teams reach an impasse?
- **Team design.** Which roles sit within value streams rather than shared services and enabling teams?
- **Resource allocation.** Where do we leverage hard-line versus dotted-line reporting?
- **Funding.** Which part of the matrix owns the funding? How does the money flow?
- **Talent.** Where do we place our high performers?

Design decisions such as the ones above, in aggregate, should clearly signal what dimension of the matrix represents the organizational center of gravity. This could be product lines, geographic regions, customer groups, or business functions. Again, there is no single right answer, but the more these power dynamics are clear and aligned to the company strategy, the less friction there will be in the model and the faster teams will be able to move.

Enable leaders to work with and through others to align teams, make trade-off decisions, and enable flow

Achieving organization agility requires a well-designed set of forums and routines that facilitate the right conversations with the right people on a nearly continuous basis. Over time, companies that are building muscle in this area should notice a regular operating rhythm and pace to the business. Collaborating and making the decisions that drive execution also require a regular and predictable set of forums to identify systemic bottlenecks and resolve blockers to progress and flow. It may seem counterintuitive, but we find that strategic flexibility requires a very high degree of discipline.

In the credit union example, new routines were developed to manage all the new conversations and connections now required. No longer could the head of mortgage lending unilaterally make decisions that always optimized only for mortgage lending. The goal was to make decisions that optimized for customers and their needs. That would mean, for any new product, the call center had to be prepared to service it, risk to manage it, and marketing to brand it. This required a new bi-weekly forum to be established, led by the segment teams, to make sure products and channels were closely aligned on the priorities and, in particular, work sequence. If mortgage lending was working on something new this week, but marketing wouldn't get to it for six months, no value would be created for anyone. If the products and channels couldn't agree through collaboration, the segment teams could break the tie and drive alignment.

This example is not meant to be prescriptive, but rather illustrative. Effective organization design helps determine the lens through which key decisions are made, and no two companies will do it the same way.

For the telecom company, the focus from the third year was also on designing more effective connections and cadences. After addressing the underlying organization architecture, attention turned to horizontal flow and speed to value for customers. It soon became clear to the product leaders in the company that teams were spending considerable time waiting for resources to be allocated or funding to be released, or were just otherwise in a holding pattern because of misaligned priorities or work sequencing. The big shift was for product directors and other functional leaders to spend much more time together—using data—to help address downtime and resolve bottlenecks that prevented teams from moving fast. The entire business performance framework had to be revisited—new metrics, dashboards, business forums—so that the leaders at this level had a dedicated place and time to come together to weigh trade-offs and make informed, data-driven decisions.

Cultivate the right talent and servant leadership mindsets to fill the extremely challenging roles in the matrix

There is no doubt that leaders in these middle layers, tasked with driving collaboration and overcoming complexity, occupy particularly challenging positions. This group of leaders, collectively, must see agility as the goal. During the transition, some might see their role as reduced, lacking the single-point accountability, control, and full set of resources they once had. But this would be an overly simple, and incorrect, interpretation of what is changing. We are, in fact, asking experienced and tested leaders to become chameleons of sorts—contextual leaders who recognize when different situations call for different approaches and decisions. Leaders who recognize that, sometimes, business situations are straightforward and require a more top-down management approach, but, for situations that are complex, where the solution is undefined, a servant leadership approach is critical. And this is the opposite of command and control.

Organization agility demands the continuous resolution of conflict over priorities, resources, and other blockers to speed. Having the necessary forums and routines will mean little without the right leaders in the right roles. These leaders must be able artfully to advocate for an informed perspective with their peers, but also be willing to compromise and commit to an alternative path once a decision has been made. If agility is the goal, these leaders must be willing to advocate consistently for the best interests of the *enterprise* above all else. For some organizations, this will require new leadership muscle.

With regards to talent management and development, there will be a few key shifts to consider. First, organizations need to focus more on assessing leader fit—fit to the culture, the model, and the values of enterprise agility, such as servant leadership. Leaders are required who are motivated to win in a complex, dynamic, team-centric environment. Second, the needs of the individual leader will need to be managed more closely. Ensuring fairness with metrics and rewards is critical to preserving motivation, especially when there is a very high degree of interdependence among groups. Organization agility requires that leaders can remain confident that they will be rewarded for being enterprise leaders. The third shift is a new focus on consistency, reinforcement, and discipline. The most senior leaders, those overseeing these general managers and VPs tasked with managing in the matrix, need to consistently reinforce the new principles of agility. This battle is won over the course of everyday interactions and decisions. Agility must become part of the organizational DNA, and this tone is set from the top.

Leverage a single source of truth for executional data to make fast and informed decisions

Without a single source of truth for enterprise data, decision-making in organizations with strong horizontal components is likely to remain heavily influenced by siloed thinking, subjectivity, internal politics, and the HIPPOs in the room (highest-paid person's opinion). Pace will slow substantially. The leaders in the matrix who are the critical enablers of organization agility must have reliable, transparent data and insights if they are to weigh trade-offs across the vertical and horizontal components and make optimal decisions for the enterprise as a whole. Of course, there are many types of data, but for organization agility, we are choosing to focus on the executional and business performance data that supports day-to-day conflict resolution so critical to preserving speed.

Also required is the ability to translate the data into helpful insights that can be democratized and used for decision-making. This means, for example, being able to represent data visually on dashboards in a meaningful way. "Good" looks like *predictive* information that doesn't tell us that we have already missed revenue this quarter but does tell us where a problem exists that will impact our financials in the future, while there is still time to correct it. Again, advancements in AI are making this much more achievable.

Our clients often tell us how valuable it would be to have this transparent "single source of truth", but few can do this well today. Technology and data experts inside companies are faced with reconciling a myriad of tooling, datasets, and processes from different parts of the business. There are significant issues with data nomenclature and taxonomies that can make it a challenge even to compare apples with apples. There is no doubt that achieving this goal will take time and investment, but organization agility depends on the company's ability to take the personal and emotional out of decision-making. This model cannot work without reliable and transparent business performance data.

We don't have to wait for perfect data to make important steps forward, however. In parallel with investment to build the longer-term data infrastructure, leaders can right now make shorter-term gains by acquiring better data analytics and visualization capabilities, driving the habit of using data to make decisions, and role-modelling such behaviors for teams across the organization.

Design for team agility

Small teams have become the fundamental unit of work and value creation in organizations of every size. When designed well, teams contain the capacity and capability to meet the challenges of today's incredibly fast-paced and complex business environments. Everything else in the organization, therefore, should be set up to serve, support, and empower these teams to do their work as effectively and efficiently as possible. We give particular attention here to portfolio and organization agility to ensure that those layers and leaders are set up to be in service to the teams—providing clarity, prioritizing work, allocating resources, and removing blockers.

Much of the energy and new thinking about teams has come from the software industry, codified in Agile methodologies. Scaling these models and principles across the broader organization and for work beyond software and technology is possible but not always straightforward. Our focus here is to introduce some core tenants of team-level agility that can be applied broadly.

Put high-performing, autonomous teams at the center of the organization and ensure they are set up for success

The science of teams in the workplace has been well-studied, offering more insight than we could possibly cover within a chapter. Two books, however, stand out to us for their applicability and readability. First, *Drive* by Daniel Pink makes a strong and fascinating case for rethinking motivation in the workplace (or in any context).[16] Pink's research concludes that the three elements of intrinsic motivation are autonomy, mastery, and control—all elements that a well-designed work team can effectively provide. Second, *Leading Teams* by Richard Hackman identifies the conditions that leaders can put in place to increase the likelihood of team effectiveness: the ability to create a real team (clear task, boundaries, authority) with a compelling direction, operating in a supportive context, and with ample coaching available.[17] From these authors, and many more, we know enough now about the potential of well-designed teams to want everyone in the organization to feel part of one—even a team with homogenous skills (that is, not cross-functional, such as an HR center of excellence). The following list summarizes what executives should know about basic team design:

- **Team size is important.** Five to twelve members, typically, to encourage strong bonds and mutual trust. Amazon famously designs its teams to adhere to the "two pizza team" rule,[18] meaning that the team should be small enough to be fed by two pizzas.

- **Teams should be stable and persistent.** They should have dedicated members (preferably full-time) that work together on an ongoing basis to avoid constant storming, forming, and norming and accelerate cycles of learning.

- **Teams should be designed for autonomy.** Each team should have the skills and tools to be able to deliver work as independently as possible. This may mean that teams require people with competencies across functional disciplines.

- **Teams need a clear purpose, scope, and set of boundaries.** Each team should have a clear and unique "mission" with (ideally) end-to-end responsibility for a product, experience, or part thereof. When this is the case, most of the required collaboration can be contained within the team. The team's mission should be transparent, so it is clear to all who the team is there to serve.

When these basic conditions are met, teams can make significant contributions towards the primary capabilities of enterprise agility that we defined earlier in the chapter. This shift towards distributed teams represents a major change for many companies, so we will spend a little more time explaining why teams are such an important asset for sensing, adapting, and responding.

Sensing

Teams play an important role in gathering the voice of the customer and serving as the early-alert system, recognizing even subtle changes in needs and preferences. Teams can stay closely connected to customers (external and internal) by being immersed in market, product and channel data, net promoter score surveys, and frequent customer interactions. This intimacy ensures the product and service offerings the team develops will align to what customers really want and reduces wasted effort and unnecessary capital expenditure.

Adapting

Teams can easily and quickly respond to changes they have sensed by adjusting the backlog of work and priorities accordingly or by requesting new skills and resources. Connected and empowered teams should have flexibility and autonomy to define how and when they will deliver new work, provided they stay within established guardrails. No longer having to wait for prescriptive leadership instructions, or heavily governed or gated processes, teams should be able to "go until told to stop" (as opposed to "stop until told to go").

Responding

Well-designed and empowered teams can execute with speed. Their intense focus on a single meaningful piece of a more complex puzzle shortens learning cycles. Cross-functional membership enables greater collaboration and fewer formal handoffs (think basketball team versus relay race), reducing wait time and waste. Iterative delivery models (lots of smaller "bets") also increase the speed and frequency of getting new ideas to the market. The focus on the customer (internal or external) encourages teams to put work into what is truly resonating with customers and terminating work that is not.

Leverage modular product and technology architectures to facilitate team design decisions

Organizations are shifting away from deploying people to a series of temporary projects that fracture individual attention spans and muddy accountability. The trend is towards focusing the work of a team around a purpose and scope that is fully contained, has measurable business impact, and can be managed end to end. A role of organization design is to make it easy to form persistent teams that have clear ownership over a scope of work that has clear boundaries and represents a source of value to the customer.

To do this at scale requires a structured approach—ideally based on an organization's product and technology architectures. While many companies have made significant progress towards completing this work, we have worked with several others that still have a very incomplete or unstructured view of all the offerings they have in the market or the underlying technology required to support them. A product and technology architecture has the benefit of providing a structured breakdown (taxonomy) of the organization's key assets that require ongoing ownership and support.

Ideally, these assets are somewhat self-contained and decoupled from one another, (that is, they are "modular"). A smartphone, for example, will break down into a camera, display, battery, enclosure and other discrete, modular parts. Having a clear modular architecture for products and enabling technologies supports agility in many ways. First, a modular architecture provides a clear blueprint for mapping stable teams to discrete scopes of work that can be managed end-to-end. Teams are aligned to one or more of the modules, which helps create clear and unique boundaries in scope and accountability. Second, it creates a clear taxonomy for assigning work to the most appropriate team. Third, it promotes ready reuse and incremental innovation, as opposed to teams continually building new infrastructure from scratch (the latter being more likely to happen with temporary project teams). For a consumer technology company manufacturing a phone, a modular architecture would allow the company to easily organize teams and reuse parts not only across generations of a product, but also across other product lines.

Taking a modular approach, leaders can more easily identify the work that is most important, under-resourced, or that is no longer a priority and should therefore be stopped. With a modular architecture, work can be clearly visualized, organized, prioritized, and resourced.

To enable such modularity, an organization might even choose to adopt a reporting structure that mirrors how the company's products and enabling technologies break down. This idea isn't new—Jay Galbraith described the "mirror image" organization in *Designing Organizations* 25 years ago, but today the idea has taken on new meaning. We now refer to this collection of design principles described above as a "product-based" organization. And a key feature of a product-based organization is, of course, the empowered product team. We will discuss this next.[19]

Match the type of team to the need (product, platform, enabling teams)

There is another trend in current thought leadership to recognize different types of teams. For example, the excellent book, *Team Topologies*, by Matthew Skelton and Manuel Pais, refers to several types of teams found in technology and software organizations, such as (value) stream-aligned, platform, complex subsystem, and enabling.[20] These definitions go beyond basic team design and the "two-pizza" rule and differentiate teams based on several factors, such as the homogeneity of team members' skills, the customers the team serves, and how the team interacts with other teams. For the purpose of *this* book—and to fit our goal of making this topic as broadly applicable as possible—we highlight three key types of teams: product, platform, and enabling.

Product teams are responsible for designing and delivering value from a customer point of view. These teams exist to meet the needs of their customers in the most effective and efficient way possible. "Product" in this case typically refers to the business's market-facing products and services, and the underlying technologies that enable them. However, use of the term "product" has expanded inside organizations to include almost anything that can be decoupled, defined with clear boundaries, and managed end to end, such as the discrete steps of a customer journey or steps of a major enterprise process. While there are advantages to treating *all* types of work in an organization like a product, when applied too broadly, the word starts to lose meaning and can create significant confusion.

Platform teams provide common, consistent, and easy-to-consume assets *as a service,* primarily to internal customers. Platforms can come in the form of data, tools, technology systems, infrastructure, and other physical components. The objective of the platform is to optimize for scale and encourage reuse across as many internal customers as possible. Effective platforms allow product teams to work faster and more autonomously, without having to take time to develop new capabilities not central to the product team's mission.[21] While platforms are often associated with software, they also include physical assets that can be leveraged across lines of business, such as a common car chassis used in multiple vehicle models within an automotive company. An objective of organization design should be to identify as many opportunities as possible to move common work—across technology, business groups, and other functions—into common and reusable platforms wherever doing things differently across groups adds little value.

Enabling teams are all other teams within an organization that provide shared services and support the product and platform teams. This includes all the resources from the set of "enabling" functions, such as finance, HR, procurement, assurance, and more. Enabling teams are often comprised of resources with the same skillset (such as HR resources within a talent center of expertise) who can work to develop standard processes and tools, publish thought leadership, or even partner directly with product teams as needed to solve a specific issue.

A central tenet of team agility is allowing the product team to work as autonomously as possible on tasks that are core to the team's mission, while minimizing time spent recreating solutions or doing work that is outside the adjacent skills of the team. Product, platform, and enabling teams work together on distinct yet interconnected tasks that enable the organization to bring new ideas to market quickly. With a clear understanding of the types of teams that are needed, we can then begin grouping those teams and creating a bottom-up view of the organization design that will meet many of the top-down design considerations (verticals, horizontals, power dynamics, and so on) discussed earlier in the chapter.

Identifying the different types of team also helps us to understand the nature of their work and apply the most appropriate methods, tools, and ways of working. Some organizations will choose to formally adopt a methodology, such as Agile, in certain parts of the business or use one of several frameworks that scale Agile principles across the entire organization. However, even those that do not formally adopt a methodology will likely find themselves employing many of the same fundamental Agile principles, such as team size, team autonomy, end-to-end ownership, audit-based governance, and incremental value creation.

Agile, Scrum, Kanban, DevOps and Lean are just some of the common team methods and practices under the banner of "new ways of working". An organization might employ several different methodologies to match the right approach with the right context. For example, product teams managing the complexity and uncertainty involved in sensing and responding to customers often benefit from Agile-based methods that encourage experimentation, short work sprints, and iterative delivery. On the other hand, a team managing a contact center, with high volumes of more repeatable work, would likely benefit more from Lean practices that drive optimization and seek to minimize waste.

Conclusion: Achieving enterprise agility

As designers, we sense great frustration in the market around the topic of agility. The pressure to remain relevant and competitive despite the unprecedented pace of change is immense, and years of investment in methodologies such as Agile have not always delivered.

Agile methods alone are not the problem. Agile remains a highly effective set of principles for managing teams and teams at scale, but bridging *from Agile to agility* requires much more than just grassroots, team-level efforts, or initiatives isolated to the technology function. Executives who are looking to take transformative action to continuously reinvent the organization, committing to long-term relevancy and financial stability above all else, put enterprise agility at the top of their shared agenda. This means that effective team design must converge with enterprise organization design—including fit-for-purpose adjustments to structure, roles, processes, decision rights, data, metrics, and people practices—for leaders to be able to overcome the complexity of these new models and unlock speed to value.

If we were to summarize in a single word what has been missing it would be *discipline*: sufficient discipline to navigate the complexity *and* get the fundamentals right—clarity of strategic direction, alignment of priorities from top to bottom, timely resolution of conflict, and design of effective teams, for example. While this discipline is likely to exist in pockets of the organization, it is unlikely to exist more broadly. Breaking down enterprise agility into its portfolio, organization, and team components provides a much clearer road map for how this discipline can be intentionally established and consistently managed.

What we can take away from Apple, for example, is not necessarily its exact choices for organizing, but rather its management discipline and relentless focus on how the company's design enables its strategy and products. At Apple, agility is in high demand. Therefore, the company is extremely intentional about how it organizes (functionally), with lean upper-management layers, precisely to foster the type of cross-boundary interactions and decisions that it believes best drive technological innovation in its context. At Apple, there is a steady pace and rhythm to the business—extremely well-defined and well-exercised processes and cadences where leaders engage in collaborative and vigorous debate about the facts and data, as Joel Podolny and Morten Hasen detail in their article "How Apple is Organized for Innovation".[22] Above all, this organizational know-how is deeply embedded into Apple's values.

We are not expecting companies to become "like Apple" overnight. Pursuing enterprise agility is better considered a continuous journey than a project with a fixed end date and fully defined outcomes. Ironically, it is almost a certainty that a company will never fully arrive at the destination, given that the model is inherently built to change. This is why we emphasize the importance of incremental progress and highlight select design enablers that can have significant impacts in the short-term, while readying the organization for further transformation. By focusing on building the right capabilities, at the right layers, we believe all companies can eventually achieve the promised results.

Key takeaways

- Enterprise agility—the organization's ability to sense, adapt, and respond—is the result of three types of agility working together as a connected system: portfolio, organization, and team. Each is a separate design task with different Star Model implications.

- Small, autonomous teams have become the fundamental unit of work capacity and value creation in organizations of every size. When designed well, teams contain the capacity and capability to meet today's business challenges.

- Team design is a good place to focus, but it is often not enough. The difference between Agile and agility lies in an enabling organization design. Structure, roles, processes, talent, and power (including decision rights) will need to change.

- Agile and related methodologies play an important role in enterprise agility. Apply these methods in the right places according to the nature of the work.

- Enterprise agility requires tremendous management discipline and a commitment to master the fundamentals despite significant organizational complexity. This has implications for leader selection and fit for key roles.

- Models for agility cannot be "installed" nor copied from somewhere else. We consider this to be a journey where milestones mean more than the end state. There is a starting place for everyone.

Notes

1 Agile Alliance (2024) What is Agile? Agile 101. agilealliance.org/agile101 (archived at https://perma.cc/KX6N-E7Y4).

2 Galbraith, J.R. (2014) *Designing Organizations: Strategy, Structure, and Process at the Business Unit and Enterprise Levels*, San Francisco: Jossey-Bass, p. 133.

3 Galbraith (2014) p. 140.

4 Galbraith (2014) p. 131.

5 Rita, M. (2014) Management's Three Eras: A Brief History, *Harvard Business Review*, 30 July. www.hbr.org/2014/07/managements-three-eras-a-brief-history (archived at https://perma.cc/2NDS-MDYZ)

6 Apple (2023) *Apple Annual Report 2023*. app.stocklight.com/stocks/us/nasdaq-aapl/apple/annual-reports/nasdaq-aapl-2023-10K-231373899.pdf (archived at https://perma.cc/85VY-5XDC).

7 Tilley, A. and Colias, M. (2024) Apple Ends Quest to Build Its Own Electric Vehicle, *The Wall Street Journal*, February 27. wsj.com/business/autos/apple-car-project-canceled-ced2b626 (archived at https://perma.cc/GHM7-SZTS).

8 Project Management Institute (2012) What is Flow? www.pmi.org/disciplined-agile/what-is-flow (archived at https://perma.cc/2JTQ-7C6Z).

9 Kates, A., Kesler, G., and DiMartino, M. (2021) *Networked, Scaled, and Agile: A design strategy for complex organizations*, London: Kogan Page, p. 63.

10 Wang, D. and Evans, J.A (2019) Research: When small teams are better than big ones, *Harvard Business Review*, February 21. hbr.org/2019/02/research-when-small-teams-are-better-than-big-ones (archived at https://perma.cc/NX2T-X3KK).

11 Lombardo, C. (2019) Ackman Opposes United Technologies-Raytheon deal, *The Wall Street Journal*, June 11. wsj.com/articles/ackman-opposes-united-technologies-raytheon-deal-11560283358 (archived at https://perma.cc/64TG-ZX2R).

12 Kates et al. (2021) p. 67.

13 Kates et al. (2021) p. 68.

14 Clayton, C. and van Bever, D. (2014) The Capitalist's Dilemma, *Harvard Business Review*, June 30, hbr.org/2014/06/the-capitalists-dilemma (archived at https://perma.cc/UQ82-VH8R).

15 Galbraith (2014) p. 140.

16 Pink, D. (2011) *Drive: The surprising truth about what motivates us*, Edinburgh: Canongate Books.

17 Hackman, J. (2002) *Leading Teams: Setting the stage for great performances*, Boston, MA: Harvard Business School Press.

18 Slater, D. (2023) Powering Innovation and Speed with Amazon's Two Pizza Teams, Amazon blog. aws.amazon.com/executive-insights/content/amazon-two-pizza-team (archived at https://perma.cc/2MA2-5XY2).

19 Galbraith (2014) p. 81.

20 Skelton, M. and Pais, M. (2019) *Team Topologies: Organizing business and technology teams for fast flow*, Portland: IT Revolution.

21 Skelton and Pais (2019) p. 93.

22 Podolny, J.M. and Hansen, M.T. (2020) How Apple is Organized for Innovation, *Harvard Business Review*, November–December. hbr.org/2020/11/how-apple-is-organized-for-innovation (archived at https://perma.cc/FER9-7XR3).

Close the Sustainability Execution Gap

APRIL LACROIX, JENNA TRESCOTT

Contributors: Ellie Azolaty, Tim Henshaw, Jens Laue, Cyrus Suntook

The corporate sustainability movement over the past decade has promoted the idea that sustainability is not just the right thing to do but is a driver of better business performance.[1] Likewise, many companies proudly declare that sustainability is "at the heart of all we do". Yet, many of these companies are failing to deliver on these promises, finding that the reality of execution is hard.

So, the world has become increasingly skeptical of corporate sustainability. The notion that public companies might put concern for environment or diversity above shareholder return has drawn negative political focus.[2] Companies are being accused of "greenwashing" or "woke-washing" and overinflating their sustainability efforts in order to pander to consumers.[3] While many companies forge ahead publicly with their sustainability agendas, others are disclosing less for fear of backlash—a phenomenon that also has a new label: "greenhushing".[4]

Some companies are beginning to tiptoe around how they market sustainability, but evolving mandatory regulations are taking the choice out of what companies disclose. What was seen as progressive action just a few years ago is fast becoming a minimum requirement, demanding data, reporting, and operational changes in nearly all companies doing business in North America and Europe.

Organizational execution is the root of the problem and solution. When sustainability efforts fail, we have observed that it is primarily due to two execution gaps:

- Failure to link the sustainability strategy to the commercial and operational strategy
- Failure to wire sustainability into the underlying organizational system.

In this chapter, we explain sustainability in business terms, and provide an overview of the sustainability value opportunity in the context of the changing regulatory environment. We then discuss the two execution gaps, with suggestions for embedding sustainability into business strategy and the organization. The chapter closes with guidance for leaders as they implement a journey toward sustainability.

Defining sustainability

Sustainability, ESG (environment, social, and governance) and responsible business are often used interchangeably. ESG is a specific framework used by investors and other stakeholders to evaluate a company's performance. Responsible business connotes a focus on ethical business practices.

We see sustainability as the broadest lens of these, one that considers a wide range of the company's impact on the external environment as well as the long-term health of the company. Sustainability will be used as the umbrella term in this chapter, defined simply as "social and environmental performance that supports financial performance". This builds on the United Nations' definition of a sustainable organization as one that can meet its needs while not compromising the ability for future generations to meet their needs.[5] We will focus on sustainability activities that are most closely tied to business strategy and core business value versus those that are intentionally ancillary to the core, such as philanthropy. We will also explore many examples and strategies on the environmental aspects of ESG, which are most in focus for regulatory and performance management. A sustainable business is one that works for all stakeholders and is designed to stand the test of time.

Realize value through sustainability

Going forward, companies will need to demonstrate sustainability results that align with financial performance. This requires meaningful integration of sustainability into enterprise management (how priorities are set and funded) and business management (how core work gets done).

Throughout this chapter, we examine how organizational effectiveness can solve for four outcomes: regulatory compliance; sustainability performance and resilience; business value creation and differentiation; and efficiency and cost savings.

Regulatory compliance

Maintaining compliance with evolving regulatory requirements has become essential to avoid fines, penalties, and restrictions on the import or export of products. For instance, the new European Regulation on Deforestation-Free products (EUDR) will impose fines of up to 4 percent of a company's EU turnover from the preceding year if the company sources goods from deforested lands, which could amount to billions of dollars for many companies.[6] Beyond fines, there are revenue-loss implications. Additional penalties include the confiscation of revenues gained of up to 12 months.[7]

Quality, trusted data and respective controls are critical to being ready for compliance and reducing exposure to compliance-related risks. Investment includes addressing data gaps, controls, and governance. For many, regulation is kickstarting much-needed enterprise-level sustainability transformation efforts. A Bloomberg Research survey found a 10–50 percent increase in spending on sustainability data from 2022 to 2023.[8] Technology investments will be a key enabler of data quality and controls: the sustainability software market is anticipated to grow from $905 million in 2021 to $4 billion by 2027.[9] New sustainability roles focused on compliance, such as "controllers" and "digitization leads", are beginning to appear too. We provide additional context and perspective in the section "A changing regulatory landscape", page 177.

Sustainability performance and business resilience

Driving and demonstrating performance on material sustainability topics is important for reputation, risk, and resilience management, especially for investors, customers, and employees. Beyond regulators, consumers and business partners are demanding evidence that companies are meeting goals and benchmarks. B2B companies are seeing a sharp increase in customer requests for assurances or claims. Those that can't fulfill requests face putting the business at risk, while those that may gain competitive advantage or premium opportunities. We have heard many carrot-and-stick stories in food and agriculture, where B2B customers are highly reliant on emissions reductions upstream in the value chain. While one provider may face threats from a large customer to pull business if sustainability demands are not met, another is able defend business from lower-cost providers because it is able to verify reductions benefits for their customers.

Business value creation and differentiation

A focus on sustainability can create differentiation and opportunities for growth, customer acquisition, and higher-margin products and services: differentiation that can drive customer acquisition, share of wallet, and long-term relational value. The Carbon Disclosure Project estimates the value of the global market for low-carbon goods and services at $5.5 trillion,[10] including increased revenue through demand for low-emissions products and services, such as electric vehicles, shifting consumer preferences, and increased capital availability as financial institutions increasingly favor low-emissions producers.[11] The quest to capture this opportunity and demonstrate top-line growth is immature for most industries and companies.

Efficiency and cost savings

Today, most sustainability activities are carried out adjacent to the core business. This shows up as multiple stakeholders independently requesting the same data, disparate spreadsheet tracking and manual manipulation, and ad hoc and reactive processes.

As sustainability demands on the organization increase, companies will need to build business capability that will effectively scale and integrate with the core business. It is no longer possible to take a merely reactive compliance-centric approach or strategically choose to lag one's industry, and a proactive, integrated approach can only be achieved through coordinated adjustment to the organization system. The following sections of this chapter provide guidance for taking a holistic organizational approach that will both ready the organization for compliance and unlock value-added sustainability capability.

A CHANGING REGULATORY LANDSCAPE

New and evolving regulations that aim to drive integrity in disclosures are developing in earnest, both geographically and topically.

In Europe, the most cross-cutting regulation is the proposed European Union's Corporate Sustainability Reporting Directive (CSRD) which—together with the EU taxonomy—will require companies to enhance their sustainability reporting and data monitoring to provide detailed information on all material sustainability matters in their annual reports.[12] In tandem, the EU Corporate Sustainability Due Diligence Directive (CSDDD) will create legal liability pertaining to human rights and environmental violations in companies' value chains.[13] Some European countries have already implemented supply-chain due diligence requirements, for example the Supply Chain Act in Germany.[14]

EUDR is an EU-mandated regulation that will require companies to collect and verify supplier and commodity-specific information on product imports and exports.[15] These regulations have serious implications for companies with operations in Europe, whether they are headquartered there or not. EUDR penalties, for instance, can include an EU product trading ban as well as confiscation of the products or revenues gained from non-compliant items.

In both the EU and United States, extended producer responsibility (EPR) regulation makes producers responsible for the environmental impacts across a product's life cycle. This type of policy is increasingly recognized as the leading approach to mitigate product waste and is broadening in application beyond plastics and packaging materials.[16, 17]

In the United States, California has put forward the most progressive legislation of any individual state, including a series of bills that require disclosures of financial risk and Scope 1, 2 and 3 emissions, as well as specific reduction targets for 2030 and 2045.[18, 19]

In parallel, the International Sustainability Standards Board (ISSB) aims to provide the same level of rigor to sustainability reporting as there is for financial reporting.

Regulations are also driving increased rigor into sustainability and product claims. The EU's Empowering Consumers Directive aims to protect consumers from misleading and unfair practices about products by having traders provide better information on their products and the associated environmental, social, or circularity aspects of them.[20]

Defending compliance challenges requires strong data; a challenge when many home-grown sustainability functions are still in a highly manual environment. Litigation related to sustainability disclosures is rising as stakeholders and individuals are challenging corporations in court. The UNEP reported that, between 2021 and 2022, the total number of climate-change litigations more than doubled.[21] When it comes to carbon majors, not only energy companies are being implicated, but also those in food, transport, finance, and other sectors.[22]

Readying the organization for regulatory compliance is not insignificant. Some are saying we are in an "SOX-like" moment for sustainability, anticipating that the cost and investment companies will need to address incoming regulation will be at least on par with the 2002 Sarbanes Oxley (SOX) Act mandating strict reforms in financial reporting. That legislation saw companies with revenue over $5 billion spending almost $5 million in the first year of its implementation alone.[23] Under new sustainability laws, companies will face penalties and fees for regulatory non-compliance. In fact, France has introduced a provision that could jail corporate directors who don't comply with the country's adoption of the CSRD.[24]

Embed sustainability into strategy

For nearly a decade and a half, Accenture has regularly conducted a global study of CEOs' opinions on sustainability. The question, "How important is sustainability to your business strategy?" is no longer asked because, without exception, CEOs agree that sustainability is critical to the future of their business. The reasons vary, but include resilience in the face of weather events, consumer expectations, employee attraction, and a general desire to have positive impact.

However, sustainability strategies might be well-designed and have the best intentions and science behind them, but, in most organizations, they have not been well-integrated into enterprise strategies, innovation, and business planning. Typically, a sustainability team is set up at the enterprise or business unit level. The team is tasked with creating the company's sustainability strategy. The team works tirelessly to gather data, research, formulate goals and plans, and get stakeholder input and alignment, but they usually lack authority to influence enterprise strategy and management. This is particularly true when the work impacts customer-facing topics such as new offering developments that are owned by commercial and marketing teams.

The result is that sustainability becomes an adjunct activity, ancillary to overall enterprise priorities and investment. While many companies are delivering on small or pilot strategic sustainability initiatives, they are struggling where more fundamental change to the business and growth model is required. For example, in many industries, decarbonization can only be achieved through completely shifting the product growth mix. The sectors with the most significant contributions to greenhouse gas emissions associated with product mix include electricity and heat, transport, manufacturing and construction, and agriculture.[25] For example, for most packaged-goods companies and food retailers, agricultural products—in particular dairy and animal proteins—and packaging are the largest sources of their carbon footprints and can only be tackled through scaled sustainable agriculture practices and changes to the core portfolio mix.

The challenge is especially salient for companies that are getting closer to publicly stated 2030 commitments and are realizing they don't have a clear path to achieve their goals. Only 49 percent of business leaders surveyed in 2023 felt confident that their 2030 target is attainable.[26] The reality is likely even more dire given that executives often consider their sustainability initiatives to be more mature than their employees do.[27] Leaders are beginning to realize that they have addressed the easy levers and urgently need to find ways to get to the targeted outcomes at scale. As a sustainability lead from one major fashion company told us, "All of the low-hanging fruit is gone."

Embedding sustainability into strategy-making

Linking sustainability to the core business growth trajectory requires much closer integration of sustainability and enterprise strategies and management. Ideally, the standalone sustainability strategy process should help determine what topic areas are material to the business and the scale of impact the company aims to achieve. This holistic view of the sustainability agenda should then be fully incorporated into corporate planning processes, decision-making, and incentives. This involves:

- Surgically embedding sustainability targets into the strategic decisions of the company, including enterprise portfolio decisions, growth plans, and allocation of resources
- Strong upfront planning interfaces between business and sustainability teams
- The organizational muscles and incentives to allow business teams to consider sustainability alongside other objectives, such as when to select the more sustainable (but perhaps less immediately financially appealing) option.

The following sections suggest several ways to integrate sustainability into the core business strategy.

Long-term planning and patient capital

Budget and planning timelines may need to extend beyond the typical one-to-three-year payback periods to enable the significant yet valuable long-term investments required for sustainability. It is estimated that $125 trillion of climate investment is needed by 2050 to meet net zero, $32 trillion of which is required by 2030, and many of these investments do not have returns under three years.[28] A sustainability director from a major construction supply company recently shared that "priorities rise to the top based on the needs of business—and it is hard to care about recycling or product end-of-life if it's not an immediate need for the business".

Product portfolio reinvention

Products can be made more sustainable in several ways. They can be reformulated through more sustainable inputs and ingredients. More sustainable product formats can be used, such as concentrates or powders that use less water and packaging; or, the delivery model of the product can be redesigned, for example from one-time products to models in which products can be serviced and reused. Finding the right shifts requires innovation and testing of concepts akin to any other product or service innovation. In addition to sustainability, the consumer experience, pricing model, and positioning must be optimized to provide an at-par or superior product experience.

This requires a strong bridge between marketing and sustainability—two teams that don't naturally interact in most companies. One approach to building the bridge is to weave sustainability into broader portfolio planning and management. This can entail integrating sustainability KPIs into portfolio analysis, growth, and optimization decisions, alongside other measures such as profitability. The sustainability organization serves in a topic advisor role closely interlocking with commercial teams; or, sustainability roles can be more directly created within those teams. Some retail companies are adding entire layers of sustainability professionals to merchandising and marketing teams. Beyond liaising and collaboration, this approach embeds the skillset into operations through more direct roles, such as sustainability product manager, to accelerate the maturity curve and bring greater value in the short term. At Interface, a sustainable carpet pioneer located in Atlanta, the chief innovation officer is also the chief sustainability officer, aligning teams and incentives to bring sustainable product design to market.[29]

The auto industry is one case that demonstrates how companies can pursue successful growth mix shift while proving the business case to shareholders. Many industry leaders have pledged that around 40 percent of their new cars worldwide will not use gasoline by 2030—with clear progress being reported. Jaguar is nearing completion of its goal to transition entirely to electric vehicles by 2025, recently announcing that it will stop building cars (except for SUVs) by the end of 2024 in preparation for its all-electric revamp.[30] While industry data is showing mixed reports on electric vehicles' profitability, they are projected to account for 50 percent of all cars sold globally by 2035.[31]

The food industry is another sector that is starting to reevaluate long-standing portfolios, as pressure mounts for accelerated protein transition. The Non-State Actors Pillar of the Food Systems & Agriculture Agenda for COP28 called on companies to increase the availability of alternative proteins by 2030, develop a protein transition plan, support farmers through inclusion in sustainable protein sourcing, and promote customer choice of these proteins. Some companies are orienting portfolios as part of an integrated strategy for achieving such goals. Others are setting portfolio targets to drive sustainability goals. Multinational retailer and wholesaler Ahold Delhaize requires all of its European food brands to establish protein ratio targets, encouraging them to introduce more plant-based protein products and help customers make more sustainable choices.[32] Albert Heijn, its supermarket brand in the Netherlands, has committed to achieving 60 percent plant-based protein sales by 2030.[33]

Business performance metrics

Internal carbon market and pricing structures are excellent examples of how to embed sustainability targets into strategy through performance metrics. Some organizations are including a carbon budget as part of any project setup process. Managing to your carbon budget then becomes just as important as managing to your time and financial budget, and enables the organization to compare and aggregate the carbon intensity of various projects across the enterprise. At Microsoft, for example, business divisions pay an internal carbon fee for all Scope 3 emissions; part of a plan to be carbon negative by 2030.[34]

While imperfect, converting environmental and social impacts into monetary values can help to clarify trade-offs. For example, the French luxury group Kering consistently ranks as an industry leader for sustainability.[35] It publicly shares its methodology for quantifying environmental impacts of business activities, what it calls the environmental profit-and-loss tool (EP&L).[36] The EP&L rollout within the group has helped translate environmental impacts into monetary terms and support in decision-making such as evaluating materials, processing activities, and sourcing locations.

These methods can also make visible the benefits of sustainable products and materials that are not accounted for in conventional P&Ls. For example, savings from circular business models that redeploy products (reducing raw material extraction and product cost) would not be accounted for over product lifetimes in a traditional set of metrics. A life cycle accounting approach includes the full range of inputs, outputs, and processes associated with a product or service for a comprehensive view of positive and negative profit impacts.

Team and individual incentives

To make sustainability part of strategy, we find that it must be integrated into each leader's role and business-as-usual remit, and equal to meeting other individual targets, such as those related revenue growth or cost management. For example, chief commercial officers should be accountable for bringing forward sustainable products and services, and chief information and digital officers should be accountable for building the data backbone and digital services to support sustainability. Companies have two primary tools to incentivize sustainability performance: financial compensation directly tied to sustainability metrics, and integration of sustainability objectives into overall performance management.

Typically, compensation tied to strategic goals is reserved for the most senior executives, but sustainability goals that can be relevant for multiple levels in the organization, be that a people leader held accountable for ensuring their people feel safe and well at work, or a budget holder considering the sourcing of any new purchases, or project managers organizing to an internal carbon budget alongside a time and financial allocation. Mastercard, for example, has tied executive pay to progress on its sustainability priorities, as well as bonus calculations for all employees, to corporate performance on emissions, financial inclusion, and closing the gender pay gap.[37, 38] In 2024, the LEGO Group tied annual employee performance management to company-wide emissions reductions across factories, offices, and stores. While significant compensation might not be directly tied to these goals, embedding them into broader performance management structures signals to all that sustainability is truly part of the business strategy and relies on shared accountability across the organization.

INGREDION   Embedding sustainability into business strategy

Ingredion has successfully integrated sustainability into the fabric of the company's strategic and innovation agenda. As its sustainability strategy matured, the company shifted the sustainability function from operations where it was sitting with functions like quality, engineering and safety to the commercial part of the business.

The move repositioned sustainability from a function focused primarily on mitigating risk, viewed as a cost center to the business, to a value driver linked to customers and supporting growth of the business. Ingredion's sustainability initiatives, such as supporting farmers in carbon reductions, are now being deployed as a portfolio of differentiated customer solutions that are helping drive and defend business, insulating against competition. As Brian Nash, Vice President of Corporate Sustainability, describes it, "We have completely changed our approach so that sustainability is embedded in the enterprise growth strategy."[39]

Embed sustainability in innovation and transformation

With the exhaustion of the low-hanging fruit, even well-funded and prioritized strategic sustainability initiatives can struggle to find their way to scale. The economics, markets, or infrastructure may not yet be mature, or they may require major operational, cultural, and business model changes with new collaborative approaches.

For example, circular models, including product take-back and resale, rental, and refillable packaging, hold a lot of promise to improve impact, but bringing them to life is highly complex, requiring new and interconnected capabilities across the value chain. Products need to be designed for circular life cycles (to be easily used by many customers, or easily repaired and recovered), sales teams need to promote new end-to-end offers, and customers need to see value in participating. This may require standing up infrastructure for collection, reverse logistics, sorting, processing, and redeploying these new inputs back into manufacturing and operations. Some of these new business models require partnering with third parties on operational back-end activities for trade-in, cleaning, and so on, or with retailers or even peers to help build markets.

Companies are building foundational structures to entrench circular principles within the organizational culture and across functions. For example, Cisco realized that transforming to a circular model requires enterprise-wide changes to how a company thinks about its product design, supply chain, reverse logistics, and go-to-market models. In 2019, the company created its Circular Design Principles, which provide guidance on how to design products and packaging to improve sustainability performance across the product life cycle. Cisco also set a goal to incorporate these principles into all new products and packaging by 2025. Aligning to implement the principles and measure progress was a massive, cross-functional effort that required an integrated strategy. Circular design requirements are now documented in the new product development process, associated management tools, and all new designs are required to be scored prior to being released to production.[40]

Figure 6.1 shows the types of value chain modification that support circular models for product reuse and recollection.

Figure 6.1 Example of circular value chain transformation

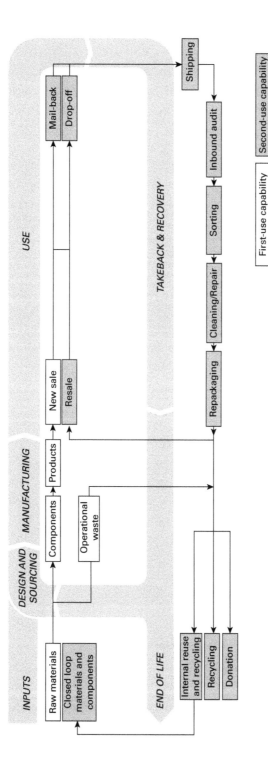

NOVO NORDISK   Building a circular value chain

Novo Nordisk, as part of its ambition to achieve net-zero emissions across the entire value chain by 2045, established a medical device recycling program called ReMed$_{TM}$, focused on reducing waste plastic from the company's products.[41] The global ReMed$_{TM}$ program was developed through local pilots that tested different innovative approaches, partnerships and customer engagement specific to the markets they were tested in. Take-back and recycling represents a radically new business model in the life sciences sector. A key to Novo Nordisk's success was the ability to establish new forms of collaboration with existing partners across the value chain, from wholesalers through to healthcare professionals, alongside building net-new capabilities and partnerships such as in recycling infrastructure for used devices.

Large companies that recognize the complexity of bringing truly sustainable innovations to life are investing in a range of new functions and units to catalyze and coordinate this work. These take a variety of forms.

Forward-looking research

A dedicated group focused on identifying, testing and developing innovative strategies and solutions to address emerging sustainability challenges can serve in a consultative capacity or jointly team up with business units on innovative solutions or pilots. This team may sit within sustainability or it may be independent of those groups to protect its ability to think long-term and creatively. It may be well-connected externally and collaborate closely with R&D, operations, marketing, and corporate strategy to help mobilize transformative changes that would not come to be without deep topical expertise and a mechanism for collaboration across the organization.

Incubator/internal venture capital fund

An internal corporate incubator is a specialized program that can support the development and growth of sustainability-focused projects. These initiatives might come directly from the business or from center-led research. The incubator provides resources, mentorship, and funding to teams who are working on innovative solutions to promote sustainability that may not gain traction within the normal operation of the business. Sustainability ideas can then be embedded into the right business unit once they have proven their merit. The incubator may even need to sit outside the sustainability function to protect its focus and remit, particularly when the investment required to launch new sustainable business models does not meet the standard requirements of the capital investment or finance teams. For example, in order to accelerate capabilities and drive its strategy to reduce landfill to zero, building components producer Owens Corning founded an innovation laboratory to pilot capabilities for new recycling processes and enable the development of more extensive take-back programs and end-of-life solutions for customers. As Owens Corning develops and learns from these programs, it will bring the capabilities into its production environment and asset network.[42]

Industry collaboration

Industry collaboration involves sharing knowledge, resources, best practices, and technologies among companies, with the goal of fundamentally changing sustainability dynamics in the industry. It can also involve collective action, such as demanding that industry suppliers increase the production of more sustainable materials and making a joint commitment to procure that. For example, Catena X is a partnership with companies including BMW, SAP and ZF that provides an open-data ecosystem for the automotive industry to support product carbon-footprint tracking, battery and product passports, traceability of parts, and master data management.[43]

Open innovation

The world is not short on great ideas for sustainable business models. There has been a proliferation of sustainability-focused startups and small-to-medium-sized enterprises with strong concepts but without the resources and reach of larger companies. A mechanism to identify, assess, and test collaboration in concert with startups can help mature companies leapfrog in sustainable business model development and source valuable expertise. Enel North America, for example, runs the NextHy Booster, a program to test and scale green hydrogen solutions in a partnership that provides entrepreneurs with financing, data, and expertise.[44]

The challenge of sustainable innovation

Sustainable product and packaging initiatives highlight the organizational tensions of bringing sustainable innovation to scale. Alongside efforts to shift to more sustainable material inputs (such as sustainable plastics or alternatives), many companies are trying disruptive models, such as reusables. While exciting in concept, these efforts require wholesale customer behavior change as well as cross-functional capabilities that support new sales models that shift from one-time to recurring revenue.

For example, the LEGO Group has expanded its focus on sustainable materials to exploring circular business model opportunities to earn revenue from recirculating bricks. The group acknowledged that recycled PET, one of many prototype materials it has been working on to replace virgin ABS plastic, would not be put into full-scale production. While some observers were quick to call the effort a "failure", the company used it as an opportunity to highlight the challenge of innovating sustainable products: "This is the nature of innovation – especially when it comes to something as complex and ambitious as our sustainable materials program. Some things will work, others won't." The group is applying those learnings as it continues to develop new materials and explore other ways to make LEGO bricks more sustainable.[45]

Build sustainability in business capabilities

Sustainability teams typically focus their efforts by topic, such as climate, packaging, or human rights. This topical lens is important, but a narrow focus can overlook cross-cutting opportunities to leverage core organizational capabilities. For instance, many sustainability goals in areas such as human rights, deforestation, and decarbonization all rely on suppliers making changes. This can result in burdensome and disjointed requests from each topic team to suppliers. The next step in maturity is to transition from a topical to an organizational mindset that takes a cross-business capability view.

Business capabilities are the organization muscles built across the organization that create competitive advantage. They don't live in one business unit, geography, or function. Embedding sustainability goals into established business capabilities makes them easier to understand and achieve. The following capabilities are a foundational set of organizational muscles relevant to many companies.

Supplier due diligence, management, and trust

Integrating sustainability into sourcing, supplier due diligence screening, and ongoing performance monitoring is one of the most important capabilities for becoming sustainable. It enables implementation of sustainability policies (such as supplier code of conduct, no deforestation, human rights) and initiatives that are necessary to drive performance improvement such as Scope 3 carbon reductions (indirect emissions up and down stream in the value chain) through supplier selection and ongoing engagement programs. Optimally, this work can be deployed through core procurement functions and processes to support seamless and trusted supplier relationships.

End-to-end sustainability data and performance monitoring

Tracking and understanding sustainability data from sourcing to distribution is critical to driving proactive performance management at production sites and in transportation. The capability to effectively manage key metrics such as energy, carbon, water, and waste supports progress on commitments and enables traceability of sustainability information for product- and customer-level reporting. These capabilities are increasingly being built out as distinct sustainability IT departments, reporting up to the CIO, but operating independently in recognition that there are both enterprise-level connections and new and unique data structures necessary to organize new technology solutions.

Integrated external reporting and disclosures

With the influx of both mandatory and voluntary reporting needs, organizations are establishing the same level of quality, accuracy, transparency, and auditability for sustainability metrics as they have for financial metrics. Other capabilities include preparing financial-based sustainability metrics for mandatory disclosure (such as percentage of revenue from products or services related to economic activities that can be considered environmentally sustainable); financing or bonds linked to sustainability outcomes; voluntary disclosures to raters, rankers, and investors; management reporting on performance and returns on investment; and board communications. As this is part of finance's core skillset, finance has a role to play in ensuring the robustness of the data and integrating metrics and activities with ongoing financial processes.

Sustainable product and service development and differentiation

Integrating sustainability into core business offerings and go-to-market activities is central to realizing strategic opportunities for business growth and resilience. This includes upfront integration into product and service design, business development plans, and enablement of sales and marketing teams. For instance, enabling and incentivizing sales teams to sell a product as a service versus a one-time sale and/or equipping them with the information and pricing tools to monetize sustainability premiums.

Wire sustainability into the organizational system

Sustainability needs to be hardwired into core business, systems, and processes because: its implementation is distributed; its distribution depends upon collaboration across organization boundaries; and it requires enterprise-wide sustainability data. Each can present challenges to established ways of working and power dynamics.

Distributed implementation

Sustainability outcomes rely on business delivery and capabilities that are highly distributed across the organization. If sustainability goals are truly part of the business strategy, it is likely that all parts of the organization will have a role to play. Corporate-level direction—often in the form of a chief sustainability officer—relies on implementation in the markets, business units, and functions. One sustainability leader admitted: "I have no control over implementation. That's terrifying." Center-led coordination is usually required at the enterprise level to ensure intentional and integrated decision-making so that sustainability teams don't need to rely on informal relationships or create duplicate work that shadows the core business. Neither is usually successful.

Collaboration across boundaries

Sustainability requires a high degree of cross-functional coordination and interaction. For example, product carbon-footprint capabilities span the full material journey from procurement to sales. Similarly, developing end-to-end circular product and service offerings means connecting end-of-life product supplies, product design, and commercial sales and customer management. Such new ways of working are impossible to establish without formal management processes and networks.

Most companies have made some degree of directional improvement towards enterprise integration, such as establishing cross-business working groups and creating sustainability roles outside of the core sustainability team so they understand the teams they are part of and have credibility in that business to navigate how to really make things work and drive change. For instance, one leading lifestyle and innovation brand established a sustainable product director role within product innovation with a dotted line to the sustainability lead.

However, many business teams are being asked to perform sustainability activities, but, often, they are not answerable or rewarded for the outcomes. When loosely embedded into other teams, sustainability will always feel like an "other" or extracurricular activity. As a result, many sustainability teams are trying to understand and report performance for areas they don't control rather than proactively managing performance.

Enterprise-wide data

Sustainability is a significant generator and consumer of enterprise data in the form of internal scorecards, mandatory disclosures, and voluntary disclosures such as requests from raters and customers. Many key performance indicators, such as carbon calculations, rely on the consolidation and analysis of metrics that are sourced from different parts of the business.

Without integration, sustainability data is often managed reactively, resulting in inefficient shadow processes or duplicated systems. This can lead to issues in data quality, trust, and lag time that all impede use by broader business stakeholders in decision-making. The decentralization and ad hoc nature of sustainability data management also means that most companies do not have a consolidated view of their sustainability performance and investments, making it challenging to deliver and demonstrate value. For example, Whitney Mayer, Head of Global Sustainability and ESG at Hershey, shared with us: "As our reporting needs increased, we realized we were spending a disproportionate amount of time gathering data versus managing in order to improve performance." Hershey is now implementing a multiyear ESG data and technology program that will address compliance while enabling greater value through performance management. According to Mayer: "We are collaborating with our technology colleagues to develop process and technological solutions that address data collection, quality and automation needs at the enterprise level. Our ESG data and technology strategy is foundational to understanding and taking action on the most material ESG risks and opportunities for our business."

In the remainder of the chapter, we discuss organizing approaches to overcome these issues and realize the value of integration.

Embedding sustainability in the organization structure

Across industries, we have observed an optimal set of organizational options for creating accountability for sustainability work.

Role of the board

Commitment to sustainability goals and connection to business strategy starts with the board. The board connects purpose to strategy and capital allocation decisions. The board ensures that sustainability is incorporated into the company's governance and risk management conversation. Sustainability can be embedded into standard committees, such as a corporate governance committee, or be its own standalone committee. For instance, Accenture's Nominating, Governance & Sustainability Board Committee oversees "ESG performance, disclosure, strategies, goals, and objectives and monitoring evolving ESG risks and opportunities".

Enterprise sustainability leadership and governance

Most organizations now have a chief sustainability officer (CSO) or equivalent leader who oversees the sustainability agenda for the company. The CSO role is poised for a dramatic evolution in a similar fashion to chief information officer (CIO) changes years ago. At first, the CIO was seen as a librarian, managing data files and sources of information but not accountable for driving business performance through technology assets. Today, CIOs produce insights, tools, and capabilities that drive top- and bottom-line value. The CSO is similarly evolving beyond writing the annual sustainability report or periodic sustainability strategy refreshes. Much like the journey of a CIO, we believe the CSO of the (near) future will be seen as a true strategic driver of value and competitive advantage. We are seeing this position designed as a standalone role or combined with other executive roles, such as the Interface example mentioned earlier.

One of the other initial decisions that companies need to consider is where to place executive authority for sustainability within the organization. For the standalone CSO, it is becoming more common to report directly to the CEO to establish appropriate authority, access, and accountability.[46] Other companies give CSO accountability to one or more functional leaders that bear the greatest responsibility for driving sustainability value. For example, if sustainability is a significant part of the company's commercial strategy, sustainability leadership may sit with the chief commercial, strategy or marketing officer, as in the Ingredion example discussed earlier. In contrast, in heavy industries, it is common for sustainability to roll up to the chief operations officer. Additionally, with the increasing focus on regulatory reporting, the chief financial officer is now taking on more sustainability responsibility and may oversee the entire function.

A combined approach has its benefits as the sustainability agenda is supported by a C-suite member with additional influence and authority over key parts of the business. A CSO focused exclusively on sustainability and reporting directly to the CEO may benefit from strong leadership support but runs the risk of being siloed among C-suite leaders and having less authority over key parts of their agenda. The right fit depends upon the company's industry, sustainability maturity, sustainability ambition, and underlying organizational structure. Figure 6.2 shows the most common variations on sustainability leadership roles and configurations.

Figure 6.2 Common variations on sustainability leadership roles and configurations

A. Standalone chief sustainability officer on executive committee

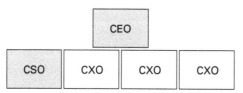

B. Combined sustainability + dual role on executive committee

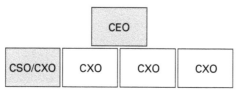

C. Standalone head or VP of sustainability to executive committee member

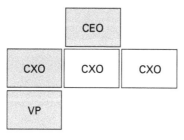

Leadership roles and accountabilities

While the role of chief sustainability officer is a strong integrating mechanism from the top, providing enterprise governance and directing the agenda, the majority of the actual work of sustainability usually sits in the functions and business units. For each goal and objective on the sustainability agenda, there are three options for where accountability lands: with the CSO; with the corporate function that is most relevant to the topic; or with the business unit that must ultimately provide the resourcing and implementation of the goal. For example, a chief procurement officer, overseeing a company's Scope 3 carbon reductions and supplier due diligence programs, could be the leader responsible for execution of those outcomes; or, the business unit leader that is responsible for the majority of related emissions might be accountable.

Only one leader should have accountability. When accountability is spread across multiple members of the executive team, we find that it tends to dilute ownership and can hamper execution. At the same time, given many sustainability outcomes have cross-business interdependencies, a strong level of coordination is critical. Clear accountability doesn't mean that others aren't involved or don't have metrics around the goal. It just means that one executive has to do the work to ensure the system supports meeting the goal.

As sustainability responsibilities become more distributed, it is becoming critical for all leaders in the business to gain fluency in sustainability, just as it is important for sustainability leaders to be fluent on the business.

The central sustainability function

Most companies require a center-led function to manage all the components of the sustainability agenda, including facilitating the strategy definition process, regulatory compliance, performance tracking, internal consulting, and change management. The degree of centralization—the amount of work that ultimately gets driven by the central team as opposed to being distributed across the business—depends on the sustainability priorities for the business and the underlying operating model of the company. For a company that operates with a very lean corporate center (typically having a very loosely related portfolio of businesses), we would expect to see a similarly lean corporate sustainability team that relies on business units to design and execute specific initiatives, within the frame of a corporate agenda. Conversely, a company that already operates multiple centers of expertise and services to link closely related business units would likely choose to build sustainability expertise centrally in order to provide hands-on support to business units. Time and maturity also influence this decision. Companies

Figure 6.3 Example of centralized governance, distributed implementation

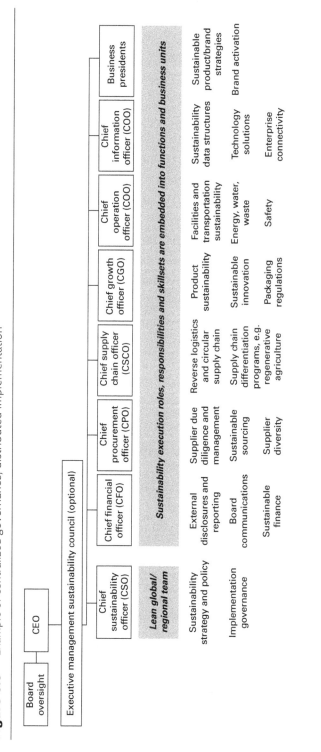

early in their sustainability journey might house more execution-related capabilities in their central team at first to build deep expertise and scale, and then distribute those to their natural home within the company as the skills and processes mature.

Whether they are involved in implementation or not, the central team typically facilitates setting sustainability strategy and commitments, reporting, and standards. They work with the business to "write the rules" for implementation. For instance, one team at a pharmaceutical company developed requirements for supplier due diligence and selection. The team codified the expectations, and now the business units run the checks as part of their everyday sourcing process. At another company, the sustainability team provides customer-specific sustainability information, such as the carbon footprint of a product, designing the right calculations and methodology, but sales and commercial teams engage customers on their requests and make any related pricing determinations. Over time, as capabilities mature, more sustainability capabilities—including those previously run by a central team or within the corporate layer—can be moved directly into customer-facing, product, and operating teams. Figure 6.3 shows an example structure that maintains a small, centralized team while distributing implementation roles into business areas accountable for implementation.

Embedding sustainability in processes

Process integration is the key to truly embedding sustainability into everyday business management by reducing duplicated work and fragmented implementation. Many of the sustainability capabilities described earlier are similar to existing business processes, so, if they are not integrated, sustainability teams end up running parallel processes to track, report on, and attempt to manage sustainability goals. Collecting and processing data for reporting and scorecard management can be incredibly time-consuming and there are often redundancies, even within sustainability teams that ask suppliers for information in a non-standard or ad hoc way. In addition, companies may have limited touch-points to engage suppliers and need to be consolidated in their requests and engagement.

When sustainability is not integrated into business performance management, sustainability teams try their best to influence decisions, but they often feel they are on the sidelines. Take, for example, tracking the end-to-end carbon footprint of a product. Sustainability leaders need a clear view to report performance. Sales stakeholders have a business need for the overall result, which will help them fulfill information requests, avoid discounting, and potentially differentiate themselves with customers, thereby creating a business opportunity (such as securing premiums, longer contracts, providing new sustainable services). However, for site-level operations managers—who are nonetheless essential for providing the data and performance—the question may be less pressing.

The power of process integration is the ability to write the rules for sustainability at the enterprise level—in this case carbon tracking and management—into the activities of the business that should perform them. In essence, sustainability requirements get written into the work and decisions of other teams. It is important to help teams understand the *why* behind sustainability requirements. Being able to connect the work to the bigger picture value—in the case of site managers, the ability to drive business with customers—also helps with motivation and a sense of purpose.

Here, the notion of value streams is useful, whether it is the customer experience journey or high-impact workflows such as ideate-to-launch or integrated business planning. Rather than sustainability as an add-on activity, it is a part of the work. This often requires redesigning handoffs and decision rights as work moves, from marketing and consumer insights to research and product development, on to sourcing and manufacturing, and through to sales and delivery.

Ultimately, the goal should be to avoid having the sustainability team running any parallel processes to the value streams that cut across the organization. This approach also enables redesign of the organization for the future versus hiring new resources to carry out the new capabilities.

ARCHER DANIELS MIDLAND   Enterprise sustainability transformation

Archer Daniels Midland (ADM), a global leader in innovative solutions from nature, is scaling sustainability across full value chains—farm to distribution—to help decarbonize the multiple industries it serves. Achieving impact at scale across highly global and complex supply chains is being made possible through integration of sustainability into the company's organizational system. ADM has a small, centralized sustainability team that provides strategy and governance over sustainability activities, but the bulk of sustainability activities are executed across the organization. The team defines sustainability initiatives and requirements, while it is the business and functional teams that own those requirements, tied to their existing work.

ADM has been recognized for rapid success in scaling its global regenerative agriculture program, which is driving adoption of sustainable practices toward a more resilient food system. Paul Scheetz, Director of Climate Smart Ag Origination at ADM, notes that, as the program developed, "the sustainability organization has provided the rulebook, and we (the business) execute the playbook". The program is driven by a commercial team within ADM's largest business, Ag Services & Oilseeds, as a business imperative. According to its president, Greg Morris, "sustainability is driving our strategic efforts to get closer to our producer customers and create value across our broad range of customers".[47]

To drive its broader sustainability vision, ADM is leveraging its enterprise transformation initiative to embed sustainability into standard processes and the digital backbone of the company. The future state of data-needs from customers and investors requires empowering the business and end-to-end supply chain. According to Alison Taylor, ADM's Chief Sustainability Officer, "We need to build a system that will be accessible throughout the enterprise and be owned by the enterprise, not one business unit or function."[48]

Embedding sustainability in data tracking and management

New regulations are greatly expanding the scope and expected rigor in data disclosures on sustainability topics.[49] For most companies, however, data collection and processing on sustainability is highly manual and disjointed. It is often tracked across spreadsheets by various topical owners, which only grows inefficiency and risk of error with regards to increasing data and compliance needs. An added complexity is that sustainability often depends on outside input from suppliers and other stakeholders in the value chain.

The confluence of new requirements is triggering many companies to take an enterprise approach to acquiring, managing, and controlling sustainability data. In some cases, existing master data management strategies and tools can be expanded to cover sustainability performance metrics and improve data quality. Creating an enterprise source data foundation for automated data processes can put in place the necessary controls for data auditability and reduce risk of error. Some companies are building centralized data hubs and utilizing source systems to create centralized repositories for sustainability data. For those embarking on data and systems transformations, many are beginning to build sustainability requirements into solution design. Kristy Folkwein, Chief Information Officer of ADM, has championed sustainability integration into the global solution design and rollout of its ERP system: "We are embedding sustainability solutions into our core technology and processes to help make better decisions faster across the business. Our foundational capabilities will position the company for continued success in business compliance, sustainability value and social impact."[50]

In addition to sustainability-focused data lakes and tools, existing enterprise tools can also service critical sustainability needs. Manufacturing execution systems that connect, monitor, and control manufacturing systems and data flows on the factory floor can help collect and analyze data related to material use to identify efficiencies such as idle time and water and energy consumption. Enterprise resource planning systems that combine core business processes such as accounting and purchasing in a single tool can measure and manage carbon emissions and water, assess and rate supplier sustainability performance, and support forecasting. Many client relationship management interfaces also have features such as carbon accounting tools to share greenhouse gas emission details with clients and customers.

In addition to enterprise solutions, given the current solutions landscape, most companies are also deploying specialized solutions for sustainability priorities, such as carbon accounting, product footprint, packaging, and chain and custody. Many of these solutions can support reporting and compliance while also driving step changes in performance analysis capability.

HARNESSING GENERATIVE AI TO ADVANCE SUSTAINABILITY

Emerging digital technologies, including GenAI, are rapidly becoming important enablers of sustainability. Numerous use cases are being explored to apply GenAI to sustainability. They range from more incremental with large efficiency gains to possibly major performance accelerators. The following are examples of promising ways to leverage GenAI in order to:

- Extract, collate, and tailor sustainability information into external reports, disclosures, and responses to customer and supplier questionnaires

- Apply predictive analytics to automatically adjust sustainability target glide-paths based on near-time tracking of metrics
- Run sophisticated, automated supplier risk assessments, climate scenarios, and resilience planning
- Advance circular value-chain capabilities, such as waste sorting and remanufacture, route optimization, and inventory management
- Accelerate the speed of sustainable R&D, process optimization, design and innovation.

While these new technologies can be impactful, they are also hugely energy intensive. It is estimated that training a large language model with 213 million parameters generates the same CO_2 emissions as 315 return flights from New York to San Francisco, so it is crucial to find ways to reduce this footprint.

With GenAI's rapid evolution, its uses can also have potential ethical implications that directly impact people's lives. When enterprises adopt AI, they should practice responsible AI in designing, developing, and deploying AI with good intentions to empower employees and businesses, and fairly impact customers and society, allowing companies to engender trust and scale AI with confidence.

Embedding sustainability in talent development

There is currently a sustainability skills shortage in the market, with new sustainability roles continuously being created, and demand for sustainability skills far outstripping supply.[51] Furthermore, given the need for sustainability to play such an integrated role across the business, people who intimately know the business *and* possess the requisite sustainability skills are even scarcer. Indeed, many sustainability roles initially start as "side of desk" or passion projects and may not be formally recognized in an individual's role and responsibilities, resulting in a level of effort and new learning that can quickly burn out dedicated and knowledgeable individuals.

New talent development models are required to meet the needs of the organization, starting by bringing skills into the center sustainability organization, creating the right roles that formally recognize the work being done, and then spreading them out to embed the skills and roles across the business as capabilities mature. Options include investing in upskilling talented individuals who want to take on a more sustainability-focused role through formal learning programs or certifications. There has been a proliferation of executive-targeted courses on sustainability, as well as business schools embedding sustainability into their core executive education courses.[52] On-the-job learning is also possible, with internal and external rotations to learn from teams with more advanced sustainability knowledge. External partnerships and secondments enable individuals from an external organization to come in for a defined period of time to build the internal capability. Some organizations are even leveraging a "fractional" CSO—particularly useful if they need the external expertise without the full-time cost.[53] Given the material talent gaps in this space, in addition to upskilling, companies need to think about how they access and create talent in key areas, such as sustainability data systems and management.

From a role perspective, sustainability responsibilities and associated skills need to be codified in role descriptions, skills taxonomies, and performance reviews to help individuals' evaluation and recognition. While many may be interested in the work, if the effort is not formally recognized, it just adds to the unpaid labor burden that many already face.

Conclusion: Closing the sustainability execution gap

The sustainability landscape is continuously evolving, so organizations similarly need to continuously evolve to keep pace. In particular, the costs and challenges of preparing for dozens of major sustainability regulations are vast, as can be the penalties for inaction. Necessary actions span new capability, process, and workflow development and data and technology integration, alongside upskilling, structuring, and empowering the broader organization to manage sustainability hand in hand with business performance.

There is no standard roadmap for building a sustainable business, but effective leaders can give their organization a compass point to follow, supported by effective operating model design, to turn intent into reality. A holistic view of the sustainable organization is summarized in Table 6.1.

Table 6.1   A holistic approach to embedding sustainability

Organization element	Key question	Target state	Business outcomes
Strategy	How will sustainability investment create value for the core business?	• Material sustainability risks and opportunities are integrated into enterprise strategy, priorities, and performance management	• Compliance/ minimized cost of non-compliance • Business value creation and differentiation • Business and operational resilience
Capabilities	How can sustainability capabilities get embedded across the organization?	• Multi-benefit capabilities are integrated with business and functions • Formalized processes guide sustainability execution	• Efficiency through streamlined work • Proactive performance management where work occurs
Structure and Governance	How will sustainability teams be structured, and responsibilities be distributed?	• A central function guides activities and governs performance • Sustainability responsibilities and accountabilities are distributed across the business	• Improved sustainability outcomes and performance • Efficiency through streamlined roles
Metrics and rewards	How are people incentivized to deliver sustainability?	• All employees are rewarded based on short- and long-term financial and non-financial targets	• Engaged employees driving sustainability value across the business • Ability to make investments with longer-term return

(continued)

Table 6.1   (Continued)

Organization element	Key question	Target state	Business outcomes
Data and technology	How do we advance sustainability data and management?	• Sustainability data collection, processing, and storage are automated with necessary controls • Regular visibility into sustainability data for reporting and proactive performance management • The right data is available to the right people at the right time and format to facilitate more sustainable decision-making	• More granular, frequent data capture, tracking, and quality controls for reporting, compliance and decision-making • Sustainability considerations reflected in day-to-day decision-making
Talent	How do we upskill the business to drive sustainability business objectives?	• Sustainability skillsets are embedded into business and operations roles	• More effective cross-functional collaboration, risk mitigation and innovation through empowered teams • Staffing efficiencies from integrated roles

Implementation tips

Designing the organization to execute on sustainability strategies is a process. We have observed a number of successful ways to accelerate adoption and change:

- Use **compliance as a catalyst**. Much of the work needed for compliance can also enable value-adding activities. Leverage the investment needed for compliance to create and set up the processes, organization, and systems that will enable broader transformation.

- **Get on the transformation train.** Link into enterprise transformation programs that can help deliver sustainability outcomes. Embedding a sustainability workstream into the broader company operating model, process, or technology transformation will be more efficient and cost-effective than attempting it separately. These kinds of programs can provide the tracks that enable the sustainability train to access cross-functional opportunities.

- **Spend time on upfront translation around the what and why.** Cross-team engagement is heavily reliant on understanding what needs to be done. It is challenging to translate sustainability needs into business requirements and technology solutions. Because requirements will be distributed across multiple teams, it is important to connect everything back to the broader *why* and business outcomes that are relevant to different parts of the organization.

- **Anticipate power struggles.** Many of the changes discussed in this chapter are ripe for emotional reaction. Decision-making and control are likely to shift. Questions may surface such as: Who owns what? What happens to my role as it gets distributed? Do I want to accept accountability for work done elsewhere? Will sustainable business models cannibalize my business unit? Meanwhile, some leaders may not fully agree with the goals. Approach sustainability like any transformation and factor in change management strategies to mitigate tensions and resistance.

- **Engage hearts and minds.** Embedding a sustainability mindset in the organization will be a key aspect of making sustainability stick. Projects and priorities come and go, but, for sustainability to be a core part of how business is done, you will require a shift from expecting a specific leader or initiative to drive sustainability to making it a core part of how employees think, make decisions, and see the purpose of the business.

Key takeaways

- Now is a SOX-like moment for sustainability, requiring transformation of how sustainability is operated and managed as a compliance and performance driver.

- Opportunities for sustainable growth can be realized through the adoption of organizational structures that embed sustainability into commercial priorities and teams.

- Clear lines of accountability for the sustainability agenda should be established among those with the authority and influence to drive sustainability goals, initiatives, and business models.

- Sustainability capabilities and processes should be integrated within the core functions of the business to embedding sustainability into the day-to-day activities and decisions of the company.

- Investment in technology and data will drive efficiency, reduce risk, and create value through data and analytics-driven management of sustainability.

Notes

1   World Economic Forum (2022) *Why Sustainability is Crucial for Corporate Strategy.* weforum.org/agenda/2022/06/why-sustainability-is-crucial-for-corporate-strategy (archived at https://perma.cc/4LAZ-YNMR).

2   Kim, R.C.H. (2021) Rethinking Corporate Social Responsibility Under Contemporary Capitalism: Five ways to reinvent CSR. https://doi.org/10.1111/beer.12414/v2/review2 (archived at https://perma.cc/58HC-AXUE)

3   Collins, S. and Northrup, L.M. (2022) The Legal Risks of Greenwashing are Real. news.bloomberglaw.com/environment-and-energy/the-legal-risks-of-greenwashing-are-real (archived at https://perma.cc/Y4DV-B9UW).

4   South Pole (2022) Going Green, Then Going Dark – One in four companies are keeping quiet on science-based targets. www.southpole.com/news/going-green-then-going-dark (archived at https://perma.cc/JB5N-MEKK).

5   United Nations (n.d.) *The Sustainable Development Agenda.* un.org/sustainabledevelopment/development-agenda-retired (archived at https://perma.cc/7JP4-BYNG).

6   European Union (2023) Regulation (EU) 2023/1115 of the European Parliament and of the Council of 31 May.

7   S&P Global (2023) Global Impact of the EU's Anti-Deforestation Law, August 31.

8   Bloomberg (2023) *ESG Data Acquisition & Management Survey 2023,* Bloomberg and Adox Research.

9   Verdantix (2023) Market Size and Forecast: ESG reporting software solutions 2021–2027 (global), January.

10 CDP (n.d.) Climate Change. cdp.net/en/climate (archived at https://perma.cc/62S9-2MTX).

11 CDP (2018) Global Climate Change Analysis 2018. cdp.net/en/research/global-reports/global-climate-change-report-2018 (archived at https://perma.cc/4NE6-8TFW).

12 European Commission (n.d.) Corporate Sustainability Reporting. finance. ec.europa.eu/capital-markets-union-and-financial-markets/company-reporting-and-auditing/company-reporting/corporate-sustainability-reporting_en (archived at https://perma.cc/63TN-VPEZ).

13 European Commission (n.d.) Corporate Sustainability Due Diligence. commission.europa.eu/business-economy-euro/doing-business-eu/sustainability-due-diligence-responsible-business/corporate-sustainability-due-diligence_en (archived at https://perma.cc/X9LK-YWX5).

14 Federal Ministry of Labour and Social Affairs (2023) Supply Chain Act. bmas. de/EN/Europe-and-the-World/International/Supply-Chain-Act/supply-chain-act.html (archived at https://perma.cc/2CJZ-6LYQ).

15 European Commission (2023) Regulation on Deforestation-free Products. environment.ec.europa.eu/topics/forests/deforestation/regulation-deforestation-free-products_en (archived at https://perma.cc/2WZ8-3647).

16 Resource Recycling (2023) In Our Opinion: How EPR picked up steam in 2023, 5 August. resource-recycling.com/recycling/2023/08/02/in-our-opinion-how-epr-picked-up-steam-in-2023 (archived at https://perma.cc/Y3QF-UDRY).

17 OECD (2023) *New Aspects of EPR: Extending producer responsibility to additional product groups and challenges throughout the product lifecycle*, OECD iLibrary. oecd-ilibrary.org/environment (archived at https://perma.cc/EU8E-ML8Q).

18 Harvard Law School Forum on Corporate Governance (2023) California Enacts Major Climate-Related Disclosure Laws, October 22. corpgov.law. harvard.edu/2023/10/22/california-enacts-major-climate-related-disclosure-laws (archived at https://perma.cc/632C-V3U8).

19 Governor Newsom, G. (2024) California Releases World's First Plan to Achieve Net Zero Carbon Pollution.

20 European Union (2024) Directive (EU) 2024/825 of the European Parliament and of the Council of 28 February.

21 United Nations Environment Programme (2023) Climate Litigation More than Doubles in Five Years, Now a Key Tool in Delivering Climate Justice, July 27.

22 Higham, C. and Kerry, H. (2022) Taking Companies to Court Over Climate Change: Who is being targeted? LSE and Grantham Research Institute, May 3.

23 Solomon, D. and Bryan-Low, C. (2004) Companies Complain About Cost of Corporate-Governance Rules, *The Wall Street Journal*, February 10.

24 Garden, L. (2024) France Will Jail Corporate Directors Who Fail to Adhere to New CSRD Requirements, Trellis, January/July. trellis.net/article/france-will-jail-corporate-directors-who-fail-adhere-new-csrd-requirements (archived at https://perma.cc/JC6U-ZDNN).

25 Ritchie, H., Rosado, P., and Roser, M. (2020/2024) Breakdown of Carbon Dioxide, Methand and Nitrous Oxide Emissions by Sector, Our World in Data.

26 Accenture (2023) UN Private Sector SDG Stocktake, September 14. accenture. com/us-en/insights/sustainability/getting-sdgs-back-on-track (archived at https://perma.cc/RYN4-JS25).

27 World Economic Forum (2022) How Stakeholder Alignment on Sustainability Unlocks a Competitive Advantage, February 1. weforum.org/stories/2022/02/ how-to-strengthen-sustainability-by-engaging-with-stakeholders (archived at https://perma.cc/9V5X-PV7H).

28 GFANZ (2021) *Race to Zero: Financing Roadmaps.* gfanzero.com/ netzerofinancing (archived at https://perma.cc/E6WG-4UW8).

29 Interface (n.d.) Corporate Governance: Person details.

30 Hood, B. (2024) Jaguar Will Stop Building Its Gas-Powered Cars in June in Preparation for Its 2025 Electric Revamp, *Robb Report*, March 4.

31 International Energy Agency (IEA) (2024) *Global EV Outlook 2024.* iea.org/ reports/global-ev-outlook-2024 (archived at https://perma.cc/C4S2-M3JP).

32 Ahold Delhaize (2023) Ahold Delhaize: Investing in our planet, April 22. aholddelhaize.com/en/news/ahold- delhaize -investing-in-our-planet (archived at https://perma.cc/BE4G-P92B).

33 Ahold Delhaize (2022) *Climate Plan.* aholddelhaize.com/media/4eofwbza/ ahold-delhaize-climate-plan-november-2022.pdf (archived at https://perma. cc/6HDM-WTTT).

34 Smith, B. (2020) Microsoft will be Carbon Negative by 2030, Microsoft, official blog. blogs.microsoft.com/blog/2020/01/16/microsoft-will-be-carbon-negative-by-2030 (archived at https://perma.cc/8GU4-E7A8).

35 Kering (n.d.) Sustainability: Measuring our impact: Ranking. kering.com/ en/sustainability/measuring-our-impact/ranking (archived at https://perma. cc/XDK7-RTQD).

36 Kering (n.d.) EP&L: Environmental measurement tool for sustainable luxury. kering.com/en/sustainability/measuring-our-impact/our-ep-l (archived at https://perma.cc/TUU7-D2JA).

37 Miebach, M. (2021) Why We're Tying Executive Compensation to Our Sustainability Priorities, Mastercard Newsroom, March 24. mastercard.com/ news/press/2021/march/why-we-re-tying-executive-compensation-to-our-sustainability-priorities (archived at https://perma.cc/2858-HB7Y).

38 Mastercard (2023) Corporate Social responsibility & Sustainability Program. mastercard.com/global/en/vision/corp-responsibility.html (archived at https:// perma.cc/A72L-P9XU).

39 Accenture (2024) Interview. Unpublished.

40 O'Donnell, J. (2023) Kinaxis Provides Tool For Sustainable Supply Chain, *TechTarget*, June 21. techtarget.com/searcherp/news/366542537/Kinaxis-provides-tool-for-sustainable-supply-chain (archived at https://perma.cc/FA6M-F9SV).

41 Novo Nordisk (n.d.) Sustainable Business: Introducing ReMed. novonordisk. com/sustainable-business/zero-environmental-impact/recycling-used-devices. html (archived at https://perma.cc/YA9M-RZ78).

42 Owens Corning (2023) *Making the Difference: 2023 Owens Corning Sustainability Report.* owenscorning.com/en-us/corporate/sustainability/docs/2024/2023-Owens-Corning-Sustainability-Report.pdf (archived at https://perma.cc/P9NE-G6AK).

43 Catena-X (n.d.) Catena-X. catena-x.net (archived at https://perma.cc/K8JZ-5KDG).

44 Enel (n.d.) NextHy Booster with Power to Hydrogen. enelnorthamerica.com/about-us/newsroom/search-videos/video/2023/03/nexthy-booster-program-with-power-to-hydrogen (archived at https://perma.cc/VSD8-937M).

45 Vasil, A. (2023) Lego Says It Hit a Recycled Plastic Stumbling Block. Do Its Claims Stack Up?, *Corporate Knights,* October 4. corporateknights.com/category-circular-economy/lego-recycled-plastic-stumbling-block (archived at https://perma.cc/U52C-4D9C).

46 Michel, M. (2024) Increasing Influence: 66% of new Chief Sustainability Officers report to CEO, CSO Futures, January 9. csofutures.com/news/chief-sustainability-officers-report-to-ceo-cso-futures (archived at https://perma.cc/YU6L-82DW).

47 See, for example, *Nutraceuticals World*, July 21, 2023, ADM expands regenerative agriculture program in North America.

48 Accenture (2024) Interview. Unpublished.

49 Workiva (n.d.) CSRD Data Points & Disclosure Requirements. workiva.com/uk/blog/csrd-disclosure-requirements#:~:text=CSRD%20standards%20require%20companies%20to,can't%20hide%20from%20ESG (archived at https://perma.cc/73A5-FTS9).

50 Accenture (2024) Interview. Unpublished.

51 LinkedIn (2023) *Global Green Skills Report 2023.* economicgraph.linkedin.com/research/global-green-skills-report (archived at https://perma.cc/4YAX-NPGU).

52 Bleizeffer, K. (2023) INSEAD Revamps Its MBA Curriculum, Putting a Heavy Focus on Sustainability, *Poets & Quants,* May 6. poetsandquants.com/2023/05/06/insead-revamps-its-mba-curriculum-putting-a-heavy-focus-on-sustainability (archived at https://perma.cc/X5DV-F7JR).

53 Penrhyn-Jones, S. (2023) Fractional Sustainability Leadership: A game-changer for SMEs, The Now Work, November 6. thenowwork.com/fractional-sustainability-leadership-a-game-changer-for-smes (archived at https://perma.cc/E4E2-C4GE).

The Reinventor Organization 07

SANAM GILL, KENT MCMILLAN

Contributor: Yaarit Silverstone

In the face of ever-accelerating disruption, the buzz around reimagining traditional organizational constructs and practices is louder than ever. It is crucial, however, to differentiate between the allure of ideas simply because they are new and the implementation of innovative, yet practical, operating models.

A theme throughout this book has been that leaders who look to the future are continually building new organizational capabilities in the face of uncertainty and technological advancements. Instead of focusing on backward-looking activities like redesigning, reorganizing, or restructuring, they are looking ahead and reinventing their strategies and business models. They are deliberately setting a new performance frontier for their companies and the industries they operate[1] in—one where continuous reinvention is key. This involves adapting to market dynamics, embracing new technologies, and staying aligned with the evolving expectations of customers, employees, and society.

This final chapter sets out the key features of these organizations and provides guidance on how to leverage them to build a reinventor organization.

Seven features of the reinventor organization

Becoming a reinventor organization means creating a world where humans and machines truly work in harmony, teams and skills are the new currency, and people feel engaged, supported and energized. The operating models of these organizations, from our research and hands-on project experiences, have seven key features (summarized in Table 7.1). While few companies have achieved all seven, front-runners—from startups to industry incumbents—provide insight on what is possible. We will define each feature, the key shifts required in the operating model to embody it, the benefits it brings, and what needs to be in place to achieve the full potential of the feature.

Table 7.1   The seven features of the reinvention organization

1	**Connected and empowered**	Unite the organization through shared data and insights, with clarity on purpose and direction, trade-offs, and guardrails that enable big bets and empower people to act
2	**Adaptive and scaled**	Organize around customer needs for innovation and speed, and platforms for efficiency and scalability, built on modular data and technology architectures, continuously sensing and adapting to the market
3	**Integrated around outcomes**	Rewire the organization around multidisciplinary teams that work across boundaries and hierarchies to find and deliver end-to-end 360-degree value for external and internal customers
4	**Automated and augmented**	Use data and technology as the primary way to get work done and amplify human creativity and decision-making, enabling a paradigm shift in productivity and intelligence of the organization
5	**Skills and aspiration driven**	Build teams with the skills and aspiration to deliver on the company's strategy through a radically more granular understanding of the skills and sophisticated combinations of people and technology
6	**Ecosystem powered**	Partner deeper and faster for innovation and competitiveness, enabled through simple digital interfaces, that deliver for customers and multiply the value of the ecosystem
7	**Always pursuing performance**	Proactively self-disrupt how work gets done to achieve new performance frontiers, enhancing organizational capabilities and inspiring employees as co-creators of change

1: Connected and empowered

Reinventors unite the organization through shared data and insights, with clarity on purpose and direction, trade-offs, and guardrails that enable big bets and empower people to act.

A connected and empowered organization enables individuals, teams, functions, and business units to build, work, and learn together where required. Leaders achieve this through weaving and sharing data and insights throughout the organization and by empowering the teams to act with a clear direction and guardrails.

An example is Supercell, a Finnish mobile game developer known for its daily company-wide updates on how the world is reacting to its offerings. Leaders share metrics such as new user acquisitions, active daily users, player spending, and player return rates.[2] Such total transparency gives everyone in the company a common understanding of the world Supercell is competing in and the product-to-customer fit (or not) it is achieving. Teams have the visibility and ability to stop development of a game not achieving market fit, or to use one game's performance to inform the development and marketing strategies of another. To work this way requires a single version of the truth, radical transparency, and clarity on how data should be managed, who can see what, and with any associated risks managed.

The benefits of such connections are only realized when leaders and teams can act at speed on the data and insight in alignment with the company's purpose and direction. This "freedom in a framework" requires establishing a clear global direction and one set of standards, within which individual organization units are given the flexibility to operate. In this way, organizations gain high degrees of connectivity across units, without unnecessary controls.[3]

Luxury hotel brands demonstrate this approach well. They have global standards that must be adhered to at every property to deliver on the promise of luxury, while empowering employees to personalize the experiences at each hotel to reflect their guests' preferences and expectations.

Operating in this manner necessitates mutual trust among organizational units. For instance, once the corporate center or regional layer sets guardrails—such as predefined capital expenditure limits as part of the annual planning process—individual units should not need to seek repeated approvals for decisions that fall within these parameters. These units should independently manage their expenditures, while reporting progress during quarterly business reviews, thereby maintaining transparency and allowing the center to verify that plans are being executed as agreed.

Further, organizational units and teams must be empowered to collaborate directly, reducing reliance on hierarchy. Fjeldstad et al. reinforce this view in "The architecture of collaboration",[4] emphasizing three critical elements: organizational units and teams must have the autonomy to self-organize; the infrastructure must enable seamless resource sharing; and clear protocols and processes must be in place to support effective multi-actor collaboration. Accenture is an example of this model, where teams operate with a high degree of autonomy, utilize shared methods and knowledge bases, and follow well-defined protocols for mobilizing and delivering projects.

These ways of working hinge on getting the metrics right: creating complementary performance units and aligning team and individual goals and measures. Companies such as Google and Salesforce have accomplished this by designing wider P&L performance units that enable bigger bets and strategic investments, while minimizing internal competition over "enterprise resources". At the same time, they employ frameworks such as objectives and key results (OKRs) to drive performance and accountability at all levels, ensuring team and individual goals are ambitious, strategy aligned, and transparent to all, while granting teams the autonomy to achieve them in their own ways.

Connected and empowered organizations thrive on a foundation of data, trust, and enabling mechanisms such as integrated planning and performance management. This results in a more engaged, responsive, and aligned workforce that can make informed decisions quickly wherever they are.

Key operating model shifts

- Flatten the organization and empower teams.
- Apply a "freedom in a framework" approach to governance.
- Enable teams to collaborate directly, reducing reliance on hierarchy.
- Allow for shared data and transparency across divisions, functions, and layers.
- Set a clear direction with complementary metrics and incentives across organizational dimensions (units and layers).

2: *Adaptive and scaled*

Reinventors organize around customer needs for innovation and speed, and platforms for efficiency and scalability, built on modular data and technology architectures, continuously sensing and adapting to the market.

Adaptive and scaled organizations are defined by their ability to anticipate and meet customer needs in the face of an ever-increasing pace of change and an unrelenting competitive landscape. They achieve this by being customer "obsessed" and by applying modern product- and platform-based operating model approaches.

To deliver on this goal, product units and teams solve for their customers' needs through an emphasis on speed and responsiveness. They are asset light and embrace agile ways of working, with empowered cross-functional teams that work in short, iterative cycles to develop, test, and refine products. A hallmark of these teams is their curiosity and commitment to continuous improvement, which ensures they drive ongoing innovation and remain aligned with evolving customer needs.

Platform units and enabling teams emphasize integration and scalability, and provide foundational infrastructure and services. However, organizations that are oriented this way don't simply use platforms to lower costs; they use them to make it easier for product units and teams to develop new offerings, make deeper insights, and get to market faster. Reinventors take advantage of advances in technology that are radically reducing coordination and scaling costs, which enable them to deliver ever-more seamless customer experiences, while opening up their platforms for multiple parties to contribute and benefit from the shared data and infrastructure.

Chinese multinational technology company Alibaba sets its front-end product units and teams (such as Taobao and Tmall) to focus on understanding demand and creating customer-orientated products and services. Meanwhile, shared middle (such as payments and customer profiles) and back-end (for example storage and computing) data and technology platforms enable more personalized recommendations and reduce duplication. This drives better conversion rates and sales growth and enhances profitability, while also enabling any small business to set up on Alibaba's e-commerce platforms in a matter of days or weeks.[5]

Modular organizational structures and systems are the backbone of adaptive and scaled organizations. Each module has distinct accountabilities and most of the capabilities to deliver them, minimizing coordination costs across organizational units and teams. This is counterbalanced through an approach of "aligned autonomy" that allows modules to operate interdependently while remaining connected to achieve the organizations goals.

Amazon showed the power of this approach when it mandated the modularization of its teams and software.[6] This sped innovation and generated new revenue streams, enabling the retail business to launch thousands of experiments daily to optimize product assortment, pricing, and sales funnel.

Further, the company expanded stock-keeping units to over 12 million through its marketplace by sharing its e-commerce platform and logistics capabilities with third-party vendors. The company even created a new business in AWS that rapidly monetized the scalable digital infrastructure and is now the company's largest income generator.[7]

However, only when these ways of working are combined with an open and dynamic strategy can reinventors truly sense, respond, and adapt at scale. This requires moving away from traditional top-down annual planning processes to a more inclusive approach that relies on continuous feedback and real-time data from across the organization and beyond, leveraging AI and big data for insights, forecasting, and scenario modelling and actively seeking input from the front line, customers, and external experts.

Organizations that are successful in this way recognize that customer needs and market conditions are constantly evolving, requiring them to continuously configure and reconfigure their capabilities to achieve a competitive edge. They have the ability to quickly assemble, deploy, and redeploy teams on any dimension, supported by flexible systems that can track success and attribute financial impact as the organization adapts.

Key operating model shifts

- Set up an open and dynamic, data-driven strategy development process.
- Apply modern product- and platform-based operating model approaches.
- Embrace agile ways of working at three layers: portfolio, organization, and team.
- Take advantage of the latest modular data and technology architectures.
- Ensure structures, systems, and performance reporting can be reconfigured easily.

3: Integrated around outcomes

Reinventors rewire the organization around multidisciplinary teams that work across boundaries and hierarchies to find and deliver end-to-end 360-degree value for external and internal customers.

Organizations that are integrated around outcomes fulfill increasingly sophisticated customer demands with consistency and speed. They achieve this by taking a value-stream approach, where multidisciplinary teams work together around common goals, powered by data and the right technology, to deliver end-to-end for the customer.

These value streams include the full life cycle of activities and muscles coming together to deliver on the most critical outcomes for the customer.

They are customer-centric, emphasizing efficiency, effectiveness, and continuous improvement, cutting across traditional departmental or functional boundaries to focus on the overall flow of value through the system. Typically, value streams materialize as the highest-impact customer experiences or journeys or the most high-impact workflows. In consumer-packaged-goods companies, for example, the fundamental value streams such as insight to plan, ideate to scale, plan to deliver, and engage to consume drive disproportionate value for the customer.

What work to do is driven by multidisciplinary teams in the value stream, and *how* to do the work remains in homeroom functional disciplines. This ensures collaboration is concentrated within, rather than across teams, encouraging innovation and increasing the clock speed of the organization.

Consider ride-sharing platforms such as Uber and Lyft. Typically, they select function and geography as their primary and secondary structural building blocks. This enables them to create a global product while adapting to local customer preferences, driver requirements, and regulatory environments. However, the functional and geographic silos risk the very strategy of an asset-light organization—to create value through an integrated solution and a seamless customer experience. To solve this, they leverage value streams and agile ways of working, and, given the multisided nature of their platforms, they implement both customer-focused and driver-focused value streams, for example passenger booking, driver dispatch and ride matching, payments, and ratings for customers; and income opportunities, driver support and resources, vehicles, and partnerships for drivers. With the product largely digitized (the app and platform) and outsourced (the drivers and their vehicles), a significant portion of the companies' teams focus on innovation and problem-solving, applying agile ways of working. This principle applies equally when work is digitized in an organization.

Incumbent data and software organizations, such as banks and insurance companies, have also embraced this type of thinking as they seek to be more customer-centric and faster to market. Take, for example, the more consumer-centric idea of "moving house" as a solution, rather than the product-centric "mortgage products" approach. BBVA, Citibank, and ING, and many more, are well down this path using customer journey value streams and agile ways of working in the development and management of largely digital, consumer-centric offerings.

The logic is also being embraced by physical product and asset-based companies. Consumer goods companies continue to explore ways to organize around customer and consumer journeys, and are already having success with high-impact workflows such as integrated business planning and new product development. For example, one global consumer goods company is reinventing one of its biggest categories around its six most critical end-to-end value streams to improve customer outcomes and business performance. It is fully rewiring the organization, with clear ownership of continuous improvement by each value stream. While there are common threads, every organization will need to find the right value streams and balance of where it applies multidisciplinary teaming and agile principles.

Key operating model shifts

- Rewire the organization around the highest-impact end-to-end value streams (customer journeys and workflows).
- Establish multidisciplinary teams that work together towards a common goal.
- Ensure the *what* of work is driven by the teams in the value stream.
- Measure outcomes and lifetime customer value, rather than activity.
- Create shared success metrics and incentives that are cross-functional.

4: Automated and augmented

Reinventors use data and technology as the primary way to get work done and amplify human creativity and decision-making, enabling a paradigm shift in productivity and intelligence of the organization.

Automated and augmented organizations embrace complexity, and challenge traditional operating model and organization design trade-offs such as agility versus scale. They achieve this by digitizing their business models, offers, and core value chains, and by reshaping how work is done to unlock new levels of productivity. They seek, through the application of advanced technologies such as Generative AI, to raise the collective intelligence of the organization.

In this new world, machines have gone far beyond simple low-value task automation and collaboration tools. They have become assistants, peers, and even managers, completing increasingly complex tasks at ever-faster speeds. The latest large language models of Chat GPT and Gemini, for example, are even exhibiting nascent abilities to perform tasks requiring reasoning and planning,[8] and we are seeing increasingly intelligent processes that are self-learning and healing, as well as the dawn of autonomous AI agents.

While businesses often find that initial growth and scale bring efficiencies, they also see diminishing returns as their operating model buckles under the weight of the added complexity of new products, markets, and customers.[9] However, operating models powered by data and technology can manage this heightened complexity at a significantly lower marginal cost compared to traditional organizations, disrupting the long-standing correlation between linear head-count growth and business outcomes, allowing businesses to scale without proportional increases in staffing. A useful example is Ocado, a UK online grocery retailer and online grocery platform (it also offers its capabilities to other retailers). Its warehouses are the most robotic in the industry and it uses data and analytics to enable retailers and consumer goods companies to predict demand and reduce waste, significantly enhancing joint planning.[10] An outcome is that previously unwieldy and unrewarding industry complexities now present opportunities. Ocado's deep automation means that if it needs to onboard additional customers or product lines, it does not need a fully stacked team for each. Instead, data from new customers or product lines is seamlessly integrated into existing systems, meaning any additional head count brought in can focus on providing better service to customers.

Organizations that are designed with data and technology at the core discover untapped sources of value, enhance their offerings, radically reduce costs, and seamlessly connect capabilities with others. They push the boundaries of traditional design trade-offs, such as global versus local, using advances such as AI-driven mass-personalization of offers and experiences, based on individual customer profiles. Leaders take on what was once impossible or cost prohibitive and radically challenge themselves to find where humans and machines add value together.

Wealth management is another example of an industry that has seen considerable rapid reinvention. Digitized value chains are enabling digital wealth management specialists and "robo investors" to develop more personalized services and offerings and to deliver these new offerings more quickly and efficiently than ever before. Beyond simply raising effectiveness and efficiency, this has resulted in greater democratization of wealth management, making it more accessible to a wider customer base. The outcomes are new revenue streams for wealth management providers, while also bringing customers greater flexibility and choice.

Advanced technologies such as generative AI and hyper-automation will have far-reaching consequences on the shape of the organization and how it operates. When much of execution is automated, the real work of humans will be that of innovation, human contact, and complex problem-solving. Consider how a fintech loan company automates the full process, from application, credit assessment, pricing, and offer through to putting the money in your account. In this type of organization, people can be fully focused on designing new loan products and solving issues (such as when an algorithm fails).

To truly exploit automation and augmentation, reinventors will need to create an environment of trust between humans and machines. A first step is to consider digital actors, as Jeremy Heimans puts it in his research, to be "autosapiens" that are part of the team.[11] Second is to design the technology to interact and learn with humans. For example, while the United Parcel Services' routing algorithms issue a central plan to drivers, the drivers can share input on local conditions and make decisions to change the route.[12]

Key operating model shifts

- Digitize the business model, products, and core value chain.
- Implement intelligent self-learning and healing processes and AI agents.
- Design organizations for the collective intelligence of people and machines.
- Start with software and algorithms, rather than structures, as the organization grows.
- Ensure human agency and responsible AI ethics are built in.

5: Skills and aspiration driven

Reinventors build teams with the skills and aspiration to deliver on the company's strategy through a granular understanding of the sophisticated combinations of people and technology.

Organizations driven by skills and aspirations value having a real-time picture of the current and future landscape. Leaders tap into internal and external signals of how the work and workforce is evolving. They capture workers' skills based on their experience and exposure, overlayed with their aspirations, combined with an in-depth understanding of where people and/ or machines are the best fit for the work.

Professional services firms have always been skills-focused organizations as, without the right combination of skills on any project team, the desired client outcomes cannot be delivered. Accenture uses a global skills taxonomy and centralized skills and aspirations database, and proprietary algorithms, to identify proficiencies, predict required team structures, and drive intelligent talent matching and development. This focus on skills increases the mobility of talent, optimizes capacity, better matches talent to the job to be done, and ensures targeted investment across every dimension of the talent strategy.[13]

These types of organization can respond better to the volatility companies are facing today. We have observed that organizations do this by deconstructing jobs into granular parts and specific skills, rather than constructing broad-based jobs in an environment of talent shortages. They hire for and assign tasks to specific people and create personalized learning paths based on their individual skills and aspirations, rather than job titles. In this way, organizations can unlock pools of hidden talent within and beyond the organizational border, retaining skilled people through internal growth opportunities, and drive higher levels of engagement and effectiveness.

However, it is not simply a question of matching individuals to tasks. Skills- and aspiration-driven organizations embrace the dynamics of teams and how humans work with machines. Reinventors not only match talent with the right skills to deliver on a task; they optimize for team outcomes. This requires putting together a team with the right combination of skills, while balancing the needs of other teams and enabling the dynamics that make a team greater than the sum of its parts. Consider the example Simon Sinek gives of the Navy Seals' team building, where they have found it better to choose a medium performer with high trust over a high performer with low trust.[14]

Further, only by harnessing the collective intelligence of humans and machines to create, as Tom Malone puts it, "superminds" can reinventors truly set a new performance frontier.[15] Malone offers the example of the corporate strategic planning process: small groups of specialists and the management team make decisions on where they play, how they win, and what it will take to win. Using collaboration tools and clear line of sight to the required skills, a wider pool of input from those best placed to shape the future are involved in the process. Machines augment the process by supporting the team in generating and evaluating strategic options based on previous patterns and actions taken, so creating teams of humans and machines.

In this new world, not only the human but the technology is learning and changing, creating the opportunity for people and machines to continuously learn together, as, for example, an AI sales coach, where a sales agent uses AI to refine their pitch with real-time feedback while the AI updates its algorithms based on what strategies work.

Skills- and aspiration-driven organizations make use of sophisticated talent marketplaces that enable rapid and non-stop matching of internal and external talent to teams and the work to be done, increasing organizational agility by making more informed source, skill, borrow, and retain decisions. Cisco's Talent Cloud is such a mechanism—matching people with the right skills and reputation to suitable assignments.[16] This enables Cisco to achieve greater agility by flexibly porting talent as required, improving the retention and satisfaction of employees.

Key operating model shifts

- Create a real-time understanding of people's skills and aspirations.
- Continuously assess where people and/or machines are the best fit for tasks.
- Establish the infrastructure to match teams of people and machines to the work.
- Build systems that enable people and machines to learn together—cybernetic.
- Develop the ability to onboard and train people and AI agents.

6: Ecosystem powered

Reinventors partner deeper and faster for innovation and competitiveness, enabled through simple digital interfaces, that deliver for customers and multiply the value of the ecosystem.

Ecosystem-powered organizations dynamically assess where and how they can create value, and who they can partner with to generate that value. They have multiple partners, each with complete clarity on the role they will play and how value is generated for the wider ecosystem.

Partnering is not new, so what is different now? Historically, companies were closed systems, with solid borders that clearly defined what happened inside the organization versus outside. Relationships with external partners were guided by competitive thinking, with partnerships based on who could offer the lowest price for the required goods or services.

However, companies such as Haier—a $35 billion appliance manufacturer with 75,000 employees—are redefining what it means to partner. Haier's core belief is that "more collaboration will happen when more boundaries are broken, and more valuable relationships are established".[17]

Haier creates an environment where all stakeholders, internally and externally, are integrated into one large ecosystem where they work to create more value for the customer. The larger ecosystem consists of microenterprises. All parties sign a collective contract and share benefits based on how much value they create collectively for customers. This leads to improved goods and services for customers, and means Haier gets a share of the revenues generated by all other stakeholders that have joined the ecosystem. Through its Hai Chuanghui (HCH) entrepreneurship acceleration platform, Haier has successfully incubated 7 unicorns (a startup valued at over $1 billion) and 102 gazelles (fast-growing enterprises that maintain exceptional and consistent growth over a prolonged period).[18]

Choosing where and how to partner goes back to the capabilities an organization is building in order to deliver its strategy. Organizations have typically chosen to own the work that is a core competency and differentiator, and partner with others for commodity activities or where partners may have scarce or expensive expertise. Apple and Nike, for example, both keep product design very close while choosing to partner for manufacturing.

There is now a shift towards using multiple partners even to build core sources of value. This requires organizations to nurture a diverse ecosystem of partners. Take the example of Verizon and how it chose to build the 5G economy. It did this by forming strong partnerships across its value chain. Device manufacturers help ensure that Verizon's network can support all devices; cloud providers and system integrators help develop Verizon's mobile edge computing (MEC) ecosystem; and customers test new use cases.[19] Each partner is managed differently to achieve the right level of cooperation and so that the right information is shared at the right time, while keeping intellectual property safe.

The half-life of competitive advantage is getting shorter and shorter, and this requires organizations to continually assess where to play and how to win. In those choices, they will need to determine where the value is in their industry's value chain, what the organization's distinctive capabilities are, and, therefore, which partners can support them best, where, and how. Consider Vodafone's partnerships with Microsoft and Accenture. With Microsoft, Vodafone can scale its Internet of Things business and grow its enterprise business for small and medium-sized businesses (SMEs)[20], delivering a core part of Vodafone's business, not just service provision. While, with Accenture, Vodafone will accelerate the commercialization of its shared services operations (Finance, HR, IT, etc.), allowing for significant efficiencies and the transformation of its core business.[21]

Ecosystem trust is built on clear standards and principles, alignment on what activities different parties will be responsible for, and when different partners should be used (for example innovation phase or scale-up phase). The Alibaba and Tencent models work this way. Alibaba takes a commission on everything that passes through it without competing with ecosystem participants. In return, ecosystem participants get full access to Alibaba's services and a high volume of customer data. Data sharing drove value for all in the ecosystem when more than 3,000 Chinese companies were able to rapidly scale the production of medical supplies, such as masks and protective equipment, during the Covid-19 crisis.[22] For example, data sharing enabled the demand requirements to be communicated to those companies that could meet the need. They in turn confidently met the demand, knowing their products were not going to go to waste. Alibaba earned the commission for the traffic flowing through and so benefited too.

Key operating model shifts

- Continuously assess where, how, and with which partners to create value.
- Establish robust but flexible partnering models and interfaces.
- Consider multi-party relationships (rather than only one-to-one) to create network effects.
- Make the organization's data and technology more accessible and interoperable.
- Measure total ecosystem value, with shared risk and reward.

7: *Always pursuing performance*

Reinventors proactively self-disrupt how work gets done to achieve new performance frontiers, enhancing organizational capabilities and inspiring employees as co-creators of change.

Organizations that always pursue performance reinvent every part of their organization over time. They continually seek new and different ways to deliver value. These organizations don't ask for benchmarks; rather, they redefine what the top quartile will be for their industry by investing in leading-edge capabilities that will differentiate them in the market. Leaders of these organizations harness disruption and shape new performance frontiers, creating a culture of experimentation and learning where every employee has a role and a voice and feels, collectively, empowered to challenge the status quo. Meanwhile, executives break down boundaries across the enterprise and treat reinvention of the business and how work gets done as equal to operational execution.

This is not a one-off activity, but a permanent state of reinvention where change itself is a distinctive capability; where organizations maintain a constant focus on initiatives that drive the most impact, with regular restocking of the pipeline with new initiatives.[23] Dell took this approach following its privatization. Establishing the Dell Agenda held the backlog of strategic imperatives essential to the company's transformation that would be addressed at regular executive leadership team meetings. As items on the agenda were achieved, new items were added to ensure the transformation remained ongoing. In this way, initiatives driving the strategic imperatives would be dynamically aligned and prioritized based on the strategy and value delivered. Seeing transformation became a part of daily leadership practices.[24]

Further reinventors break down the change and take a "do, learn, do" model, recognizing that to achieve results in complex organizations is challenging when taking a top-down approach alone. Haier demonstrates this approach, with CEO Zhang Ruimin believing in an approach of "running more trials and replicating the most successful ones faster" to accelerate organizational transformation.[25] In this way, the organizational change emerges as an iterative process of experimentation and learning. Such organizations also focus on making employees part of the journey, rather than *taking* them on the journey. When executive leaders simply declare the problem and announce a solution, they risk alienating the employees they need to embrace it and who would execute the mission, and they short-change the opportunity to find better, more systemic, solutions and sustainable change. The very act of co-creation delivers results faster and increases employees' resilience to change.

Corporate transformation offices are often established as a catalyst to this enterprise capability. These tend to have a small, experienced teams that serve as facilitators to and coaches for change initiatives. They have a focus on enterprise value and outcome, rather than deliverables and milestones. Through this, they can provide assurance to the senior management team that the organization is focused on executing the strategy. They embrace flexibility responding to the fast-changing business environment and build a change muscle throughout the organization. These are not traditional project management offices that focus on coordination and compliance.

True reinventors go one step further. They create accountability throughout the organization and build the muscles to continuously improve the way work is done. McDonald's, for example, is always seeking to create the perfect McDonald's burger. Through the application of data-driven workflow analysis, waste and quality improvements are continuously identified and implemented.[26]

Companies that get this right actively manage their organizational system in service of the company's strategy. This requires the cultivation of four key operating model and organization management muscles:

1 Ensuring all elements of the operating model are aligned with the organization's objectives

2 Planning the workforce and monitoring organizational effectiveness and efficiency

3 Proactively hacking the organization, identifying opportunities for optimization and innovation, including running experiments and scaling successful experiments

4 Laying the organizational data foundation to underpin analysis and link to results.

With this in place, AI and GenAI have the potential to identify patterns and generate hypotheses that leaders can use to model scenarios, forecast potential impact, and assess the trade-offs at play. At the most advanced, they can build a digital twin of the organization to test hypotheses in a virtual environment as a guide to faster and better decision-making. BP has this aspiration. It has already found that employees who work for great team leaders are 15 "points" more engaged than those who see their team leader less often and receive less feedback.[27] Using AI, GenAI, and digital twin technologies, BP could model the exact leadership behaviors and approaches to test with, drive greater engagement, and then roll out more widely.

Key operating model shifts

- Create a culture of challenging the status quo and of experimentation and learning.
- Continuously assess and prioritize investments and change initiatives.
- Ensure change itself is a distinctive capability and everybody plays a role in it.
- Make leaders accountable for reinvention and execution.
- Use data and digital twins to hack the organization for performance.

Put the seven features to work

Shareholders, boards, activist investors, and even employees are pressing leaders to redefine how their organization will work in the face of changing technological and global economic dynamics. Yet, when companies boldly claim they will dramatically increase growth while halving their workforce, obliterating hierarchy, and dissolving organizational silos, they raise more questions than they answer. Only with ambition, humility, and pragmatic thinking will companies be able to shape the organization of the future and decide how they will get there in the face of ever-accelerating disruption.

Consider the pressure today to break down functional silos. Dissolving functions to create cross-functional units is attractive on the surface, but many discover the simple reality that trading one set of silos for another is hardly a panacea. Today's agile models provide the benefits of center-led functional groups that deliver efficiency and deep capability, as well as cross-functional teams organized around value streams that relentlessly focus on customer needs. Shared organizational platforms and digital technology make this possible.

Look again at Haier, with its microenterprise model that fully embraces the agile organization.[28] Small teams are fully accountable for their customer segments and leverage shared sales, design, manufacturing, and support services. Each cross-functional team actively engages its internal and external partners, with its entrepreneurial acceleration platform bringing together internal and external stakeholders to achieve value for the entire ecosystem. Powered by this model, revenue for Haier's core appliance business has grown by an average of 19 percent per year from 2003 to 2023.[29]

Another example is Moderna, where its mRNA technology is becoming a business platform, a centerpiece for drug development, business strategy, and potential commercial partnership that extends the reach of the company well beyond its own captive organization. What if Moderna, as an asset-light player, could achieve the revenues of, say Merck or Pfizer, with a fraction of the employees and the structural costs?

Selecting the right value streams—whether customer journeys or high-impact workflows—is essential to make these new models effective. There are trends, but no standard set of value streams, and certainly no single correct set that will remain applicable indefinitely. Based on our experience, it is crucial to identify five to eight value streams that have the highest impact on activating the unique business model and the strategic growth plan for your organization. A focus on the end customer is the key. Value streams should be designed with the internal or external customer in mind, working backwards from their needs and identifying the full set of activities and muscles required to deliver against these needs.

In parallel, the democratization of data and advances in technology such as GenAI are making it easier and cheaper every day to achieve a radical reduction in the cost of complexity as work is consumed by algorithms, and the transparency of data and insights enables decisions to be made anywhere in the organization. This is particularly evident with the rise of AI agents and agentic architectures, where AI agents will act autonomously within set parameters, adapting dynamically to real-time data and changing business conditions. The following further explores the potentially explosive impact and implications of this rapidly emerging phenomenon.

The rise of AI agents and supporting agentic architectures—which enable these AI agents to function autonomously and interact with their environment, other agents, and humans—are poised to revolutionize operating model and organization design.

Imagine a pharmaceutical company where a single research director oversees the work of thousands of AI agents, each specializing in molecular analysis, clinical trial design, and regulatory compliance. A new drug concept is uploaded, and within minutes, a coordinator agent initiates compound simulations, while another scans vast datasets of medical literature and previous trials. Simultaneously, a compliance agent ensures the design aligns with global regulatory frameworks. This is not a dream—it's the emerging reality of a new AI agentic architecture. Jensen Huang of Nvidia says they are already using agents at the heart of their chip designs and envisions a future where his 50,000 employees work alongside 100 million AI agents, amplifying productivity and scaling intellectual labor.[30]

This shift demands a radical rethinking of organizational design. The traditional linear hierarchy, built around managing human effort, gives way to decentralized networks of AI agents working in parallel. Human roles shift from execution to innovation and governance, directing agents and validating outcomes. With AI agents independently optimizing processes, enhancing decision-making, and facilitating seamless collaboration across teams and functions. As AI agents take on the bulk of operational tasks, organizations could potentially achieve what once required tens or even hundreds of thousands of employees with just a few hundred. This model accelerates and collapses processes, lowering costs and boosting agility. In this world, organization design evolves from structuring human roles and processes to engineering ecosystems of human–AI collaboration, balancing autonomy with alignment to strategic goals and metrics.

The implications for CEOs are profound. Smaller, nimble organizations will be able to compete at a scale previously reserved for the largest enterprises. The focus pivots to assembling ecosystems of interoperable agents and fostering innovation through adaptive and modular structures. Organization design becomes an ongoing process of tuning and recalibrating AI-driven workflows, much like continuously refining software. Business leaders and organization design practitioners will need to master new tools to map dependencies between agents, define their scope of action, and ensure they seamlessly integrate alongside people to deliver on evolving business strategies. In this new era, the success of an organization will hinge less on its size and more on the sophistication of its agentic architecture, requiring a deeply integrated approach to strategy, organization and technology.

The vision of this agentic architecture is already taking shape. Nathan Warren, and Daniel Bashir explore this shift in Azeem Azhar's Exponential View blog, "Towards Billions of Agents".[31] Their insights have informed our thinking and provide valuable context for understanding how AI agents are set to redefine organizational scale and capability.

While decisions at the heart of the enterprise operating model, such as the value streams to organize by and that will anchor the business, provide a degree of stability, companies simply cannot anticipate today the precise nature of change that lies ahead. The winners in AI-powered business will create the capability to regularly hack the organization for growth and performance. They will embrace big-bet transformation as well as incremental optimization and innovation of their operating model to create a permanent process of reinvention.

Picture a company that is transforming its top-down operating model to enable it to shift from selling products to selling solutions, such as the journey Rolls-Royce[32] went on when it moved from selling engines and maintenance contracts to per-hour of engine running time, or Cisco, which now sells network solutions and services rather than hardware alone.[33] What if a company like this, at the same time, continuously and meticulously identified and analyzed, through ongoing experiments, the performance of its maintenance and operations teams, testing potential organization design scenarios (people, processes, and systems) and interventions, thus harnessing a dual engine of top-down and bottom-up reinvention?

Leaders of organizations that embrace this approach don't fret that business units and functions are continuously iterating and transforming their operating models. They recognize this as healthy and that it takes multiple pathways of exploration and change to achieve ever-higher levels of performance. However, they don't simply leave the operating model changes to chance or the whim of each organizational unit leader: they set the conditions for success, grounded in the company's strategy.

With a well-understood set of principles for the operating model and organization design, agreement on the capabilities required to win, and clarity on the roles and accountabilities of each major component of the operating model, change can be managed continuously.

Conclusion: The reinventor organization

Rethinking operating models is not merely about adopting new structures and systems but embracing a reinvention mindset. The seven features outlined in this chapter offer a blueprint for a new type of organization that continuously reinvents itself, morphing with market dynamics, embracing new technology, and staying in tune with customer, employee, and societal expectations.

The advent of advanced technologies such as GenAI and new ways of working presents a pivotal moment in organization design, enabling businesses to push the barriers of organizational trade-offs, achieve radically higher levels of productivity, and even create new sources of value. This potential can only be fully realized, however, through operating models that consistently integrate these changes into the very fabric of an organization's customer journeys and organizational workflows, with people and machines working in harmony.

This transition is not trivial—it involves curiosity, imagination, and unlearning decades-old practices that made the leaders of today successful. It also requires investment in leading-edge capabilities and deft management

Figure 7.1 The reinventor organization Star Model

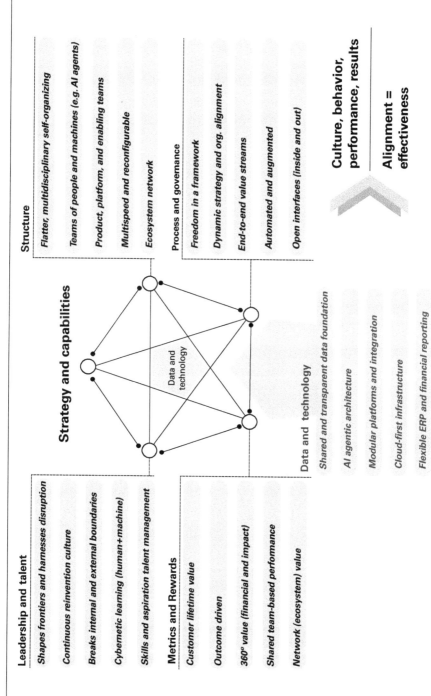

Leadership and talent

Shapes frontiers and harnesses disruption

Continuous reinvention culture

Breaks internal and external boundaries

Cybernetic learning (human+machine)

Skills and aspiration talent management

Metrics and Rewards

Customer lifetime value

Outcome driven

360° value (financial and impact)

Shared team-based performance

Network (ecosystem) value

Strategy and capabilities

Data and technology

Structure

Flatter, multidisciplinary self-organizing

Teams of people and machines (e.g. AI agents)

Product, platform, and enabling teams

Multispeed and reconfigurable

Ecosystem network

Process and governance

Freedom in a framework

Dynamic strategy and org. alignment

End-to-end value streams

Automated and augmented

Open interfaces (inside and out)

Data and technology

Shared and transparent data foundation

AI agentic architecture

Modular platforms and integration

Cloud-first infrastructure

Flexible ERP and financial reporting

Culture, behavior, performance, results

Alignment = effectiveness

SOURCE Adapted from Jay Galbraith

of the six enduring operating model challenges. In addition, the periodic redesign of an organization's operating model, every three to five years, is no longer sufficient. The world is moving too fast, and technologies like GenAI are developing too rapidly, necessitating a shift to an accelerated and ongoing approach to redesign that reshapes the organizational architecture and ways of working every day to set a new performance frontier.

Only a "systems thinking" approach to aligning all the elements of your organization—including the data and technology architecture—with the company's strategy will deliver on the promise of these reinventor organizations. Figure 7.1 provides a snapshot of how each element of Galbraith's Star Model, adapted in recognition of the role of data and technology, will need to be realigned to deliver on the vision set out in the seven features.

QUICK REINVENTOR DESIGN TEST

How do you know if you are ready to be a reinventor organization? Take a few minutes with your leadership team to consider the following questions.

Fundamentals

- Are you taking a deliberate strategy of setting new performance frontiers for your company and the industry in which you operate, or settling for the benchmark?
- Is your operating model able to morph with market dynamics, embrace new technology, and stay in tune with customer, employee, and societal expectations?
- Do you continually review your operating model, taking a "systems thinking" approach to align all elements with your company's strategy?

Features

- Is your organization united through shared and transparent data and insights, with clarity on purpose and direction, trade-offs, and guardrails?
- Are you organized around customer needs for innovation and speed, and platforms for efficiency and scalability?
- Do your teams work across organizational boundaries and hierarchies to deliver value for external and internal customers?

- Are you using data and technology as the primary means to get work done and to amplify the human creativity and decision-making of your leaders and teams?
- Do you build teams based on a deep understanding of people's skills and aspirations and sophisticated combinations of people and machines?
- Is your ecosystem strategy clear and are you set up to multiply its value, with simple and digital interfaces that enable you to engage faster and deeper?
- Are you proactively and continuously self-disrupting how work gets done to achieve new performance frontiers for your company and industry?

Notes

1   Accenture (n.d.) Total Enterprise Reinvention.
2   Yeung, A. and Ulrich, D. (2019) *Reinventing the Organization*, Boston, MA: Harvard Business Review Press, Chapter 10, Information sharing.
3   Kates, A., Kesler, G., and DiMartino, M. (2021) *Networked, Scaled, and Agile: A Design Strategy for Complex Organizations*, London: Kogan Page.
4   Fjeldstad, Ø.D., Snow, C.C., Miles, R.E, and Lettl, C. (2012) The Architecture of Collaboration, *Strategic Management Journal*, 33 (6).
5   Yeung and Ulrich (2019).
6   Swann, M. (2024) How to Drive Change Through Long-Term Strategy, *Forbes*, April 15. forbes.com/sites/forbestechcouncil/2024/04/15/how-to-drive-change-through-long-term-strategy (archived at https://perma.cc/S7WE-SNJQ).
7   Novet, J. (2024) Amazon's Cloud Margin Widens on Accelerating Revenue Growth, CNBC, April 30. cnbc.com/2024/04/30/aws-q1-earnings-report-2024.html (archived at https://perma.cc/L6QD-EJAZ).
8   Murgia, M. and Criddle, C. (2024) OpenAI and Meta Ready New AI Models Capable of "Reasoning", *Financial Times*, April 9.
9   Iansiti, M. and Lakhani, K.R. (2020) *Competing in the Age of AI*, Boston, MA: Harvard Business Review Press.
10 Edwards, J.S. and Rodriguez E. (2018) Knowledge Management for Action-Oriented Analytics, in S. Hawamdeh and H.-C. Chang (eds), *Analytics and Knowledge Management*, New York: Auerbach.
11 Heimans, J. and Timms, H. (2024) Leading in a World Where AI Wields Power of Its Own, *Harvard Business Review*, January.

12   Baertlein, L. (2018) New UPS Navigation Tool Aims to Save Time and Money with Each Turn, Reuters, December 4.

13   Accenture (2023a) *Becoming a Skills-Driven Organization.* accenture.com/content/dam/accenture/final/accenture-com/document/Accenture-Becoming-a-Skills-Driven-Organization-Report.pdf (archived at https://perma.cc/WA5B-H8C6).

14   Sinsek, S. (2019) *The Infinite Game*, New York and London: Penguin.

15   Malone, T.W. (2019) Corporate Strategic Planning, in *Superminds: How Hyperconnectivity is Changing the Way We Solve Problems*, London: Oneworld Publications.

16   Gifari, F. and Madhakomala R. (2023) Education and Training (Diklat)-Based Human Resource Development to Increase Employee Creativity: Literature study, *Journal of Advances in Accounting, Economics, and Management*, 1 (2).

17   Haier (n.d.) About us. haier.com/global/about-haier (archived at https://perma.cc/B2CF-7R7E).

18   Haier Europe (2024) Haier Group in a nutshell. staging.haier-europe.com/about-us/who-we-are (archived at https://perma.cc/E69Z-G5ZZ).

19   Verizon (2022) Investor Day 2022 (edited transcript). verizon.com/about/sites/default/files/2022-03/Investor-Day-2022-Transcript.pdf (archived at https://perma.cc/Y569-NPQJ).

20   Microsoft (2024) Vodafone and Microsoft Sign 10-year Strategic Partnership to Bring Generative AI, Digital Services and the Cloud to More Than 300 Million Businesses and Consumers, Microsoft News Center, January 15. news.microsoft.com/2024/01/15/vodafone-and-microsoft-sign-10-year-strategic-partnership-to-bring-generative-ai-digital-services-and-the-cloud-to-more-than-300-million-businesses-and-consumers (archived at https://perma.cc/A93R-T8A9).

21   Accenture (2023b) Vodafone announces strategic partnership with Accenture to accelerate the commercialization of its shared operations, Accenture Newsroom. newsroom.accenture.com/news/2023/vodafone-announces-strategic-partnership-with-accenture-to-accelerate-the-commercialization-of-its-shared-operations (archived at https://perma.cc/89LR-W7L9).

22   Prashantham, S. and Woetzel, L. (2020) 3 Lessons from Chinese Firms on Effective Digital Collaboration, *Harvard Business Review*, August 10.

23   Accenture (2023c) *Total Enterprise Reinvention.* accenture.com/content/dam/accenture/final/accenture-com/document/Accenture-Total-Enterprise-Reinvention.pdf (archived at https://perma.cc/73AZ-TYM5).

24   Mankins, M. and Litre, P. (2024) A New Model for Continuous Transformation, *Harvard Business Review*, June 4.

25   Hamel, G. and Zanini, M. (2020) Haier – The Road to Rendanheyi, in *Humanocracy: Creating Organizations as Amazing as the People Inside Them*, Boston, MA: Harvard Business Review Press.

26 Garg, H. and Purohit, S.R. (2022) Sustainable Value Stream Mapping in the Food Industry, in S. Sehgal, B. Singh, and V. Sharma (eds) *Smart and Sustainable Food Technologies*, Singapore: Springer.

27 Accenture (2023d) *The CHRO as a Growth Executive.* accenture.com/content/ dam/accenture/final/capabilities/strategy-and-consulting/talent-and-organization/ document/Accenture-CHRO-Growth-Executive.pdf (archived at https://perma.cc/ 9TSX-XG55).

28 Hamel, G. and Zanini, M. (2018) The End of Bureaucracy, *Harvard Business Review*, November–December.

29 Haier (n.d.) Annual Reports. smart-home.haier.com/en/gpxx/?id=yjbg&spm= inverstor.en_home_pc.irheader_20200506_2.2 (archived at https://perma. cc/4ZXX-F3KV).

30 Gurley, B. and Gerstner, B. (2024) "Ep17. Welcome Jensun Huang." BG2 podcast, October 13. https://open.spotify.com/episode/0pt8FAP3UKdZhgKHf AWPdC (archived at https://perma.cc/2Y3S-NTN2)

31 Azhar, A. (2025) "Towards Billions of Agents". Exponential View Blog, December 4. https://www.exponentialview.co/p/from-chatgpt-to-a-billion-agents (archived at https://perma.cc/ W23A-BZ37)

32 Rolls-Royce celebrated 50th anniversary of Power-by-the-Hour (2012).

33 Cisco to sell everything-as-service—even core networking hardware—and cut costs by a billion bucks (2020).

INDEX

Note: Page numbers in *italics* refer to tables or figures.

Looking for another book?

Explore our award-winning
books from global business
experts in Human Resources,
Learning and Development

Scan the code to browse

www.koganpage.com/hr-learning-
development

More from Kogan Page

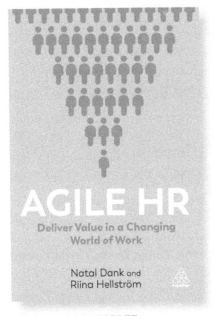

ISBN: 9781789665857

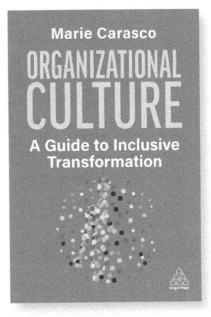

ISBN: 9781398614994

ISBN: 9781789667912

ISBN: 9781398608665

www.koganpage.com

EU Representative (GPSR)

Authorised Rep Compliance Ltd, Ground Floor, 71 Lower Baggot Street, Dublin, D02 P593, Ireland

www.arccompliance.com

www.ingramcontent.com/pod-product-compliance
Lightning Source LLC
Jackson TN
JSHW071036280225
79898JS00006B/6